CW00492085

Admiral Lord Howe

ADMIRAL LORD HOWE

by

David Syrett

Foreword by James Bradford

SPELLMOUNT
Staplehurst

British Library Cataloguing in Publication Data:
A catalogue record for this book is available
from the British Library

Copyright © David Syrett 2006

ISBN 1-86227-262-X

First published in the UK in 2006 by
Spellmount Limited
The Mill, Brimscombe Port, Stroud, Gloucestershire GL5 2QG

Tel: 01453 88300; Fax: 01453 883233

E-mail: enquiries@spellmount.com
Website: www.spellmount.com

1 3 5 7 9 8 6 4 2

The right of David Syrett to be identified
as the author of this work has been asserted by him
in accordance with the Copyright, Designs
and Patents Act 1988

All rights reserved. No part of this publication may be
reproduced, stored in a retrieval system or transmitted in
any form or by any means, electronic, mechanical,
photocopying, recording or otherwise,
without prior permission in writing from
Spellmount Limited, Publishers.

Printed in Great Britain by
Oaklands Book Services
Stonehouse, Gloucestershire GL10 3RQ

Contents

List of Maps

Index of Ship Names

Foreword

Richard Howe, 1st Earl Howe, was one of the greatest admirals of the late eighteenth and early nineteenth centuries when Great Britain's Royal Navy achieved supremacy at the climax of the Age of Sail. Lord Howe played key roles in moulding the Navy both as an administrator and as a squadron and fleet commander. Indeed, Howe rose to a position of prominence rapidly. His father, Emanuel Scrope Howe, 2nd Viscount Howe, died when Richard was ten, but his mother, Mary Sophia Charlotte, daughter of the mistress of King George I, was able to advance her son's career after he entered the Navy at age fourteen. In less than a decade Richard rose to post-captain and commanded the flagship of a British squadron in the West Indies.

After seeing action during the wars of mid-century, Howe entered Parliament in 1762. He served as treasurer of the navy from 1775 to 1770, a period of decline after the great victories of the Seven Years War. During the American War of Independence Richard Howe commanded naval forces in North America while his younger brother, Major General William Howe, commanded the British Army in the colonies. For two years he blocked attempts by Le Comte d'Estaing and the French navy to aid the colonists but this success was overshadowed by his frustration at failing to negotiate a peace settlement with the Americans. In 1778 Richard Howe resigned his position and did not serve in the Royal Navy again until Lord North left as Prime Minister in 1782. During the autumn of that year Howe returned to active duty as commander of the Channel Fleet that relieved the siege of Gibraltar. Ashore from 1783 to 1788, Howe served as First Lord of the Admiralty during another time of naval retrenchment. In 1788 King George III recognised his services by granting him the title Baron and Earl Howe. At the outbreak of war with France Howe returned to sea duty and led the Channel Fleet to victory over the French at the battle of the Glorious First of June (1794). Ever popular with sailors in the Royal Navy, 'Black Dick' as the seamen called him, helped end the Spithead Mutiny in 1797, the year he retired as 'Admiral of the Fleet', the highest rank in the Royal Navy.

With such a distinguished career, one would expect Richard Howe to have been the subject of several biographies, but this is not the case, largely because of a paucity of extant personal papers. For over a century Sir John Barrow's *The Life of Richard, Earl Howe, KG, Admiral of the Fleet, and General of Marines* (1838) remained the standard biography. During the twentieth century Troyer S Anderson, *The Command of the Howe Brothers During the American Revolution* (1936), and Ira D Gruber, *The Howe Brothers and the American Revolution* (1972), analysed the impact of Richard and William Howe on the war in America. His brother was the subject of Bellamy Partridge's *Sir Billy Howe* (1932), but Richard never received a full biography.

David Syrett is the perfect person to fill this gap in naval and Revolutionary War bibliography. A prolific author who conducted extensive archival research on both sides of the Atlantic, he is the author of volumes on *Shipping and the American War, 1775–88* (1970); *The Royal Navy in American Waters, 1775–1783* (1989); and *The Royal Navy in European Waters during the American Revolutionary War* (1998). David died unexpectedly while this volume was in press and it thus constitutes one of the last of his many contributions to Anglo–American naval history. Born in 1941, David Syrett earned BA and MA degrees from Columbia University and his PhD from the University of London. He taught at Queen's College, CUNY, for over thirty-five years during which time he guided the graduate work of numerous students as well as producing seven books and dozens of articles on Anglo–American naval history that focused on two eras, the late eighteenth century when Britain and America shifted from being allies during the Seven Years War to opponents during the War of American Independence, and the mid-twentieth century when the United States and Britain fought together as allies in the Battle of the Atlantic against the German U-boat menace. In this latter field, David produced *The Defeat of the German U-Boats: The Battle of the Atlantic* (1994). An active member of the Naval Record Society, David edited three volumes for the society's publication series: *The Siege and Capture of Havana, 1762* (1970), *The Commissioned Sea Officers of the Royal Navy 1660–1815* (with R L Di Nardo, 1994), and *The Battle for the Atlantic and Signals Intelligence: U-Boat Situations and Trends, 1941–1945*. David was a member of the Royal Historical Society, served as John F Morrison Professor of Military History at the US Army Command and General Staff College, 1981–2, and was, at the time of his untimely death, a distinguished Professor of History at Queens College. In his most recent publication, 'A Study of Peacetime Operations: The Royal Navy in the Mediterranean, 1752–5' (*The Mariner's Mirror*, vol. 90 [2002], 42–50), as with his biography of Richard Howe, David returned to the eighteenth century.

The Library of Naval Biography provides accurate, informative, and interpretive biographies of influential naval figures – men and women who have shaped or reflected the naval affairs of their time. Each volume explains the forces that acted upon its subject as well as the significance of that person in history. Some volumes like this one on Richard Howe, explore the lives of individuals who have not previously been the subject of a modern, full-scale biography, while others will re-examine the lives of better-known individuals adding new information, a differing perspective, or a fresh interpretation. The series is international in scope and includes individuals from several centuries. All volumes are based on solid research and written to be of interest to general readers as well as useful to specialists.

James C Bradford, Editor
The Library of Naval Biography

Preface

Admiral Lord Howe, in the course of a long career as an officer in the Royal Navy, took part in many of the great naval events of the 18th century. As a midshipman, Howe was on one of the ships which attempted to accompany Anson around the world. Then, as a captain, Howe fired the first shot at sea in the Seven Years War and led the British attack at Quiberon Bay. During the American War Howe served as commander in chief in America and conducted the third relief of Gibraltar. And in the French Revolutionary War, Howe fought and won the Glorious First of June and was instrumental in ending the great mutiny at Spithead in 1797. No other flag officer of the Georgian Royal Navy served as long in so many different wars and varied circumstances as Howe. Yet there is only one book-length and out of date biography of Howe.[1] With the exception of the admiral's period of command during the American War,[2] Howe has been little studied by historians of the 18th-century Royal Navy.[3]

A biographer of Admiral Lord Howe is confronted by a number of difficult problems. One of these is the fact that, whether in spoken or written communications, Howe is the most inarticulate of all the major figures of 18th-century British history. Anecdotes abound about his perplexing and obscure employment of the English language and the admiral's speeches in Parliament are legendary for their confusing and bewildering syntax. Howe's letters, whether public or private, are written in a style which is so opaque, guarded and convoluted as to render them at times almost beyond comprehension. Compounding all the problems of a confused and muddy style, when writing and speaking, is the fact that Howe at times is almost pathologically secretive about the reasons why he acted as he did on specific occasions. His official dispatches to the Admiralty, for example, leave little or no doubt as to what he did, but more often than not these documents fail to explain the reasons for his actions. Further, there is evidence that Howe, at times, told less than the whole truth about some of his activities.[4] Under these circumstances, it is not surprising that historians are left, even after consulting the existing records, with a number of unanswered questions concerning Howe.

A scholar's ability to understand Howe is made even more difficult by the disappearance of many of his papers. The largest known collection of

Howe's private papers was lost at the beginning of the 19th century when the library at Westport House, Westport, Ireland was destroyed by fire.[5] The admiral himself also destroyed documents. On 9 July 1778, in an instance which must have been repeated many times, Howe wrote to William Eden: 'I acknowledge the receipt of yours of yesterday and have destroyed it.'[6] Some years later Howe appears to have also engaged in what is now called 'weeding'. On 30 May 1791, for example, Howe wrote that he was 'Employed lately in destroying Letters & Papers accumulated at the Admiralty, & which are not necessary to be retained.'[7] Even though there are a number of Howe letters scattered about in various manuscript collections in the United States[8] and Great Britain the fire in Ireland and Howe's destruction of his papers have produced a situation in which almost no manuscripts concerning the admiral's private life have survived. This biography, therefore, is about Howe's career as a navy officer and public figure.

This book would not have been possible without the assistance of a number of people and institutions in Great Britain and the United States. I wish to thank the staffs of the University of London's Institute of Historical Research; The National Archives (formerly the Public Record Office); the British Library; and the Rosenthal Library of Queens College, City University of New York. I am immensely thankful for the assistance rendered over the years by Ms Marianne Conti and Ms Evelyn I Silverman of the Inter Library Loan Department of the Rosenthal Library of Queens College. I wish also to thank Dr Mary Ellen Condon for providing me with microfilm of the Keppel Papers. I also wish to thank the late Dr Richard Boulind who before his death provided me with transcripts of Howe's letters to Sir Roger Curtis which are in the Huntington Library. Research for this book was supported in part by the City University of New York's PSC-CUNY Research Award Program.

I am, of course, responsible for any sins of commission and omission.

David Syrett
New York

Notes

1. Sir John Barrow, *The Life of Richard, Earl Howe, K G, Admiral of the Fleet, and General of Marines* (London, 1838).

2. Cf. Troyer Steele Anderson, *The Command of the Howe Brothers during the American Revolution* (New York, 1936); Ira D Gruber, *The Howe Brothers and the American Revolution* (New York 1972).

3. An exception on a small scale is Roger Knight, 'Richard Howe, 1726–1799', *Precursors of Nelson: British Admirals of the Eighteenth Century*, Peter Le Fevre and Richard Harding, eds (London, 2000), pp. 297–299.

4. W H Moomaw, 'The Denouement of General Howe's Campaign of 1777', *English Historical Review* (July, 1964), vol. 79, pp. 498–512.

5. Gruber, *The Howe Brothers and the American Revolution*, p. 371.

6. American Philosophical Society, The Sol Feinstone Collection of the American Revolution, Howe to Eden, 9 July 1778.

7. HL, Howe to Curtis, 30 May 1791.

8. Cf. David Syrett, 'A Check List of Admiral Lord Howe Manuscripts in United States Archives And Libraries' *The Mariner's Mirror* (Aug. 1981), vol. 67, pp. 273–284.

CHAPTER I

Early Career

It is said that Admiral Lord Howe, because of circumstances of birth, enjoyed a close relationship with the royal family. The future admiral, styled the Hon. Richard Howe, was the third but second surviving son of Emanuel Scrope Howe and was born in London on 8 March 1726. Richard Howe's grandfather was Scrope Howe, a long-serving Member of Parliament for Nottinghamshire, a Whig, and a vehement opponent of popery. Voting in the Convention Parliament to place William III on the throne, Scrope Howe was made groom of the bedchamber by the new king and created Viscount Howe of the Kingdom of Ireland. His son, and Richard Howe's father, was Emanuel Scrope Howe, 2nd Viscount Howe in the peerage of Ireland and for ten years a Member of Parliament for Nottinghamshire. Richard Howe's mother, considered by some to be the illegitimate daughter of George I, was Mary Sophia Charlotte Kielmansegge, the daughter of the Countess of Darlington and the mistress of George I. Mary brought to the marriage the sum of £1,500 per year.[1] Nevertheless, Emanuel Scrope Howe, in 1732, encountered financial difficulties and, on the advice of the Duke of Newcastle, resigned his seat in the House of Commons to be appointed governor of Barbados. The governorship was said to be worth 'a good £7,000 a year' but Emanuel Scrope Howe did not live to see much of the money for he died in the West Indies in 1735.[2]

Little is known of Richard Howe's early life that can be documented. Apparently he did not accompany his father to the West Indies for he was admitted to Westminster School in 1732[3] and later probably attended Eton College.[4] Nevertheless, on Richard Howe's lieutenant's passing certificate,[5] which is badly torn, he is listed as having served in the merchant ship *Thames*, William Merchant, Master, for some three years before entering the Royal Navy. If this was the case then Richard Howe did not attend Eton. The most likely explanation for this apparent discrepancy is that the entry in Howe's certificate is fraudulent and designed to show on paper that he had the required sea time to qualify for a lieutenant's commission. It was not unusual for more than the whole truth to be entered on a lieutenant's passing certificate.[6] Richard Howe's two brothers, George

Augustus and William, both attended Eton.[7] It is highly unlikely that Richard Howe owing to his family background, would be removed from school at the age of 10 and be sent to sea before the mast on a merchant ship. Unfortunately, in the absence of information supported by documentation, not much can be said with certainty about Richard Howe's childhood.

There were in 18th-century England very few careers that a person such as Richard Howe, coming from an aristocratic family, could pursue without a loss of status. Business and trade were out of the question and, before the rise of the modern professional classes, to be a surgeon was to be one step above a barber. That left the armed forces of the crown and the church. The government, especially the army, was the employer of last resort for the sons of aristocratic families in Hanoverian England. Richard Howe would become an officer in the Royal Navy while his two brothers George Augustus and William would become officers in the army. On 16 July 1739, at the age of 13, Richard Howe's name was entered as an ordinary seaman in the muster books of HMS *Pearl*.[8] HMS *Pearl*, commanded by Captain Edward Legge, was at Sheerness and it is possible that Howe remained at Eton[9] and never actually served on the ship.

Richard Howe had a horrific introduction to active service in the Royal Navy. Captain Legge was transferred from HMS *Pearl* to the command of HMS *Severn* and on 3 July 1740 Howe joined that vessel as a midshipman. A 50-gun ship, HMS *Severn* was part of the squadron under the command of Commodore George Anson, which sailed from St Helens on 4 September 1740 on a voyage into the Pacific Ocean to attack the Spanish.[10] Several months later, on 10 April 1741, when attempting to round Cape Horn and enter the Pacific Ocean, Anson's ships encountered a series of violent storms. For days on end the British ships battled mountainous seas and storms blowing from the north-west. HMS *Severn* became separated from Anson and was forced back into the Atlantic Ocean. Legge believed, until sighting Cape Frio, on 1 June 1741, that HMS *Severn* had entered the Pacific Ocean. This was a classic example of the mistakes inherent in determining longitude by means of dead reckoning. On 30 June 1741 a shattered HMS *Severn* limped into Rio de Janeiro in Brazil.[11] The vessel was badly damaged, especially in the masts and standing rigging, and there were barely enough men remaining on their feet to work the vessel. Months before, scurvy and other diseases had broken out among the crew and some 430 men had died and had been buried at sea.[12] After the ship was repaired and her crew had regained their health, HMS *Severn* returned, by way of Barbados, to England arriving at Spithead on 6 May 1742.[13] More than forty years after the event a hostile critic would play down the hardships suffered by Howe claiming that the young man, while on board HMS *Severn* had not messed and bunked in the gun room with the other midshipmen, but rather had eaten with Captain Legge and slept in the captain's cabin.[14] Nevertheless, for Howe, as well as for every other man in the ship, HMS *Severn*'s attempted passage to the South Seas must have been a grim and terrifying experience.

On 24 August 1742 Howe was posted as a midshipman to the 70-gun ship of the line HMS *Burford*.[15] In the autumn of 1742 HMS *Burford* was sent to the West Indies arriving at Barbados on 17 December 1742.[16] Several weeks later on 18 February 1743 Howe took part in his first battle, when HMS *Burford* led a British squadron, under the command of Captain Charles Knowles, which attacked the city of La Guaira on the coast of Venezuela. In this battle, which was a bloody British defeat, HMS *Burford* lost twenty-six men killed, including her captain, Franklin Lushington, and the vessel was badly damaged.[17] Shortly after the abortive attack on La Guaira Howe was discharged from HMS *Burford*.[18]

For a successful career in the Hanoverian Royal Navy a young man such as Howe required the patronage, or in the parlance of the 18th century, the 'interest' of a senior officer. In the case of Midshipman Howe it is not wholly clear just how this was brought about, but it was usually by means of a relative or family connections that the patronage or interest was obtained. Howe had entered the Royal Navy under the protection of Captain the Hon. Edward Legge, and Captain Charles Knowles would see that Howe was promoted to lieutenant. On 10 March 1742 Howe became a midshipman on HMS *Suffolk* which was commanded by Captain Charles Knowles. Several months later, on 10 July 1742, he was moved to HMS *Eltham* commanded by Captain Edward Pratten.[19] And then on 8 October 1743 Midshipman Howe was again transferred out of HMS *Eltham* into the ship of the line HMS *Superb* whose new master was Captain Charles Knowles.[20] While serving as a midshipman on HMS *Superb* Howe was promoted and commissioned as a lieutenant in the Royal Navy.

On 24 May 1744 Howe appeared before a board of three post captains,[21] meeting at English Harbour, Antigua on board HMS *Argyle* to be examined on his qualifications to be promoted. To gain a commission as a lieutenant in the Royal Navy a midshipman was required not only to pass an oral examination on seamanship and navigation, but also had to produce certificates showing that he was 'not under twenty years of age' and had served at sea for at least six years.[22] Howe's lieutenant's passing certificate[23] states that he had served at sea for eight years and four months and that he was 20 years of age. Obviously this is less than the whole truth. Howe was only 18 years old and further, if the three years' alleged service at sea in the merchant ship *Thames*, which was probably fictitious, is subtracted, then the total time spent at sea can only be four years eleven months (16 July 1739 to 24 May 1744). Additionally, the time Howe actually spent at sea can probably be further reduced by about a year if the time that he is listed as having been on HMS *Pearl* was actually spent at Eton College. Nevertheless, Howe did produce the necessary certificates at the examination and no enquiries were made about his age. Passing the examination, Lieutenant Howe was immediately commissioned and the next day was assigned to serve on board HMS *Comet*. For Howe to pass the examination and be commissioned as a lieutenant when under age and without the required amount of time at sea was not unusual. The porters at the Navy Office sold false certificates to young gentlemen aspiring to be lieutenants[24] and Maurice Suckling, a contemporary of Howe and a future Comptroller of the Navy, was commissioned a lieutenant when 19 years of age with only five years and five months time at sea.[25] The surviving documentation of promotions of midshipmen to lieutenants in the 18th-century Royal Navy is littered with false certificates and dummy muster book entries.[26]

Howe did not remain for very long on HMS *Comet* for on 12 August he was transferred to HMS *Severn* where he served as 2nd lieutenant until he was promoted, on 28 October 1744, to 1st lieutenant of that vessel.[27] Howe left the West Indies and returned to England, probably as a lieutenant on board HMS *Mercury* though the documentary record is unclear. On 12 August 1745 he was appointed 5th lieutenant of the 1st rate HMS *Royal George*.[28] HMS *Royal George*, for the most part, remained in England,[29] and on 5 November 1745, Howe was promoted to the rank of master and commander,[30] having served as a lieutenant for only a year and a half before being promoted and given command of a ship.

The rank of master and commander was the forerunner of the modern rank of commander and the men who held this rank were placed in command of small warships such as sloops of war. Howe himself was ordered to take command of HM Sloop *Baltimore* and to blockade the west coast of Scotland to prevent the Jacobins from importing arms and other warlike supplies.[31] For the next seven months Howe in *Baltimore* cruised off the west coast of northern Britain on blockade duty. On 3 May 1746 HM Sloop *Baltimore* in company with HMS *Greyhound* and HM Sloop *Terror*, off the west coast of Scotland near the Sound of Arisaig, intercepted two large French privateers. A battle ensued, but the British warships were over matched and were forced to break off the action and withdraw. Howe was slightly wounded in the head and for a time 'was a little disordered'. This was the only time that Howe was wounded during a career in the Royal Navy which spanned four wars and more than fifty years. HM Sloop *Baltimore* was badly damaged in this battle, especially in the masts and standing rigging, and lost two men killed and another three men wounded.[32]

On 10 April 1746 Howe had been promoted to post captain and directed to take command of the 6th rate HMS *Triton*.[33] However, it was not until 16 July 1746, at Carrickfergus Road in Northern Ireland that Howe actually took command of HMS *Triton*,[34] when he became a post captain. This was an important step in the career of a navy officer, for not only did post captains command ships of the line, but unlike the ranks of lieutenant and master and commander, a person holding the rank of post captain could by seniority alone advance to flag rank. And then, if one lived long enough, an officer could again by seniority advance through all the grades of admiral to obtain at a very old age the rank of admiral of the fleet – the highest rank of all.[35] When Howe obtained the rank of post captain he was 20 years old and had been in the commissioned ranks of the Royal Navy for only a little under two years. This rapid promotion was not uncommon, for the Hon. August Keppel and John Rodney, who were both on extremely fast tracks for promotion, spent less than a year as lieutenants and masters and commanders. Nevertheless, Howe's promotion to post captain was rapid. It took the Hon. Samuel Barrington, Philip Affleck, and Charles Middleton two, four and five years respectively to achieve the rank of post captain, while Maurice Suckling did not reach post captain until ten years after first being commissioned as a lieutenant. Similarly, Richard Hughes spent eleven years a lieutenant and master and commander before being promoted to post captain.[36] It is difficult to generalise about promotion to post captain in the 18th-century Royal Navy for in many instances it depended upon not only interest and family connections, but also on ability and being in the right place at the right time. Nevertheless, in the case of Howe, it is clear that interest and family connections were decisive. Rapid promotion at a young age to the rank of post captain was one of the benefits of being well born in 18th-century England. Richard Howe was not only by birth a member of the aristocratic clique which governed Hanoverian England, but even though his father had died some years before, the Howe family was not without interest for it remained, especially in Nottinghamshire, a political force.[37]

After Howe had assumed command, HMS *Triton* was assigned to blockade duty off Scotland and escorted convoys up and down the east coast of Britain until the vessel, on 2 January 1747, entered Sheerness Dockyard.[38] When the dockyard refit was completed *Triton* was ordered to escort the trade to Lisbon and then, after a stay of not longer than fourteen days, to return, with 'any remittances of money' that the British merchants in Portugal desired to send to England.[39] On 27 April 1747 HMS *Triton*, with HMS *Dolphin*, escorting twelve merchant ships, sailed from Spithead and after a fast passage arrived off Lisbon on 4 May.[40] At the beginning of his return passage to England, off the coast of Portugal on 18 May, Howe met HMS *Ripon*. The captain of *Ripon* was the same Francis Holburne who had examined Howe for lieutenant. Holburne was ill and had concluded that because of the state of his health he could not carry out the orders he had received from the Admiralty to proceed to West Africa and then on to the West Indies. At Holburne's request, Howe exchanged ships becoming captain of HMS *Ripon* and assuming responsibility for carrying out the commission. This would enable Holburne to return to England in HMS

Triton to regain his health.[41] The Admiralty would later approve of Howe transferring into HMS *Ripon* and on 11 September issued a commission appointing him to the command of that vessel.[42]

The main objective of HMS *Ripon*'s mission was to show the flag among the natives and European traders along the coast of West Africa. Howe in *Ripon* arrived at Gambia on 9 June 1747 and then proceeded to sail south down the coast of West Africa, stopping at such places as Sierra Leone along the way, arriving on 13 September at Cape Coast Castle. After a stay of several months, *Ripon* departed from West Africa and proceeded westward across the Atlantic arriving, on 27 January 1748, at Carlisle Bay, Barbados. After a stay of seven months in the Leeward Islands, Howe then sailed to Jamaica arriving on 5 October. Three weeks later Charles Knowles, now a rear admiral and commander in chief of the British naval forces in the West Indies, arrived at Jamaica with his squadron.[43] The next day Knowles, in a grand act of patronage, appointed Howe captain of his flag ship the 80-gun HMS *Cornwall*.[44] The War of the Austrian Succession was over and the strength of the Royal Navy's squadron in the West Indies was being reduced. Howe was ordered to return to England and in July of 1749, after arriving at Chatham, HMS *Cornwall* was paid off.[45]

When Howe came ashore Britain was at peace and the Royal Navy's strength was being reduced from a wartime footing to a peacetime establishment. In times of peace the mission of the Royal Navy was in many respects that of a maritime constabulary. Tasks which had very little to do with fighting a major maritime war, but were nevertheless of vital importance to a nation with a growing economy and extensive overseas trading and political interests, were in peacetime undertaken by the Royal Navy. Showing the flag and exploring distant seas, testing new equipment, transporting money for the government and British merchants, gathering intelligence, protecting British commercial interests, settling minor disagreements with foreigners, and fighting pirates were some of the tasks which loomed large on the agenda of the peacetime Royal Navy. Obviously a smaller number of ships of a reduced size were required to carry out these peacetime functions than to fight a maritime war with a great European power with the result that there were very few commands available for officers in times of peace.

Howe was ashore some twenty months after leaving the command of HMS *Cornwall* and it was not until 1751 that he was again in command of a king's ship. On 14 March 1751, probably owing to family interest and connections, Howe was appointed to the command of the 44-gun HMS *Glory*.[46] It can be argued that taking command of a 44-gun ship, after commanding a ship of the line, was for Howe a demotion. However, given the strength of the peacetime Royal Navy the command of *Glory* was probably the only appointment available. As was the case with HMS

Ripon Howe was ordered to go to West Africa. HMS *Glory* was to be fitted and provisioned for an eight months long voyage to West Africa 'for the protection & security of the trade of His Majesty's subjects' as well as to prevent 'insults' to the British flag by the 'natives' or 'French'. Howe was also directed 'to inspect & examine the state & condition of the British forts and settlements' on the coast of West Africa. After completing these tasks HMS *Glory* was to return to England by way of the West Indies.[47]

On 3 April 1751 Howe in HMS *Glory* after taking on board a new type of compass which the Admiralty had ordered to be tested at sea, sailed from Portsmouth for West Africa. After a stopover at Madeira, Howe on 23 July arrived off Gambia and then proceeded southward along the coast of Africa to Sierra Leone where he arrived on 7 August. While at Sierra Leone the standing rigging of HMS *Glory* was repaired and Howe assisted a British merchant ship by supplying that vessel with a cable. On 24 August Howe departed from Sierra Leone and sailed south and then east along the coast of West Africa arriving, on 19 September, at Cape Coast Castle. There he found that the English and Dutch merchants operating in this part of West Africa were fighting a mini-war using the natives as proxies. Howe, after being informed of the situation by the English merchants resident in the region and being further told that 'it would be of great prejudice to the English ... if not in the end ruin of their trade' if an end was not put to this conflict, sailed in HMS *Glory* to the main Dutch trading post in the region at Elmina Castle. Negotiations were opened by Howe with the Dutch authorities and it was quickly agreed that the fighting should end, all prisoners be exchanged, and that all disagreements including claims, property and 'jurisdiction' should be referred to Europe for settlement. However, the dispute with the Dutch became protracted by a disagreement over the differences in the meanings between the English and Dutch versions of the agreement. Finally both sides agreed on the wording of a French text. While waiting for the agreement with the Dutch to commence, Howe forced a French merchant ship to cease trading and to leave a part of the African coast claimed by the British. On 3 November 1751 HMS *Glory*, with just enough provisions remaining for the voyage across the Atlantic, sailed from Cape Coast Castle for the West Indies. Howe arrived at Carlisle Bay, Barbados on 25 December 1751 and then proceeded westward arriving at Port Royal, Jamaica on 21 January 1752. After a stay of only three days, HMS *Glory* left Jamaica for England arriving at Spithead on 22 April 1752.[48] That same day Howe sent to the Admiralty a report on his proceedings enclosing another report on the 'State and Condition' of the English trading posts and forts on the west coast of Africa.[49]

Several months after returning to England from West Africa and the Caribbean Howe, on 3 June 1752, was appointed to command the frigate HMS *Dolphin*.[50] He was ordered to Woolwich to fit and store *Dolphin* for service in the Mediterranean under the command of Commodore George Edgcumbe.[51] The tasks undertaken by Howe and HMS *Dolphin* in the Mediterranean would be in many respects similar to those performed on the West African coast when Howe was in command of HMS *Glory*. On 24 October 1752 Howe in HMS *Dolphin* sailed from Plymouth for Lisbon and then proceeded to Gibraltar.[52] For the next year and a half HMS *Dolphin* was stationed in the Atlantic approaches of Gibraltar and the western Mediterranean showing the flag, freighting money for both the British government and merchants, gathering naval intelligence by visiting ports such as Cartagena and Toulon, to observe the activities of the Spanish and French navies, and calling at North African ports to check on the activities of the Barbary corsairs.[53] In the summer of 1754 HMS *Dolphin* returned to England, arriving at St Helens on 17 July, and on 29 August Howe left the ship turning command over to Captain Car Scrope.[54]

When Howe came ashore from HMS *Dolphin* in 1754 he was 28 years old and had served for fifteen years in the Royal Navy. However, little is known about him during these years other than the bare outline of his career as there are few surviving documents and certainly none of a personal nature. Howe's early life can be traced in the records held by The National Archives, but these only show the dates of his commissions and appointments in the Royal Navy and outline his naval service. One of the few glimpses one gets of Howe from non-official records are two brief mentions in Captain the Hon. Augustus Harvey's private journal concerning an argument over the freighting of money when he was captain of HMS *Dolphin*.[55] What is known is that Howe quickly, with the assistance of family influence, achieved the rank of post captain and that he had commanded, both in war and peace, almost every type of ship, ranging in size from a sloop of war to a ship of the line, the HMS *Dunkirk*, in the Royal Navy. In 1754 Howe, because of his experience and unblemished record, was a rising star among the younger post captains of the Royal Navy.

Notes

1. *The Complete Peerage* (Gloucester, 1987 reprint), vol. 2, nos 80, 596, 597, 599.

2. Romney Sedgwick, *The History of Parliament: The House of Commons, 1715–1754* (London, 1970), vol. II, p. 154.

3. G F Russel Barker and Alan H Steiving, *The Record of Old Westministers: A Biographical List of all those who are known to have been Educated at Westminster School from Earliest Times to 1927* (London, 1928), vol. I, p. 488.

4. Richard Arthur Austen-Leigh, *The Eton College Register, 1698–1752* (Eton, 1927), p. 184.

5. NA, ADM 6/86, f. 61.

6. Horatio Nelson, for example, was carried notarially for fourteen months on the muster books of HMS *Triumph* and was promoted to lieutenant while under age. Cf. NA, ADM 107/6, p.386.

7. Austen-Leigh, *Eton College Register*, 8. 184.

8. NA, ADM 36/2403, f. 78.

9. Cf. Austen-Leigh, *Eton College Register*, p. 184.

10. NA, ADM 51/888, 4 Sept. 1740.

11. NA, ADM 51/888, 31 Dec. 1740–30 June 1741.

12. Glyndwr Williams, ed., *Documents relating to Anson's Voyage round the World, 1740–1744* (London, 1967), pp. 88–95.

13. NA, ADM 51/888, 17 Dec. 1741, 31 Jan., 11 March, 6 May 1742.

14. *An Address to the Right Honourable the First Lord Commissioner of the Admiralty upon the Visible Decreasing Spirit, Splendour and Discipline of the Navy* (London, 1787), p. 7.

15. NA, ADM 36/435, f. 84.

16. NA, ADM 51/4133, 17 Dec. 1742.

17. NA, ADM 51/4133, 19–20 Feb. 1742.

18. NA, ADM 36/435, f. 188.

19. NA, ADM 36/4013, f. 123.

20. NA, ADM 36/4086, f. 98.

21. Captains Francis Holburne, William Lisle and Thomas Philpot.

22. *Regulations and Instructions relating to His Majesty's Service at Sea* (London, 1745), p. 15.

23. NA, ADM 6/86, f. 61.

24. Michael Lewis, *A Social History of the Navy, 1793–1815* (London, 1960), p. 163.

25. NA, ADM 6/86, p. 101.

26. Cf. Lewis, *Social History*, pp. 165–8.

27. NA, ADM 6/16, p. 525.

28. NA, ADM 6/16, p. 526.

29. NA, ADM 36/3042, f. 186; ADM 51/816, 7 Aug.–27 Oct. 1745.

30. NA, ADM 6/17, p. 17.

31. NA, ADM 2/65, pp. 373–4.

32. NA, ADM 1/2217, Noel to Corbett, 4 May 1746; ADM 51/80, 3–4 May 1746.

33. NA, ADM 6/17, p. 86.

34. NA, ADM 51/80, 16 July 1746.

35. Lewis, *Social History*, pp. 186–9.

36. David Syrett and R L DiNardo, *The Commissioned Sea Officers of the Royal Navy, 1660–1815* (Aldershot, Hants., 1994), pp. 2, 20, 223, 231, 252, 255, 384, 427.

37. Cf. Sedgwick, *History of Parliament*, vol. II, pp. 154–5.

38. NA, ADM 51/1005, 16 July 1746–2 Jan. 1747.

39. NA, ADM 2/69, p. 256.

40. NA, ADM 51/1005, 26 April–4 May 1747.

41. NA, ADM 1/1886, Howe to Corbett, 18 May 1747.

42. NA, ADM 6/17, p. 226.

43. NA, ADM 51/786, 19 May 1747–28 Oct. 1748.

44. NA, ADM 6/17, p. 484.

45. NA, ADM 3/27, July 1749.

46. NA, ADM 6/17, p. 543.

47. NA, ADM 2/74, pp. 111, 141–2.

48. NA, ADM 51/412, 3 April 1751–22 April 1752.

49. NA, ADM 1/1888, Howe to Clevland, 22 April 1752.

50. NA, ADM 6/18, p. 26. John Charnock, *Biographia Navalis: or, Impartial Memoirs of the Lives and Characters of Officers of the Royal Navy of Great Britain* (London, 1794–1798), vol. III, p. 548 mistakenly states that Howe in between commanding HMS *Glory* and HMS *Dolphin* served as captain of the *Mary* yacht. However, James Campbell was during this period captain of this ship. NA, ADM 51/3901.

51. NA, ADM 2/74, pp. 139–59.

52. NA, ADM 51/258, 24 Oct., 1 Nov., 4 Dec. 1752.

53. NA, ADM 1/1888, Proceedings with His Majesty's ship the Dolphin from 22nd day of September to the [ ]day of; ADM 1/1889, Howe to Clevland, 19 April, 10 May, 12 July 1754.

54. NA, ADM 51/258, 17 July, 29 Aug. 1754.

55. David Erskine, ed., *Augustus Harvey's Journal* (London, 1953), pp. 143, 147–8.

CHAPTER II

The Seven Years War

The Seven Years War for Richard Howe was one of the defining events of his life. Howe would fire the first shot at sea of the conflict and in 1759 his ship would lead the British squadron into Quiberon Bay to destroy the French fleet. In the course of the war Howe would show that he was not only a skilful and hard-driving captain, but also a capable and adroit commodore. By the end of the Seven Years War Howe would be a Member of Parliament, an acknowledged expert on the conduct of close blockades and amphibious operations, and considered to be one of the most promising members of the officer corps of the Royal Navy.

On 20 January 1755 Howe was appointed to command the newly-built 60-gun ship of the line HMS *Dunkirk*.[1] After fitting out, provisioning, and manning the ship at Chatham, Howe and HMS *Dunkirk* sailed for Spithead and then westward along the south coast of England arriving on 25 April at Plymouth. There Howe joined a squadron under the command of Vice Admiral the Hon. Edward Boscawen.[2] By this time, Britain and France were moving towards war. Fighting between British and French forces had begun months before in the wilderness of western Pennsylvania. Both Britain and France had responded to the clash of arms at Fort Necessity by reinforcing their troops in North America. In 1754 Britain had sent two regiments of infantry from Ireland under Major General James Braddock and in the spring of 1755 the French decided to counter the British in America by dispatching seventy-eight companies of infantry, carried in warships, to Canada. Learning of the French intentions, the British government, even though war had not yet been declared, decided to prevent the French from strengthening their position in Canada. A naval force, under the command of Boscawen, was dispatched from England to intercept the French ships carrying reinforcements in the western Atlantic before their arrival at Quebec.[3] On 27 April Boscawen sailed from Plymouth with a squadron of twelve warships,[4] including HMS *Dunkirk* to intercept the French reinforcements proceeding to Canada.

Boscawen's squadron arrived on the Grand Banks of Newfoundland in a scattered formation in conditions of limited visibility owing to periods of intermittent fog and haze. The British first gained intelligence of the French on 1 June when HMS *Dunkirk* intercepted three English fishing vessels, and the master of one of them told Howe that he had sighted, on 27 May, a French warship loaded with troops proceeding to the westward. The next day, 2 June, four French warships were sighted from Boscawen's flagship and were chased by the British. However, the French ships soon disappeared in the fog. The British continued to sail westward across the Grand Banks searching for the French ships. On the evening of 7 June Howe in HMS *Dunkirk* sighted and chased three strange sails which turned out to be three French merchant ships bound for Quebec. After releasing the French merchant ships, Howe and HMS *Dunkirk* rejoined the main body of Boscawen's squadron. That evening, just before dark, three French warships were sighted but they too escaped into the darkness before they could be intercepted. The next morning, 8 June, the French warships were again sighted to the north-west and the order was given to chase and intercept them. Just before noon, Howe in HMS *Dunkirk* overtook the sternmost of the French ships, the 64-gun *Alcide*, and demanded that the French vessel shorten her sails and heave to. When Boscawen observed that the French warships did not comply with Howe's demand, the admiral 'made the signal to engage'. HMS *Dunkirk* opened fire and fifteen minutes later, as other British warships approached the enemy vessel, the Alcide surrendered. British sailors found on board and plundered £7,600 in cash, though most of this money was later recovered by the British authorities. HMS *Dunkirk* lost in this action seven men killed and twenty-five wounded. Several hours later at 4pm the French ship of the line the *Lays* which was armed *enflute* and carrying troops, surrendered to HMS *Defiance* and HMS *Farqueur*. The third French warship, the *Dauphin Royal*, escaped.[5]

The capturing of the *Alcide* and *Lays* by Boscawen's squadron was the beginning of the Seven Years War at sea. Nevertheless, the Admiralty did not issue orders calling for the taking and destroying of all French ships and vessels encountered on the high seas until 27 August 1755[6] and war was not officially declared by Great Britain until 18 May 1756 when news of the French invasion of Minorca arrived in England.[7] For several weeks after the capture of the *Alcide* and *Lays*, Boscawen's ships searched without success the Grand Banks and the Gulf of St Lawrence for other French ships carrying reinforcements to North America.

Howe and HMS *Dunkirk* continued to operate in the Gulf of St Lawrence as a member of a squadron under the command of Boscawen during the summer of 1755 blockading the French fortress at Louisburg and hunting for French ships carrying military supplies and reinforcements to North America. There were few contacts with the enemy and the duty was for the most part uneventful.[8] On 19 October Howe sailed from Halifax, NS for England and after a stormy passage HMS *Dunkirk* on 14 November, arrived at St Helens.[9]

During the first months of 1756 Howe and *Dunkirk* served in the Channel Squadron under the command of Vice Admiral Edward Hawke. On 10 March 1756 *Dunkirk* sailed from Plymouth and for the next several weeks Howe, in company with other ships of Hawke's command, cruised in the Western Approaches of the English Channel and in the Bay of Biscay searching for French ships. During this wintry voyage no major French warships were encountered and on 8 May HMS *Dunkirk* arrived at Spithead.[10] Six days after she returned to England, the Admiralty ordered HMS *Dunkirk* to enter Portsmouth Dockyard to be cleaned, refitted and restored for Channel service.[11] While *Dunkirk* was in the dockyard, at the recommendation of Howe, 'the standing masts' of the ship were increased in length by five feet. This was just one of several alterations, made at Howe's instigation, in the masts, standing rigging, and sails of HMS *Dunkirk* designed to increase the speed and to improve the sailing characteristics of the vessel.[12] On 16 June a cleaned and refitted *Dunkirk* left Portsmouth Dockyard.[13] Whereupon Howe was placed in command of a small squadron based in the Channel Islands whose task was to protect those islands and to blockade the coasts of western Normandy and eastern Brittany from Cherbourg in the east to St Malo in the west.[14] Naval forces blockading this part of the French coast would not only have to operate off a lee shore, but also in a region known for its strong tidal currents and many submerged rocks and shoals. On 23 June 1756 Howe with his squadron,[15] escorting a convoy of transports carrying troops for the garrison of the Channel Islands, arrived at Guernsey to begin operations against the French.[16]

Howe, after undertaking a reconnaissance of the west coast of Normandy,[17] decided to mount an expedition to capture Grande Ile.[18] This island is the largest in a small archipelago, consisting of some fifty islets, known as the Iles Chausey, off the coast of Normandy, west of the small port of Granville. On 12 July Howe with several warships and five companies of troops from the garrison of Guernsey arrived off Grande Ile whereupon the fifty French troops on the island promptly surrendered without a fight. Grande Ile was captured by the British to be used as a base from which to blockade Granville and St Malo and from which to attack the French coastal shipping. However, upon inspection, Howe decided against the occupation for the island was of almost no economic value and would require a garrison of at least five hundred troops. After blowing up the fortifications on Grande Ile the British evacuated the place.[19]

With the evacuation of Grande Ile Howe deployed the ships of his squadron along the coast of France and in the Channel Islands.[20] The objective of this deployment was not only to protect the Channel Islands from attack, but also to disrupt French coastal trade and to blockade the ports of Granville and St Malo. At first Howe supervised the operations of the ships of his squadron from Guernsey, but in the middle of August he decided to go off to St Malo with HMS *Dunkirk* and 'to continue in that neighbourhood chiefly as the season and other circumstances will permit.'[21] The blockade of St Malo was especially important for the place was a known base for French privateers. Throughout the summer and into the autumn of 1756 the ships of Howe's command maintained a blockade of the west coast of Normandy and the area of Brittany around St Malo.[22] In September Howe in HMS *Dunkirk* went to Plymouth to obtain provisions, but only remained in that port for a few days before returning to the coast of France. Then on 13 October because of 'the season rendering the navigation near St Malo too dangerous for ships' Howe received orders to lift the blockade and to return to England.[23] During the summer of 1756 Howe not only gained command experience in the conduct of blockades, but also obtained first-hand knowledge of the geography of the coast of western Normandy and the area of Brittany around St Malo. This experience and information would prove to be of great value to him in future operations.

On 17 October 1756 Howe in HMS *Dunkirk* sailed from Plymouth as a member of a squadron under the command of Vice Admiral Knowles to cruise in the Western Approaches of the English Channel and the Bay of Biscay.[24] The objectives of this cruise, as with many others undertaken by the ships of the Royal Navy in the course of the naval wars of the 18th century, was to protect British trade from enemy attack, to capture enemy merchant shipping, and to take or destroy enemy warships and privateers. The results of these cruises were always problematic, for in the age before communications intelligence and aerial reconnaissance, the interception of an enemy ship on the high seas was largely a matter of luck. Because of this element of luck many of the cruises undertaken by the ships of the Royal Navy to the south-westward of the British Isles in search of the enemy were without result. Not only were the outcome of these cruises uncertain in terms of enemy vessels intercepted, but the warships undertaking them, especially during the winter months, were damaged often by adverse weather. On 19 December 1756 Howe, in company with three other warships,[25] was detached from Knowles' squadron to cruise between Cape Finisterre and The Lizard.[26] Several days later, on 24 December, Howe, after capturing a French transport carrying troops to Martinique, obtained intelligence that a French convoy was about to depart for the West Indies from Rochefort. As a result, Howe proceeded southward across the estimated track of the French convoy in an attempt to intercept it. On 4 January 1757 HMS *Lyme* running short of provisions, was detached and sent to England. Three days later HMS *Monmouth* and HMS *Vanguard* suffering from storm damage and a shortage of provisions, were also sent to England. Howe himself in HMS *Dunkirk* resolved to remain at sea searching for the French until his water and provisions ran out.[27] In an attempt to prolong the duration of the cruise Howe put into the Spanish port of Ferrol to obtain water. However, the Spanish authorities, citing Spain's 'strict neutrality' would permit Howe to take on board HMS *Dunkirk* only enough water for a voyage to England. On 8 February, therefore, *Dunkirk* anchored at Spithead.[28]

When Howe returned to England the Admiralty ordered HMS *Dunkirk* into Portsmouth Dockyard to be cleaned and refitted.[29] Once there, Howe successfully requested that the vessel be modified by the fitting of 'a false keel of 4 or 5 inches in depth' to prevent slippage to leeward when tacking.[30] When HMS *Dunkirk* had been cleaned, refitted and fitted with a false keel, she and Howe were placed under the command of the Hon. Captain George Edgcumbe of HMS *Lancaster* and the two warships were ordered to escort a number of East India ships out into the Atlantic some two hundred leagues to the westward of the Scilly Isles. When this mission was completed the two British warships were to cruise between Cape Clear and Ushant until their water and provisions were exhausted.[31] Howe and HMS *Dunkirk* sailed on 4 May 1757 from St Helens. This cruise was uneventful and they returned to England anchoring in Plymouth Sound on 19 June.[32]

While at sea cruising in the Western Approaches of the English Channel, Howe had been elected a member of the House of Commons for Dartmouth on 23 May 1757. Most of the voters of this borough were employed by the government and Howe, after being proposed to the corporation of the borough by the Duke of Newcastle, who managed Parliamentary elections for the ministry, and with the approval of the king was elected without opposition. Howe, who was a supporter of the government, because of the demands of service at sea during the Seven Years War, rarely attended the House of Commons and probably did not, during the entire course of the war, utter a word at Westminster. He would hold the seat until 20 April 1782 when he was raised to the English peerage.[33]

On 26 June 1757 HMS *Dunkirk* and Howe departed from Plymouth for Portsmouth arriving on 1 July. The next day Howe and his entire crew, on orders from the Admiralty, were discharged from *Dunkirk* and transferred into HMS *Magnanime*.[34] The French-built *Magnanime*, which had been captured by the British in 1748, was a 74-gun ship of the line and was reputed to be one of the fastest ships in the Royal Navy. When Howe took command the vessel was being fitted and stored for service.[35] Howe proposed to the Admiralty a number of what, for the time, were radical alterations to the ship's guns which were intended to improve the safety and rate of fire of the weapons. Howe wanted not only 'priming tubes' and 'flannel cartridges' issued to HMS *Magnanime* but also the cannon of the ship to be fitted with locks.[36] Priming tubes are goose-quills filled with gunpowder used to fire cannon instead of vents filled with loose gunpowder. Flannel cartridges after discharge leave little or no debris in the bore of a cannon and locks are mechanisms similar to those used to fire muskets and permit firing of cannon at a faster rate than those fired by matches. These alterations were not only designed to increase the effectiveness of *Magnanime*'s cannon, but also to reduce the number of casualties from accidental gunpowder explosions.[37] However, no action would be taken on these proposals at this time by the Admiralty, for they were about twenty years in advance of their time. It would not be until the last years of the American War that priming tubes, flannel cartridges and locks would come into general use within the Royal Navy.

The Admiralty assigned HMS *Magnanime*, after she was fitted and stored, to a squadron under the command of Admiral Sir Edward Hawke which was to undertake an amphibious attack on the French port of Rochefort on the coast of the Bay of Biscay.[38] On 8 September 1757 Howe and *Magnanime*, part of a force consisting of thirty warships including sixteen ships of the line and transports carrying 8,400 soldiers, sailed from Spithead for Rochefort.[39] The British force arrived off the Biscay coast of France on 20 September, but when Hawke ordered ships to enter Basque Road and to attack a French fort on the Isle of Aix the pilots, citing the hazards of navigation, refused to enter the area. Later Hawke would discover that even though the pilots 'made many baulks before we came in' Basque Road was 'a safe, spacious road in which the navy of England, merchant ships included, may ride without the least annoyance'. Three days later on 23 September on a flood tide, with Howe in HMS *Magnanime* leading the way, the British resumed the attack on the Isle of Aix. At 12 noon, as the British ships approached the island, the guns of the French fort opened fire. HMS *Magnanime* without firing a shot, drew within forty yards of the French fortification and then opened fire. Five minutes later HMS *Barfleur*, Captain Samuel Graves, also began to engage the French fort. After about forty-five minutes of bombardment the French surrendered. When the British took possession of Aix they found that the French fort was armed with eight large mortars and thirty cannon. Nevertheless, the attack on the French fort was not, as 18th-century battles go, a very bloody affair, for HMS *Magnanime* lost only two men killed and eleven wounded while the French garrison, which consisted of nearly six hundred men, suffered one man killed and seven or eight wounded.[40]

After the reduction of the French fort on Aix the British intended to continue the operation by making a landing on the French mainland with the objective of capturing the port of Rochefort. However, after holding two councils of war, it was decided that while a landing was possible, Rochefort itself could not be taken.[41] Having destroyed the fortifications on the Isle of Aix, the expedition returned to England arriving on 8 October at Spithead.[42]

On arrival the commanders of the expeditionary force were condemned for their indecision and incompetence. In this great wave of condemnation all the obstacles to a successful attack on Rochefort, such as shoal water and French fortifications, were overlooked and all that was seen was that the senior officers and commanders of the expedition appeared at best to have been timid and hesitant. Only Howe and Lieutenant Colonel James Wolfe had advocated continuing the operation after the surrender of Aix. According to one historian, 'had Wolfe and Howe been in control, one may affirm that had there been a failure it would at least have shed some glory on the English army and navy – and there might have been success.'[43] Howe, because of his actions, especially placing HMS *Magnanime* alongside the fort on the Isle of Aix and then blasting it into submission, was the only person on the expedition to Rochefort who appeared to be a skilful and determined commander.

After returning from the Bay of Biscay Howe requested, in order to increase the speed of the vessel, that HMS *Magnanime*'s sails be altered and that the ship's mainmast be lengthened and 'moved to the distance of about 4 or 6 feet further aft'.[44] However, before this suggestion could be acted upon, Howe and *Magnanime* were ordered to proceed to sea and to cruise in the Western Approaches of the English Channel and the Bay of Biscay.[45] Sailing from Spithead on 8 November, and arriving on his assigned station to the westward of the Bay of Biscay on 12 December, the cruise was uneventful until 30 December when Howe captured a French merchant ship. From this vessel Howe obtained intelligence that a French convoy of twenty-five merchant ships, escorted by seven warships, had sailed from St Domingo in the West Indies, on 13 November, for France. The merchant ship which Howe captured had separated from this convoy on 14 December. Upon receipt of this intelligence Howe in HMS *Magnanime* cruised, between 47°N and 49°N, in an attempt to intercept the French ships as they entered the Bay of Biscay until 8 January 1758, when with provisions running short, he was forced to return to England.[46]

Howe and *Magnanime* arrived at Plymouth on 18 January 1758. While his ship was at Plymouth Howe went to Tamerton in Devon and, on 10 March 1758, married Mary Hartopp. Howe's wife was the daughter of Chiverton Hartopp of Welby in Leicestershire. Three daughters – Sophia Charlotte, Maria Juliana and Louisa Charlotte – would result from this union.[47] On 16 April Howe and *Magnanime* sailed from Plymouth for Portsmouth and arrived at Spithead. The ship was to be refitted and restored at Portsmouth Dockyard,[48] and Howe had requested not only that the main mast be moved aft but also that the ship's 'foremast likewise [be] moved aft, from two to three feet or in any more convenient purport'.[49] While HMS *Magnanime* was being refitted and restored at Portsmouth Dockyard, the British government was formulating strategy for the conduct of the war during the 1758 campaigning season. A major element of British operations against the French in 1758 would be a series of raids conducted by British forces against the coasts of France with the objective of drawing French military forces away from Germany. William

Pitt, Secretary of State for the Southern Department, was the driving force behind British strategy in 1758 and he assumed over-all direction of the forces which would conduct the raids on the French coast. The military forces would be commanded by Lieutenant General the 3rd Duke of Marlborough with Major General Lord George Sackville as second in command. The ships of the Channel Fleet would provide distant protection to the raiding forces by blockading French naval bases in Brittany. Howe would be in command of the naval forces – warships and transports – deployed directly in support of the raiding forces.[50]

Howe was chosen to command the naval forces during the raids on the French coast probably because of the knowledge he had gained of the coasts of Normandy and the region around St Malo during 1756 and because he was the only officer to distinguish himself during the abortive raid in 1757 on Rochefort. While conducting raiding operations on the coast of France in 1758 Howe would not be under the control of the Admiralty, but rather would be directly under the command of William Pitt.[51] These arrangements, which were insisted upon by the government, were designed to enable Pitt to closely control and direct the British forces raiding the French coast. These command arrangements would cause a minor command crisis in the Royal Navy. Admiral Hawke, when confronted by Howe with orders to conduct landings of troops on the French coast, completely misunderstood the situation thinking it was a slight to his professional honour. The admiral wrongly concluded that he was being passed over by a junior officer because of the failure of the raid on Rochefort. Hawke, when Howe presented himself and his orders, refused to give the junior officer an account of the 'state of the ships I am to command'. Howe concluded from this action that Hawke was 'a good deal offended at the transports being put under my directions'. When reporting Hawke's actions to the Admiralty Howe assured their lordships that he would not make 'public mention of the incident'.[52] Hawke then, without orders and in a fluster, hauled down his flag as commander of the Channel Squadron, came ashore and remained there for the rest of 1758 whilst Anson, the First Lord of the Admiralty, then became the commander of the Channel Squadron.[53] According to Howe: 'The sudden and unexpected disappearance' of Hawke from the Channel Squadron caused 'much speculation to the *Junior officers*.' However, the uproar quickly died down with the appointment of Anson to the command of the Channel Squadron. Howe was now seen by many not as a usurper of Hawke, but rather as an agent of the First Lord of the Admiralty whose function was to settle details such as signals.[54]

The plan which emerged from the councils of government in May of 1758 called for a landing to be made in the vicinity of St Malo on the north-east coast of Brittany. It was realised by the British government that a direct assault on St Malo might be impossible for the place was heavily fortified and located on a peninsula connected to the mainland by a causeway. If St Malo could not be captured then the town might be forced to surrender by blockade and bombardment. Even if St Malo could not be captured the British might burn the place to the ground by throwing hot shot and carcass into it, destroy the shipping, and then ravage the surrounding countryside. The objective was not necessarily to occupy or capture St Malo but rather to cause a 'diversion of forces of the enemy' getting the French to assemble an army to drive away the British attackers. When the French appeared in overpowering numbers it was the British intention to re-embark their army and then to renew the attack on another French coastal region. The British intended to carry this scheme into effect by employing an army of more than 10,000 troops – fifteen regiments of foot[55] plus attached units of artillery and cavalry – embarked on thirty-two transports escorted by twenty-four warships ranging in size from ships of the line to bomb ketches.[56] It would be Howe's task to command the warships as well as the transports carrying the troops to France. When the British force arrived off St Malo Howe would then have to supervise the landing of the army on the coast of France, support the operations of the army ashore, and then re-embark the king's troops.

On 9 May 1758 Howe was ordered to take command of the squadron of ships to be employed on the raid against St Malo and was directed to hoist a commodore's broad pendant.[57] During the operations along the French coast Howe would temporarily relinquish command of HMS *Magnanime* which was considered too large a vessel for coastal raiding, and hoist his broad pendant on board the 64-gun ship of the line HMS *Essex*.[58] The squadron placed under Howe's command consisted of four ships of the line, nine frigates, four sloops, two fireships, and two bomb ketches.[59] The warships of the expedition assembled, along with the transports for the conveyance of the troops, during the first weeks of May at Spithead, whilst the troops were embarked on transports, from the Isle of Wight, during the last week of May.[60]

No established doctrine or standard operating procedures for the conduct of amphibious operations existed within the Royal Navy before May of 1758. In the War of the Austrian Succession the British conducted a number of landing operations, such as those at Cartagena in 1742 and the botched operation at Lorient in 1746, but no body of doctrine had emerged from these operations.[61] Further, the attempted raid on Rochefort in 1757 was a model of how not to conduct a combined operation. While at Spithead, as the warships and transports were assembling, Howe formulated, wrote out, and issued a stream of orders and directives covering subjects such as the embarkation of troops, signals and directions for maintaining the chain of command of the army when embarked on transports, and the regulations for the conduct of transports while at sea and at anchor. Then, during the course of operations along the French coast,

Howe periodically issued further directives and orders setting forth the measures necessary for the disembarkation, landing and re-embarkation of troops on hostile shores.[62] The intent of Howe's directives and orders was to be able to exercise effective command and control not only of the warships under his command during amphibious operations, but also to enable the Royal Navy to land the British army on enemy-held coasts. Howe's efforts formed the doctrinal basis for the conduct of amphibious operations by the Royal Navy during the Age of Sail.[63]

Not only did Howe issue all the necessary directives for the conduct of amphibious operations, but the officers and men of his squadron also had to master the use of a new type of boat to be used. Before 1758 troops involved in landing operations were carried ashore in ships' boats. The landing operations on the coast of France in 1758 would see the introduction to service of new, specially constructed landing craft known as flat-bottomed boats. There were two types.

The larger type was 36 feet long, 10 feet 2 inches in width, 2 feet 11 inches in depth amidships between keel and gunwale and was equipped with thole pins, oars and thwarts for twenty oarsmen. The smaller version was 30 feet long, 9 feet 9 inches wide, 2 feet 11 inches deep amidships and was fitted for sixteen oarsmen. Except for size and number of oarsmen, both types were essentially alike: flat-bottomed, clinker-built, with bluff bows, and steered by a detachable rudder and tiller. Two rig bolts were mounted on the keel inside each craft to hoist the boat in and out of the water. Each flat-bottomed boat was equipped with the requisite number of oars, a 40-pound grapnel, a mast, a yard, a lugsail and all the necessary sheets, lines and halyards. A half company of infantry could be embarked in each flat-bottomed boat and the boats were carried to the site of an amphibious operation on the deck of either a warship or transport.[64] According to Robert Beatson, flat-bottomed boats were developed after the raid on Rochefort, for the need of a proper landing craft was one of the lessons learned by the British from that operation.[65] It is also alleged that Howe played a role in the designing of the first flat-bottomed boats.[66] However, what little evidence there is points to a Navy Board design and then construction by private boat builders. The use of flat-bottomed boats to embark the troops on board transports from the Isle of Wight in May of 1758 was the first time that the Royal Navy employed flat-bottomed boats before the assault landing at St Malo.[67]

On 1 June the ships under Howe's command sailed from Spithead for St Malo.[68] While passing between the islands of Sark and Jersey in the Channel Islands, the transport *Richard and Ann* was lost when the vessel ran on to a rock. The transport bulged and after the troops and their equipment were transferred to another vessel, the fleet passed on through the Channel Islands arriving on 5 June at Cancale Bay to the west of St Malo on the north coast of Brittany. That evening British infantry, in flat-bottomed boats supported by warships of the Royal Navy, landed on the coast of France. The only opposition came from a small battery located to the west of the landing area. Three British seamen on HMS *Success* were killed by enemy fire as the French opposition was overpowered by naval gunfire. The next day the army's horses and artillery were landed. The British then marched on St Malo.[69] However, the town was found to be too strong to be captured without a siege and the British had to content themselves with burning the shipping at the small port of St Servan and sending reconnaissance forces eastward towards Dol. News of the approach of strong French forces convinced Marlborough that it would be prudent to withdraw.[70] On 11 and 12 June the army was re-embarked at Cancale Bay.[71] The amphibious aspects of the attack on St Malo – the landing and re-embarkation of the army at Cancale Bay – were conducted almost without a fault, vindicating all Howe's planning for the conduct of amphibious operations.

The fleet was held at Cancale Bay by bad weather until 21 June when the British force sailed northward along the west coast of Normandy passing Granville, and then the island of Jersey, to arrive off Cape La Haque on 24 June. The British ships then rounded the Cotontin Peninsula, passing the port of Cherbourg and entering the Bay of Seine to threaten Le Havre, before returning to Cherbourg.[72] On 29 June it was decided to attempt to capture Cherbourg. Troops were placed in flat-bottomed boats, but owing to bad weather the operation was called off at the last minute, as was another attempt on 3 July. The commander of the army, the Duke of Marlborough, citing shortages of water, provisions and forage, vetoed further operations against Cherbourg and demanded that the force return to England.[73] Howe and the ships of the expedition then returned to St Helens.[74]

It is true that bad weather had hampered operations since the re-embarkation at Cancale, and a shortage of supplies had brought about the return of the expedition to England. However, it is also clear that the commanders of the troops did not have their hearts in coastal raiding. Both Marlborough and Sackville wished to be transferred to the British army in Germany. According to one observer Sackville was tired of what he called 'buccaneering'.[75] Further, Howe and Sackville apparently did not get on, and according to Horace Walpole, Howe 'expressed strong aversion' to Sackville and refused even to answer the general's questions.[76]

When the expedition returned to Spithead the troops were landed on the Isle of Wight and Howe went to London to consult with William Pitt and other members of the government. The landing at St Malo and the failure to land at Cherbourg had shown the army, Marlborough and Sackville to be at best indecisive.[77] Nevertheless, the government, and especially William Pitt, had concluded that the raiding campaign had been successful in the respect that large areas of France had been threatened.

The government wished to continue the campaign by next attacking, capturing and destroying the port of Cherbourg. For the attack on Cherbourg the command structure of the force was altered when Marlborough and Sackville, using influence at court, got themselves appointed respectively commander and second in command of the British army in Germany. Ironically within a year Marlborough would be dead and Sackville would be cashiered in disgrace from the army. Lieutenant General Thomas Bligh, who had been displaced by Marlborough as commander of the British army in Germany, became general and commander in chief of the troops to be employed on the French coast. Bligh, at 74 years of age, was a little old to begin a career in coastal raiding. However, Britain in 1758 was not overflowing with military talent and Howe found that he could, unlike in the case of Sackville, work with the general.[78] After spending several days in London Howe returned to Spithead to prepare for the attack on Cherbourg.[79]

Shortly after his arrival at Spithead, Howe was informed that Prince Edward would serve on board his flagship as a volunteer during the attack on Cherbourg.[80] Prince Edward (Edward Augustus, Duke of York and Albany) was the grandson of George II and the younger brother of George III. To Howe, being entrusted with the health and safety of a royal prince was a sign of royal favour and approbation. The prestige acquired by Howe from such an event as this, while almost incomprehensible to the 21st-century man, was valuable beyond measure to a member of the governing elite of Hanoverian England.

On 25 July the embarkation of the troops from the Isle of Wight was completed, and five days later, on 30 July, Howe commanding twenty-three warships, escorting sixty-three transports carrying 10,925 troops, sailed from Spithead. Encountering adverse winds in the English Channel the British did not arrive off Cherbourg until 6 August. That same day, under the direction of Howe and supported by naval gunfire, British troops were landed to the west of the city.

The next day, with horses and artillery ashore, the British army marched on Cherbourg which surrendered without a fight upon the approach of the British. Then, after the surrender Howe moved his squadron and the transports into Cherbourg Road and for the next week the British, methodically destroyed everything of value in the city. Twenty-seven ships, warehouses, magazines and fortifications were destroyed. British military engineers even wrecked the stonemasonry of Cherbourg's bastion and jetties. Then on 16 August, before the French could assemble the forces to mount an attack to retake Cherbourg, the British troops re-embarked leaving behind a shattered city.[81]

With the evacuation of Cherbourg it was next the intention of the British to attack St Malo. However, the 'tempestuous appearance of the weather' induced Howe to proceed to Portland Road. On 21 August the force again sailed for the coast of France, but several days later, off Guernsey, due to damage caused to the ships by high winds, Howe decided to return to Portland Road where the British ships anchored on 25 August.[82] It was probably while at Portland Road that Howe learned of the death of his older brother. George Augustus, 3rd Viscount Howe, an officer in the British army, was killed in action on 6 July 1758 near Fort Ticonderoga in America. To the American troops Brigadier Lord Howe was one of the most popular of the British officers serving in America and the Great and General Court of Massachusetts Bay would erect a monument to him at Westminster Abbey.[83] George Augustus Howe died without issue and his Irish peerage passed to his younger brother Richard, who became the 4th Viscount Howe of the Kingdom of Ireland.[84]

The death of George Augustus Howe invariably raised the question of who was going to succeed to his vacated seat for Nottingham in the House of Commons. The Parliamentary fixer and intriguer the Duke of Newcastle, upon learning of George Augustus Howe's death, immediately wrote to Commodore Richard Howe, now styled Lord Howe, at Portland Road and suggested that the commodore resign his seat at Dartmouth and then run for the vacant seat at Nottingham. If Howe embraced this scheme Newcastle would use all the influence at his command to ensure that the commodore would win the seat at Nottingham.[85] What Newcastle was attempting to do was not assist Howe, but rather obtain a seat in the House of Commons for John Plumptre whose family was a long-time ally of Newcastle's in Nottinghamshire politics. In its simplest form Newcastle's plan called for Howe to resign his seat at Dartmouth to run for election at Nottingham and then for Plumptre to replace Howe in the government-controlled seat at Dartmouth. What Newcastle had not reckoned on was Howe's mother, the dowager Countess Howe, who did not care about Newcastle's schemes, and desired two sons, not one, in the House of Commons.[86] Richard Howe wrote to Newcastle by return post declining his proposal.[87] And then his mother, employing the considerable Howe influence in Nottingham, reached an agreement with the corporation of the borough whereby Richard Howe's younger brother William was elected a member of the House of Commons for Nottingham.[88]

On 31 August the expedition sailed from Portland Road, with a north-east wind, for the coast of France.[89] There has been speculation, among both contemporaries and historians, over the choice by Howe and Bligh of St Malo as a target. By the terms of their instructions from the British government, Howe and Bligh had to pick an objective on the coast of Normandy or the north shore of the Breton Peninsula. With the wind blowing out of the north any objective to the east of Cherbourg, in the Bay of Seine, would require that Howe's ships beat to windward up the English Channel. Conversely, the only place worth attacking on the west coast of Normandy and to the west along the Breton shore was St Malo.

An added advantage of St Malo as objective was the fact that Howe was familiar with the geography of the region.[90]

On 3 September the expedition arrived off St Malo. The next day, in rough seas and rain, British troops landed without opposition at St Lunaire Bay several miles to the west of the town.[91] Apparently it was the intention of the British, after landing at St Lunaire Bay, to move troops by flat-bottomed boats eastward across the Rade de Rance to occupy the village of St Servan, and then use it as a base for mounting an attack on St Malo. However, from the beginning this scheme collapsed. The movement eastward to St Servan was found to be impossible, and bad weather forced Howe to move the anchorage of the fleet and transports nine miles west to the Bay of St Cast. Instead of marching for St Cast and re-embarking when things began to go wrong, Bligh, at first encountering little resistance and perhaps over-confident, delayed, thereby giving the French time to assemble forces to oppose the re-embarkation of the army. On the morning of 11 September most of the British troops were re-embarked without undue problems. However, the French heavily attacked the British rearguard as the troops were entering the flat-bottomed boats. Howe transferred his broad pendant to the frigate HMS *Pallas* in order to personally supervise the frigates and other small warships providing gunfire support for the re-embarkation. However, the operation was a disaster, for the French almost annihilated the British rearguard. Bligh's army lost several hundred – estimates vary between five and seven hundred – officers and men killed, wounded and captured. During the evacuation from St Cast the Royal Navy lost thirty-two officers and men from all causes. All four captains[92] who were supervising the embarkation of the troops into flat-bottomed boats were captured. By noon on 11 September all the men possible had been lifted off the beach at St Cast. Bad weather then held the British ships on the coast of France and it was not until 19 September that the force arrived at Spithead.[93]

When news of the bloody embarkation of the army at St Cast arrived in London there was much criticism of the second raid on St Malo. As was the case with the first, much of the criticism of the conduct of the second raid was directed not at Howe and the navy, but rather at the army and its leaders. Howe and the navy were perceived for the most part to have saved the army from its own poor leadership in the person of Bligh.[94] While there were a numbers of errors of omission and commission committed by both of the commanders on the second St Malo raid, Howe actually emerged from the operation with an increased reputation as a skilful and forceful commander who had taken risks to rescue the army from a hostile shore. More importantly, Howe, during the coastal raiding campaign of 1758, showed himself to be not only skilled at the exercise of command, but also, in an age before staff officers, capable of conceptualising and then formulating all the orders and directives required for the successful conduct of amphibious operations.

When the expedition to St Malo anchored at Spithead, the troops were landed on the Isle of Wight and Howe's ships were re-provisioned for three months' further service.[95] However, in the midst of all the uproar over the second raid on St Malo, the government's desire for additional raids on the coast of France was waning.[96] Several months later on 13 December 1758 Howe was ordered to lower his commodore's broad pendant on board HMS *Essex* and to return to the command of HMS *Magnanime*.[97]

The year 1759, known to the British as the year of victories, was the climax of the Seven Years War. The British were victorious in a series of battles – Mindon, Lagos, Quebec, Quiberon Bay – which ended the French threat to Hanover, destroyed French colonial rule in Canada, and smashed the French navy. Howe, as one of Admiral Sir Edward Hawke's captains, would take part in the campaign of 1759 and then play a conspicuous role in the Battle of Quiberon Bay in which the French navy would be decisively defeated.

On 9 May 1759 Howe and HMS *Magnanime* were ordered to join the Channel Squadron under the command of Admiral Sir Edward Hawke.[98] As a member of Hawke's squadron, Howe in HMS *Magnanime* would take part in the almost continuous close blockade of the French fleet at Brest during the summer and autumn of 1759. In good and bad weather, *Magnanime* and the other ships of Hawke's command would remain for weeks at a time on station off the eastern end of the Breton Peninsula. At times westerly winds would threaten to drive the ships on to the rock-bound coast of Brittany and at other times the weather would force the British ships to seek shelter in Torbay. The crews of the British ships, even though the vessels were re-supplied at sea, suffered greatly from scurvy and other ills which afflicted seamen who remained constantly at sea. When a ship was worn out by the elements and constant service, she would be replaced before Brest by another vessel while being repaired in the dockyard at Plymouth before again rejoining Hawke's squadron. Week after week Hawke's squadron maintained station off Brest watching the enemy and waiting for the French to sail out of their fortified harbour to give battle. As the weeks turned into months of constant watching and waiting, tension among the British mounted almost to breaking point for it was not fore-ordained that the French would actually leave Brest.[99]

Howe and HMS *Magnanime*, during the summer and autumn of 1759, took part in the close blockade of Brest, operating off Ushant on the southern coast of Brittany, and occasionally running northward across the English Channel to Torbay. Howe, along with all the other captains of Hawke's squadron, had to contend with his share of westerly winds on a lee shore and with all the health problems associated with spending prolonged periods of time at sea. Finally, on 2 October 1759, after months of blockade duty off Brest because of the great wear and tear on his ship from the elements, Howe was forced to put HMS *Magnanime* into Plymouth Dockyard for repairs.[100]

On 12 November Howe, in a repaired and refitted HMS *Magnanime*, rejoined Hawke's squadron.[101] Two days later Hawke's squadron, including Howe in *Magnanime* sailed from Torbay to again take up the blockading station off Brest. On 16 November, off the western end of Brittany, Hawke learned from a British victualler, the *Love and Unity* that the French fleet was at last at sea. The master of the victualler informed Hawke that HMS *Juno*, on 15 November, had sighted eighteen French ships of the line and three frigates twenty-four leagues north-west of the Belle Ile steering east. From this information Hawke deduced that the French ships were proceeding to Quiberon Bay on the southern coast of Brittany and the British admiral immediately set off in pursuit of the French.[102]

As the British force approached the southern coast of Brittany from the north-west in the early hours of 20 November, Howe was ordered to range ahead of the main body of Hawke's squadron as HMS *Magnanime*, newly out of the dockyard, was one of the fastest ships in the Royal Navy. At 8am Howe sighted the French fleet, steering to the south-east towards the entrance to Quiberon Bay. Hawke's assumption that the French fleet would be found off the Morbihan coast was correct. When the sighting of the French ships was reported to the British admiral, Hawke made the signal for a general chase. The British ships were in a loose line abreast formation with Howe in HMS *Magnanime* ahead of the main body of the British squadron. Howe's ship being the closest to the enemy resulted in *Magnanime* leading the British attack.

The French, upon sighting the British to the north-west, steered to the south-east in an attempt to escape into the safety of the shoals and rocks of Quiberon Bay, believing that the British because of the navigational difficulties would not follow them. In heavy seas with 'fresh gales' the British ships led by Howe in *Magnanime* chased the French to the south-east attempting to bring the enemy to an action before they could gain the shelter of the French coast. At noon with Belle Ile bearing east Hawke made the signal for 'Every ship to Engage the Enemy as they come up'. Howe in HMS *Magnanime* in preparation for battle threw overboard not only a number of hen coops, but also the ship's launch. At 2:30pm as the French ships, in heavy seas with a gale blowing, were passing between the Cardinals and Four Shoals at the entrance of Quiberon Bay, Howe in *Magnanime*, followed by the other British ships, overtook the stern-most of the enemy ships.

When the chase ended the British and French ships, in conditions of heavy seas and decreasing daylight, engaged in a confused pitched battle within the shoals and rock-strewn waters of Quiberon Bay. Two French ships – *Thésée* and *Superbe* – sank while under attack and a third, the *Héros* struck to Howe. However, because of the confusion of battle, heavy seas and growing darkness, the British could not board the *Héros* and accept the surrender. Rather, HMS *Magnanime* had to anchor after being forced to leeward as HMS *Warspite* and HMS *Montagu* crashed into her. The

Battle of Quiberon Bay ended for Howe in the early evening when HMS *Magnanime* anchored about three miles off the Ile Dumet. All through the night distress signals could be heard over the noise of the sea, but it was not until daylight the next morning that Howe discovered just what had happened to the ships of the British and French fleets. The majority of the British squadron, along with HMS *Magnanime* were anchored off the Ile Dumet. Eight French warships could be seen inshore of the British ships anchored in the Vilaine river. Six French ships of the line were lost during the battle.[103] Eight other French ships of the line had escaped out to sea and would later seek shelter in Basque Road and Rochefort. And the *Juste* after escaping to sea, would be lost with all hands while attempting to enter the Loire river. The British lost two ships[104] wrecked on shore and several hundred men killed and wounded. HMS *Magnanime*, whose rigging was badly shot up and damaged, had one of the largest casualty lists among the British ships with thirteen men killed and sixty-six wounded. The Battle of Quiberon Bay ended all attempts by the French to challenge British power at sea for the remainder of the Seven Years War.[105]

Several days after the Battle of Quiberon Bay Howe was sent ashore to negotiate an exchange of prisoners with the French.[106] During the course of the discussions the Duc d'Aiguillon, the governor of Brittany, made what appeared to Howe to be a proposal for a separate peace between Great Britain and France without reference to the Empress of Austria. At the same time it was hinted by the French that Howe would be a proper intermediary between William Pitt and the Duc d'Aiguillon for peace negotiations. Hawke thought it best in these circumstances to send Howe to England with news of the French overture.[107] On 26 December Howe in HMS *Magnanime* arrived at Spithead.[108]

The naval war in European seas, after the Battle of Quiberon Bay, consisted for the most part of operations – cruising, blockade duty and escort work – designed to protect British trade from enemy attack and to keep the remnants of the French fleet penned up in Biscay ports. During the last years of the Seven Years War, because of the slow tempo of naval operations, Howe was able for the first time in his career as a navy officer to spend considerable periods of time ashore. Returning to England at the end of 1759 after the Battle of Quiberon Bay, he took an extended period of leave remaining ashore for several months.[109] At the beginning of 1760 Howe was made a colonel of the marines which was a sinecure worth £500 per year.[110] He did not return to active duty until the late summer of 1760 when he undertook a series of voyages in the Western Approaches of the English Channel and the Western Bay of Biscay to protect British trade and to hunt enemy commerce raiders. From the autumn of 1760 Howe, in command of HMS *Magnanime* continually cruised off Ushant, the Isles of Scilly, and to the westward of the Bay of Biscay. Occasionally the vessel would put into Plymouth, Torbay or Spithead for provisions, water and minor repairs. The objective of these cruises, which were for the most part uneventful, was to protect British trade and to suppress enemy commerce raiders. At the end of November 1761, because of the need to refit and repair the vessel after more than a year of almost continuous service at sea, HMS *Magnanime* entered Plymouth Dockyard.[111]

On 9 February 1762 HMS *Magnanime* completed her refit and left the dockyard at Plymouth.[112] Several days later the Admiralty ordered Howe to hoist his broad pendant as a commodore on board HMS *Magnanime* and to assume the command of the squadron of British ships stationed in Basque Road on the east coast of France.[113] The primary task of the British squadron in Basque Road was to blockade the remnants of the French fleet which had taken refuge in the Charente river after the Battle of Quiberon Bay. Intelligence reports placed the strength of the French forces in the Charente at three ships of the line, two frigates and a number of smaller vessels.[114] To contain this weak French force the British maintained a powerful squadron in Basque Road. For example, on 23 March 1762 the British squadron in Basque Road consisted of twelve warships.[115] Howe in HMS *Magnanime* arrived in Basque Road on 2 March to assume command of the king's ships operating in the region.[116]

Obviously the French threat to the British squadron in Basque Road was not very great given the difference in strength and numbers of the two forces. Nevertheless, always in the back of Howe's mind during the period he was in command at Basque Road was the possibility that the French might somehow manage to take a British warship by a surprise boarding from small craft or destroy a British vessel by means of fireships. Accordingly Howe gave all his ships' captains very detailed instructions regarding the stationing of guard boats and the like while in Basque Road.[117] Also, considerable sums of money and much effort was expended to obtain intelligence of French and Spanish intentions and capabilities, not only in the Basque Road region, but also along the entire coast of the Bay of Biscay.[118] However, Howe was in command of the squadron in Basque Road for only a few weeks before being recalled to England. On 19 May, at Spithead, Howe was ordered to lower his broad pendant.[119]

On 19 June 1762 Howe was placed in command of the ship of the line HMS *Princess Amelia* and a direct exchange of officers took place between *Magnanime* and *Princess Amelia*.[120] Howe was placed in command of HMS *Princess Amelia* in order that Prince Edward, the Duke of York and Albany, could fly his flag as a rear admiral from the ship. It was apparently at Howe's request that he was placed in command of the ship flying the flag of Prince Edward.[121] That Howe was given this command was a sign of royal approbation and considered to be a great honour. How long Prince Edward remained on board HMS *Princess Amelia* is not clear. But the Seven Years War was almost over and on 31 December 1762 Howe was ordered to pay off *Princess Amelia* and come ashore.[122]

Notes

1. NA, ADM 6/18, p. 122.

2. NA, ADM 51/278, 1, 17 March; 23, 25 April 1755.

3. Lawrence Henry Gipson, *The British Empire before the American Revolution. The Great War for Empire: The Years of Defeat, 1754–1757* (New York, 1958–1970), vol. VI, pp. 62, 103.

4. *Torbay, Monarch, Dunkirk, Somerset, Northumberland, Mars, Farqueur, Anson, Defiance, Nottingham, Litchfield*, 50-gun; and *Hornet* sloop NA, SP 42/37, List of HM Ships in Commission under Boscawen, 5 May 1755.

5. NA, ADM 1/481, ff. 37–8; ADM 51/287, 1–9 June 1755.

6. NA, ADM 2/75, p. 358.

7. Gipson, *The Great War for Empire: The Years of Defeat*, vol VI, p. 416.

8. NA, ADM 1/481, ff. 41, 43; ADM 51/287, July–Oct. 1755.

9. NA, ADM 1/1890, Howe to Clevland, 15 Nov. 1755.

10. NA, ADM 1/89, Hawke to Clevland, 12 March, 18, 27 April 1756; Ruddock F Mackay ed., *The Hawke Papers* (Aldershot, Hants, 1990), pp. 114, 129–32.

11. NA, ADM 2/76, pp. 430–1.

12. NA, ADM 1/1890, Howe to Clevland, 21 Dec. 1755; ADM 1/1891, Howe to Clevland, 17 May 1756.

13. NA, ADM 51/278, 16 June 1756.

14. NA, ADM 2/76, pp. 542–3.

15. *Dunkirk, Rochester, Ludlow Castle, Deal Castle, Queenborough, Dover, Happy* and *Ferret*.

16. NA, ADM 1/1891, Howe to Clevland, 26 June 1756.

17. NA, ADM 51/287, 5 July 1756.

18. NA, ADM 1/1891, Howe to Clevland, 8 July 1756.

19. NA, ADM 1/1891, Howe to Clevland, 8, 13 July 1756.

20. NA, ADM 1/1891, Howe to Clevland, 13 July 1756.

21. NA, ADM 1/1891, Howe to Clevland, 15 Aug. 1756.

22. Cf. NA, ADM 51/287, July–Oct. 1756.

23. NA, ADM 1/1891, Howe to Clevland, 5 Sept., 13 Oct. 1756.

24. NA, ADM 51/287, 17 Oct. 1756.

25. *Vanguard, Monmouth, Lyme*.

26. NA, ADM 1/1892, Proceedings with the ships of the squadron left by Vice Admiral Knowles on the Western Stations from 19 December 1756 to 3 January 1757.

27. NA, ADM 1/1892, Howe to Clevland, 3, 4, 7 Jan. 1757.

28. NA, ADM 1/1982, Howe to Clevland, 8 Feb. 1757.

29. NA, ADM 2/78, p. 70.

30. NA, ADM 1/1892, Howe to Clevland, 23 Feb. 1757.

31. NA, ADM 2/78, p. 233.

32. NA, ADM 51/287, 4 May–19 June 1757.

33. Sir Lewis Namier and John Brooke, *The History of Parliament: The House of Commons, 1754–1790* (London, 1964), vol. II, p. 647.

34. NA, ADM 51/287, 26 June–2 July 1757.

35. NA, ADM 51/3895, 3 July 1757.

36. NA, ADM 1/1892, Howe to Clevland, 16 Aug. 1757.

37. Cf. Christopher Lloyd, ed., *The Health of Seamen* (London, 1965), pp. 173–4.

38. NA, ADM 2/79, pp. 138–9.

39. NA, ADM 51/3895, 8 Sept. 1757.

40. Mackay, *The Hawke Papers*, pp. 170–82.

41. Gipson, *The Great War for Empire: The Victorious Years*, vol. VII, p. 124.

42. NA, ADM 51/3895, 30 Sept., 8 Oct. 1757.

43. Gipson, *The Great War for Empire: The Years of Victory*, vol. VII, p. 124.

44. NA, ADM 1/1892, Howe to Clevland, 10 Oct. 1757.

45. NA, ADM 2/79, p. 317.

46. NA, ADM 1/1893, Howe to Clevland, 18 Jan. 1758.

47. *Complete Peerage* (Gloucester, 1987 reprint), vol. 2, no. 600.

48. NA, ADM 51/3895, 16, 18 April 1758.

49. NA, ADM 1/1893, Howe to Clevland, 27 Jan. 1758.

50. Gipson, *The Great War for Empire: The Years of Victory* , vol. VII, pp. 132–3.

51. NA, ADM 2/1331, p. 259.

52. NA, ADM 1/1893, Howe to Clevland, 11 May 1758.

53. Mackay, *The Hawke Papers*, pp. 191–2, 202–4.

54. NA, ADM 1/1893, Howe to Clevland, undated.

55. 1st, 2nd, 3rd Battalions of Guards and 5th, 20th, 23rd, 24th, 25th, 30th, 33rd, 34th, 36th, 67th, 68th, 72nd Regiments of Foot.

56. William Kent Hackman, *English Military Expeditions to the Coast of France, 1757–1761* (unpublished University of Michigan PhD dissertation, 1969), pp. 80–2, 85, 97.

57. NA, ADM 6/18, p. 515.

58. NA, ADM 2/80, p. 343.

59. Ships of the line: *Essex, Deptford, Portland, Rochester*; frigates: *Pallas, Brilliant, Richmond, Active, Maidstone, Tartar, Rose, Success, Famborough*; sloops: *Saltash, Swallow, Diligence, Speedwell*; fireships: *Pluto, Salamander*; bombs *Grando, Furnace*. NA, ADM 2/1331, pp. 253–5.

60. Hackman, *English Expeditions*, pp. 93–5.

61. Cf. Richard Harding, *Amphibious Warfare in the Eighteenth Century: The British Expedition to the West Indies, 1740–1742* (Woodbridge, Suffolk, 1991).

62. A W H Pearsall, ed., 'Naval Aspects of the Landings on the French Coast, 1758', *The Naval Miscellany*, N A M Rodger, ed. (London, 1984), pp. 219–25, 227–31, 236–8.

63. Cf. David Syrett, 'The Methodology of British Amphibious Operations during the Seven Years and American Wars' *The Mariner's Mirror* (Aug., 1972), vol. 58, pp. 269–80.

64. The plans of flat-bottomed boats can be found in the Draft Room of the National Maritime Museum at Greenwich.

65. Robert Beatson, *Naval and Military Memoirs of Great Britain from 1727 to 1783* (London 1804), vol. II, p. 167.

66. Frederick Kielmansegge, *Diary of a Journey to England in the Years 1761–1763*, trans. Countess Kielmansegge (London, 1902), p. 257.

67. Pearsall, 'Naval Aspects', pp. 208–9, 213–15.

68. NA, ADM 51/320, 1 June 1758.

69. BL, Add. MSS 32880, f. 369.

70. Pearsall, 'Naval Aspects', p. 209.

71. NA, ADM 1/91, f. 9.

72. NA, ADM 51/320, 12–24 June 1758; BL, Add. MSS 35595, f. 223.

73. BL, Add. MSS 32881, ff. 145–6.

74. NA, ADM 51/320, 2 July 1758.

75. John Carswell and Lewis Arnold Dralle, eds, *The Political Journal of George Bubb Dodington* (Oxford, 1965), p. 373.

76. Horace Walpole, *Memoirs of the Reign of King George II* ed. John Brooke (London, 1985), vol. III, p. 24.

77. NA, 30/8/45, Howe to Pitt, 4 July 1758.

78. Hackman, *English Military Expeditions*, pp. 115–20.

79. NA, ADM 1/91, f. 27.

80. NA, ADM 1/4122, f. 164.

81. NA, ADM 1/91, ff. 53–5; ADM 51/320, 30 July–17 Aug. 1758; Hackman, *English Military Expeditions*, pp. 120–7.

82. NA, ADM 1/91, ff. 56, 58.

83. [J A Holden] 'Description of the Howe Monument, Westminster Abbey', *New York Historical Association Proceedings* (1911), vol. X, pp. 323–5.

84. *Complete Peerage*, vol. 2, nos. 597–600.

85. BL, Add. MSS 32883, ff. 58–9.

86. NA, 30/8/68, ff. 105–6.

87. BL, Add. MSS 32883, ff 190–1.

88. Sir Lewis Namier, *The Structure of Politics at the Accession of George III* (London, 1957), p. 94.

89. NA, ADM 1/91, f. 60.

90. Hackman, *English Military Expeditions*, pp. 129–32.

91. NA, ADM 51/320, 4 Sept. 1758.

92. Joshua Rowley, Jervis Maplesden, William Paston, John Elphinston.

93. NA, ADM 1/91, ff. 61–8; ADM 51/320, 5–19 Sept. 1758.

94. Hackman, *English Military Expeditions*, pp. 141–5.

95. NA, ADM 1/91, f. 68; ADM 2/81, p. 113.

96. Richard Middleton, *The Bells of Victory: The Pitt-Newcastle Ministry and the Conduct of the Seven Years War, 1757–1762* (Cambridge, 1985), pp. 84–5.

97. NA, ADM 2/81, p. 427.

98. NA, ADM 2/82, p. 529.

99. Mackay, *The Hawke Papers*, pp. 207–336.

100. NA, ADM 51/3895, May–Oct. 1759.

101. NA, ADM 51/3895, 12 Nov. 1759.

102. Mackay, *The Hawke Papers*, pp. 339–40., 345.

103. The *Formidable* had been taken by the British and the *Soleil Royal*, *Thésée*, *Superbe*, *Héros* and *Inflexible* were sunk in battle, wrecked or otherwise destroyed.

104. *Essex, Resolution*.

105. NA, ADM 51/3895, 20–21 Nov. 1759; Mackay, *The Hawke Papers*, pp. 341–50.

106. NA, 30/8/79, f. 83.

107. Julian S Corbett, *England in the Seven Years War* (London, 1992 reprint), vol. II, p. 73.

108. NA, ADM 51/3895, 26 Dec. 1759.

109. NA, ADM 1/1895, Howe to Clevland, 22 April 1760.

110. *A List of the General Officers and Field Officers, As They Rank in the Army* (London, 1763), p. 133.

111. NA, ADM 1/1895, Howe to Clevland, 26 Oct. 1760; NA, ADM 51/3895, Jan. Nov. 1761.

112. NA, ADM 1/1896, Howe to Clevland, 9 Feb. 1762.

113. NA, ADM 2/87, pp. 473–4.

114. NA, ADM 1/91, ff. 169–70.

115. *Magnanime, Buckingham, Achilles, Monarch, Superb, Nassau, Prince Frederick, Hero, Trident, Sandwich, Phoenix, Vesuvius*. NA, ADM 1/91, f. 117.

116. NA, ADM 1/91, f. 93.

117. BL, Add, MSS 34903, ff. 1–4.

118. NA, ADM 1/91, ff. 107, 112–13, 118–19, 141.

119. NA, ADM 2/88, p. 253.

120. NA, ADM 2/88, pp. 356–7, 369–70.

121. Mackay, *The Hawke Papers*, p. 387n.

122. NA, ADM 2/89, pp. 438–9.

CHAPTER III

Between Wars

At the beginning of 1763, after paying off HMS *Princess Amelia* and coming ashore,[1] Howe had, for perhaps the first time in his life, a choice of careers. He could seek, and probably obtain, employment at sea in the peacetime Royal Navy. This, however, probably did not appeal to Howe for most of the ships in commission would be small, the duty would be for the most part constabulary in nature, and there would be little opportunity of advancement or glory. Another choice would be for Howe to become a country gentleman and retire to the family estate at Langer in Nottinghamshire.[2] Howe was only 37 years old in 1763 and had spent his whole life on active duty in the Royal Navy cruising in distant seas and fighting wars, and the prospect of spending the foreseeable future in the comparative inactivity of a country gentleman probably had equally scant appeal to him. A third alternative, and one which Howe would adopt, would be to use his social status, his position as one of the best known captains in the Royal Navy, and his seat in the House of Commons to become a politician, or in the parlance of the 18th century, a man of affairs.

On 20 April 1763 Howe was appointed a junior lord of the Admiralty in a government headed by Lord Grenville.[3] Howe's appointment to the Board of Admiralty was in some ways to be expected for not only did he represent Dartmouth in the House of Commons, which was a borough with close connections with the Royal Navy and controlled by the government, but as a navy officer his knowledge of naval affairs could be utilised at the Admiralty. Nevertheless, the appointment was in some respects curious for the Grenville administration had displaced a government headed by the king's favourite, Lord Bute. Howe, who at the time was considered to be a follower of William Pitt, astonished many by accepting a place at the Admiralty in a government headed by Grenville. Howe saw himself not as a supporter of any particular government or ministry, but rather as a supporter of the king's government for he did not believe it was his duty to always follow a party line as laid down by the government. For example, in one of the few recorded votes of the period Howe voted against the government over the question of general warrants.[4] A refusal to toe the political line of the government in power and voting, on certain issues, against the ministry even though sitting for a government-controlled borough, would be a recurring theme during Howe's career in the House of Commons. Probably, even though there is no evidence on this point, what prevented Howe from being removed from the Dartmouth seat by vengeful politicians was his close connection with the king. As a member of the House of Commons Howe was a political independent and not a reliable supporter of any particular government. He was responsible only to his own political beliefs and what he considered to be the best interests of the country, the Royal Navy, and the king.

The business of the Admiralty while Howe was a member of the board was mainly routine and concerned with the administration of the peace-time Royal Navy. Howe showed himself to be a man of business missing only 111 meetings of the board out of a total of 565.[5] On 2 July 1765, several days before resigning from the Board of Admiralty, Howe was appointed by the king to the Privy Council.[6] And on 31 July 1765, amongst rumours that he would accept an appointment to the position of treasurer of the navy in a new administration,[7] Howe resigned from the Board of Admiralty.[8]

Howe apparently was not concerned with the ideological differences between administrations for he accepted an appointment, on 8 August 1765, as treasurer of the navy in the new Rockingham government. The treasurer of the navy received a salary of £2,000 per year and an allowance of £1,700 per year with which to pay the wages of the paymaster, cashier and clerks of the office.[9] The treasurer of the navy did not execute the duties of the office in person, but rather delegated the duties and day-to-day responsibilities to the paymaster of the navy who actually conducted the business of the office. Nevertheless, the treasurer of the navy was a position of great financial benefit for its holder was entrusted with considerable sums of public money which he could employ for his own 'emolument'.[10] In 1766 Howe was authorised to receive two million pounds in public money.[11] It has been maintained by some people that Howe 'refused to profit from the large sums of money which stood in his name'.[12] However, there is no proof of this statement and it seems curious that Howe would accept an office without political or any other power whose only benefit to the occupant was the use of public money if he did not avail himself of this opportunity.

The Rockingham government lasted just long enough to repeal the Stamp Act before collapsing in 1766 when a number of people, including Howe, withdrew their support in favour of William Pitt who was now known as the Earl of Chatham.[13] Howe resigned from the office of treasurer of the navy.[14] But when a new government was formed under the leadership of the Duke of Grafton and the Earl of Chatham, Howe was reappointed treasurer of the navy. Horace Walpole was astonished at Howe's actions and thought them 'an extraordinary strain of delicacy in a man' who had accepted positions in both the Grenville and Rockingham governments and then resigned declaring that 'he could not cooperate unless Mr Pitt was a minister'.[15] Howe was apparently not concerned with mere matters of political inconsistency for he remained in office as treasurer of the navy until the beginning of 1770. When the North government came to power he resigned not only from this position, but also his colonelcy in the marines[16] declaring that he had 'no obligation but to Lord Chatham and the Duke of Grafton.'[17] Nevertheless, Howe, who had resigned his offices when Lord North came to power, supported the new government by voting against the petition of the City of London calling for the dissolution of Parliament and the 'removal of evil ministers'.[18]

Britain during the autumn of 1770 was engaged in the Falkland Islands crisis and in response to the threat of war with Spain orders were issued for the mobilisation of the Royal Navy.[19] On 18 October 1770 Howe was promoted to the rank of rear admiral of the blue[20] and on 26 November was appointed to the command of the Mediterranean squadron.[21] Apparently there was in the House of Commons some opposition, which was put down by Lord Hawke, the First Lord of the Admiralty, to the appointment of so junior an admiral as Howe to such an important command as the Mediterranean squadron.[22]

Howe's flagship for the Mediterranean command would be HMS *Barfleur* which was being fitted for service at Chatham. The newly-promoted rear admiral immediately began to make arrangements for recruiting seamen for his flagship. At the same time Howe requested, in order to improve the sailing qualities of the ship, that HMS *Barfleur*'s yards be reduced in length and that a number of 'coasting anchors' as well as additional ship's boats be supplied to the vessel to enable *Barfleur* to be more easily towed and warped.[23] However, before Howe left London and HMS *Barfleur* was fitted for service, the Spanish bowed to British pressure and the Royal Navy reverted to a peacetime establishment.[24] As a result of the slowness with which the Royal Navy had been mobilised during the Falkland Islands crisis, Howe concluded that 'as a greater Security' ten or twelve ships of the line should at all times be kept fully manned and ready for service.[25]

In 1773 Howe led a movement to obtain an increase in the half pay of junior captains in the Royal Navy. On 9 February 1773, without the support or consent of the North government, he presented a petition to the House of Commons signed by a number of navy officers requesting an increase in the half pay of those captains in the Royal Navy with the least seniority. After a debate in which the proposal was opposed by Lord North and other members of the government, who did not want to set a precedent, the House of Commons voted 154 to 45 to submit the matter for consideration to a committee headed by Howe.[26] According to North 'all the Navy and Army, & Country Gentlemen and most of the placemen' voted in favour of this motion.[27] Howe's committee reported back to the House of Commons on 5 March stating that the rate of half pay for captains of the navy was governed by seniority. The twenty most senior captains received half pay at the rate of ten shillings per day. The next thirty captains eight shillings; the next forty captains six shillings; the next fifty in seniority five shillings; and all the least senior captains received half pay at the rate of four shillings per day. It was also pointed out that four shillings was less than the half pay of certain inferior officers, such as captains of marines who received five shillings per day as half pay. The logic of the situation was quickly perceived by the House of Commons and it was agreed that an address should be presented to the king calling for an increase in the half pay of the most junior captains of the Royal Navy. It was further resolved that the House of Commons 'will make good such expense as shall be incurred on that Account.'[28] The attainment, over the opposition of the ministry, of an increase in half pay for junior captains of the Royal Navy was a personal victory for Howe.

Britain's relations with the colonies in America transcended all other political issues before Parliament and the country in the decade of the 1770s. Howe's opinions on these relations before 1774 are unknown. He had never been to the American colonies and freely admitted his ignorance of American affairs,[29] his only connection with America being that his older brother, George Augustus, had been killed in action before Fort Ticonderoga in 1758 and that his younger brother, William, had served in America as an army officer during the Seven Years War. Even though Howe had been a member of the House of Commons since 1757, had been active in Parliamentary affairs since 1763, and is known between 1768 and 1774 to have spoken twenty-one times in the House of Commons,[30] almost nothing is known of his opinions on the great political issues of the time. Among the few recorded utterances of Howe in the House of Commons were outbursts such as 'I did not hear him'.[31] According to Nathaniel Wraxall:

> Lord Howe's ideas were commonly either so ill conceived by himself, or so darkly and ambiguously expressed, that it was by no means easy to comprehend his precise meaning. This oracular and confused mode of delivery, rendered still more obscure by the part of the House where he usually sat, which was on a back row at a distance from the Speaker's chair, increased, however, the effect of his oratory, and seemed to exemplify Burke's assertion that 'Obscurity is the source of the sublime'.[32]

The only recorded instance of Howe expressing an opinion on American affairs was before the end of 1774 when he said he was in favour of the

House of Commons hearing the petition from the Stamp Act Congress.[33] From the known and existing record it is virtually impossible to discern what opinions, if any, Howe had before the end of 1774 about the relationship between Britain and the American colonies.

At the end of 1774, however, Howe plunged into American affairs when he entered into secret negotiations with Benjamin Franklin over the question of relations between Britain and the American colonies. Franklin, a native of Philadelphia and the agent in London for several American colonies, was the most influential of Americans in London and was considered by many to be the spokesman for the American colonies in England. Since the beginning of 1774 Howe's sister Caroline, who lived several doors from the admiral on Grafton Street, had been playing chess and discussing politics with Franklin. On Christmas Day 1774 Caroline introduced her brother to the American.[34] The ensuing negotiations, which have for years fascinated historians, are shrouded in veils of mystery created by a lack of information. The only account is one by Franklin and a number of questions remain unanswered. What were Howe's motives for opening negotiations with Franklin? Was Howe just an independent politician acting on his initiative or were these negotiations sanctioned by the government and part of a greater scheme to achieve reconciliation between Britain and America? Or was the admiral acting as an agent for the king[35] or for an individual minister? Some people have assumed that Howe must have been acting for members of the government.[36] However, other than oblique hints[37] there is no known evidence to show who, if anybody, was sponsoring Howe during the negotiations with Franklin. Because of the lack of evidence the reasons for, and even the circumstances surrounding, Howe's opening negotiations over reconciliation with Franklin can only be guessed at.

As for the negotiations themselves Franklin reported that at the first meeting on Christmas Day 1774, Howe, after 'some extremely polite compliments' informed him that he was 'merely an independent member of Parliament' who 'wish'd for an Opportunity of obtaining my [Franklin's] sentiments on the Means of Reconciling our Difference' and that the American might find it useful to employ the admiral as a means of 'conveying my Sentiments' to the government 'without committing either them or me'. The meeting ended with Franklin agreeing to meet Howe again in a few days and to give the admiral a written statement setting forth his ideas for a settlement of the American problem.[38]

Several days later Howe and Franklin again met at Howe's sister's house on Grafton Street. Franklin had not as yet written the papers for the admiral setting forth his views on a settlement of the problems between Great Britain and America. Nevertheless, the two men had 'a good deal of Conversation on the Subject' during which Howe assured Franklin 'that there was a sincere Disposition in Lord North and Lord Dartmouth to accommodate the Differences with America and to listen favourably to any Propositions that might have a probable tendency to answer that salutary purpose'. This is the strongest, though inconclusive, evidence that members of the government might know of the negotiations. Then Howe asked what Franklin 'thought of sending some Person or Persons over [to America], commission'd to enquire into the Grievances of America upon the spot, converse with leading People, and endeavour with them to agree upon some Means of composing our Differences?' To this idea Franklin answered 'that a Person of Rank and Dignity, who had a Character of Candour, Integrity and Wisdom might possibly, if employed in that service, be of great Use'. Howe agreed with Franklin stating that the person employed on this mission should

> go with a hearty Desire of promoting a sincere Reconciliation; on the Foundation of Mutual Interests, and Mutual Good Will; that he should endeavour not only to remove their Prejudices against Government, but equally the Prejudices of the Govt. against them, and bring a perfect good understanding, &c.

At this point Caroline Howe interjected 'I wish Brother you were to be sent thither in such a Service'. Howe then took out of his pocket a paper which he gave to Franklin who quickly saw that it was a copy of a plan he himself had composed and given several days before to David Barclay, another apparently self-appointed intermediary, laying out the American terms for reconciliation between Britain and the American colonies. Howe, after Franklin admitted authorship of the document, said that the proposals contained within the paper were not acceptable as a basis for settlement and hoped that the American 'would reconsider the Subject from some Plan that would be more acceptable here'. Franklin reluctantly agreed to draw up another scheme for reconciliation even though he did not see much point to the effort for the American believed that the whole exercise 'was what the French call *spitting in the soup*'. At the insistence of Howe, in order to maintain the secrecy of the negotiations, it was agreed that Franklin would submit his paper to Caroline Howe who would then copy the document before sending it on to the admiral.[39]

At the end of 1774 Franklin sent Caroline Howe a document on reconciliation between Great Britain and America. Then when Franklin next visited Caroline Howe, on 31 December, she returned to him the reconciliation proposal saying that she had copied it and sent the document's contents to her brother in the country. In this document Franklin stated that a settlement could only be reached between Great Britain and America if the British Parliament repealed all the laws and regulations adopted since 1763 designed to tax Americans, to alter the jurisdiction of admiralty courts, to bring Americans to Britain for trial, to coerce Massachusetts, and to alter the government and boundaries of the province of Quebec. The British army and the Royal Navy must also be withdrawn from Boston. And the British government should recognise the authority of the American Congress and appoint a person to preside over that body as the representative of the Crown.[40] When Howe read Franklin's paper the admiral must have known that it was futile to continue the attempt to negotiate a reconciliation through Franklin with the Americans, for the terms set forth in the paper were for the most part, with a few embellishments, a restatement of the long-held American position. Although Howe and Franklin exchanged several letters and met again on 7 March 1775, the attempt to negotiate a settlement of the American problem in London with Franklin was over.[41] What Howe in these talks with Franklin was attempting to do, without a totally new conception of the constitutional relations between Britain and the American colonies, was to break the constitutional deadlock between the American maxim of 'no taxation without representation' and the British axiom of 'the overriding supremacy of Parliament throughout the King's dominions'. That Howe would attempt such a negotiation showed at worst a great degree of political arrogance and at best a supreme confidence in the ability of two men of good will to work out any problem no matter how difficult.

At the time of the negotiations with Franklin, Howe did not always vote with the government,[42] and considered himself a moderate who was seeking a rational solution to the American problem. In the House of Commons, in March of 1775, he supported the 'necessity' of the Coercive Acts as 'the only moderate means of bringing the disobedient provinces to a sense of their duty without involving the empire in all the horrors of a civil war'.[43] Howe, when he voted for the Coercive Acts, as did many others in Britain, misjudged the situation, for the attempt to force American obedience to Parliament by legislation exploded into war. The fighting began in Massachusetts when British troops attempted to seize American arms at Lexington and Concord. A bloody battle ensued and the British army found itself penned up in the town of Boston by American militia. With the beginning of hostilities in Massachusetts between the king's troops and American militia, royal authority collapsed throughout America. After Lexington and Concord the British were confronted with a continent in rebellion.

When news of the fighting in Massachusetts and the collapse of royal authority in America arrived in London, the British resolved to subdue the rebellion by force of arms. The decision to use force against the American rebels came easily to the British for it was a widely-held belief among the ruling elite in Britain not only that the king's army could easily defeat the Americans, but also that if the American colonies withdrew from the empire, the economy of the kingdom would be crippled and Britain would sink into the ranks of the second-rate powers of Europe.[44] The plan which emerged in London during the autumn of 1775 was to crush the rebellion in America with one great campaign in 1776 by sending an army of some 27,000 infantry supported by seventy warships to New York.[45] There were some who saw the sending of the British army 3,000 miles across the Atlantic Ocean to conquer America as a course filled with danger. Lord Barrington, the secretary at war, for instance, believed that if the king's army was committed to America, it would be destroyed piecemeal. Barrington thought that the Americans should be brought to heel by having their ports blockaded and shipping destroyed by the Royal Navy. However, objections of this kind were pushed aside in the rush to send an army to America.[46]

As preparations for dispatching an army to America got under way there were a number of people in London, including Howe and North, who believed that a further attempt should be made to reach a political settlement with the Americans. That is, in conjunction or parallel with military force, an attempt should be made to end the fighting through negotiation and to find a basis for a lasting settlement with the Americans. The idea of sending a commissioner or commissioners to America to obtain a negotiated settlement was first considered in 1774 by the then secretary of state for America Lord Dartmouth. However, due to objections from the king and the collapse of a series of negotiations with Franklin, of which Howe's talks with the American might have been a part, the effort appeared to stall early in 1775.[47]

As news of additional fighting in Massachusetts arrived in London and the government began to prepare for war, the plan to send a commissioner to America to negotiate a settlement with the American rebels appeared to have been dropped. Lord Dartmouth, the chief supporter of reconciliation within the government, had left office to be replaced by Lord George Germain, the former Lord George Sackville, who was an advocate of harsh repressive measures. Howe used the excuse of his younger brother William being promoted to commander in chief of the army in America to open a correspondence with Germain about military affairs in America. One authority believes that Howe was attempting to win Germain's confidence in order that the admiral could be appointed a commissioner to negotiate a settlement with the Americans.[48] There is little or no evidence to support such a view for the exchange of letters between Howe and Germain appears to be mostly about military affairs. What is clear is that either during or shortly after the breakdown of negotiations with Franklin, Howe gained a vision of himself as the one man who was capable of negotiating with the Americans to reach a political settlement and end the civil war within the British empire.

The government during the late summer and early autumn of 1775 had concluded that not only must an army be sent to America, but also a commissioner who would be empowered to reach a political settlement with the Americans. Probably the idea of sending a commissioner to America originated with North. The first lord of the treasury kept his desire for a commissioner to be sent to negotiate with America secret for he did not want to politically hinder the military preparations by holding out 'lights of conciliation'. William Eden, an under secretary of state, told Germain on 3 October 1775 that

> Lord North did me the honour to confide to me some months ago that he thought this would be best accelerated [concluding the war with the Americans] by giving a commission to some proper person with ample powers to settle everything in dispute with any Colony which either fear, interest, fickleness or duty, might bring into submission.[49]

Several weeks later, on 26 October, when the government proclaimed its American policy, George III stated in the king's speech:

> I shall give authority to certain persons upon the spot to grant general or particular pardons and indemnities, in such manner, and to such persons as they shall think fit; and to receive the submission of any province or colony, which shall be disposed to return to its allegiance. It may be also proper to authorize the person so commissioned to restore such province or colony so returning to its allegiance, to the free exercise of trade and commerce, and to the same protection secrecy, as if such province or colony had never revolted.[50]

The French ambassador in London reported to Paris that when he had brought up the subject of commissioners to negotiate with the Americans North's 'face lit up and [he] replied in his own terms: "Sir it is the only real solution. When negotiations will only take place, then everything will be over." However, he still counts on 70 warships of various sizes and 25 thousand men for the expedition to America'.[51] There is little doubt that North agreed with the sending of a commissioner to America even if he might not be the original author of the policy.

With the announcement in the king's speech of the intention to appoint a commissioner to negotiate an end of the war with America, London became alive with speculation as to who would be appointed to the position. Among those whose name was most conspicuous in these speculations was Howe.[52] Unknown to the public and apparently at the instigation of Dartmouth, who had approached North on the subject, the government had already appointed Howe who had accepted the position.[53] Yet even after accepting the appointment as a commissioner Howe continued to display what could be at best considered an ambivalent attitude towards the fighting in America. As an example, on 20 November 1775 Howe, during the debate on the American Prohibitory Bill, stated in the House of Commons, that 'He did not know any struggle an officer could have, serving on the present occasion, so powerful as that between his duty as an officer and his duty as a man.' When pressed by Charles Fox to clarify this statement Howe said that 'If he was commanded, it was his duty to obey and he could not refuse to serve.'[54] However, in the first week of December 1775 a chance event and his own self-esteem would wholly alter Howe's role in the British effort to end the war with America.

On 7 December 1775 Admiral Sir Charles Saunders died, vacating the position of lieutenant general of the marines, a sinecure worth about £1,200 a year. Lord Sandwich, the first lord of the Admiralty, after gaining permission from North who had forgotten that he had already promised the sinecure to Howe, gave the vacancy to Rear Admiral Sir Hugh Palliser. Howe was enraged and threatened not only to go to the king and resign all his offices, but also to get his younger brother William, the commander in chief of the army in America, to resign as well. North recognised that he had promised the lieutenant generalship of the marines to Howe, but with the assistance of Germain, succeeded in dissuading the admiral from immediately resigning. To placate Howe and to avoid a major crisis, North concluded that another sinecure must be given to the admiral. It was decided to persuade Admiral the Hon. John Forbes to resign from his generalship of the marines which was a sinecure worth £2,000 per year. Howe would then be appointed to the position and Forbes would be compensated with an equivalent pension. This scheme only made matters worse for Forbes refused to resign and Vice Admiral the Hon. Augustus Keppel, a member of the political opposition who believed that the lieutenant generalship of the marines should have been his, claimed that the Admiralty was disregarding the services of senior admirals for both Palliser and Howe were junior rear admirals. As the quarrel over the lieutenant generalship of the marines became public knowledge and threatened to alienate both Howe and Keppel, the government desperately sought to placate both admirals. Finally, after a series of Byzantine negotiations and manoeuvres a workable formula was hit upon which would apparently satisfy both Keppel and Howe. In the event of a general European war Keppel would become commander in chief of the Channel Fleet and Howe would be promoted to vice admiral and be appointed commander in chief of the squadron in America.[55]

The appointment of Howe as commander in chief of the squadron in America generated for the government additional problems. If Howe was to be commander in chief in America then something would have to be done for incumbent Rear Admiral Molyneux Shuldham. North suggested that the American command should be divided and Shuldham be given a separate command in the Gulf of St Lawrence. Howe, however, wanted the whole American command, would not accept North's compromise, and again threatened to resign. To break this deadlock North enlisted the aid of the king, believing that any break with Howe would be politically damaging to the government, for the admiral's appointment to the American command was known to the public. On 2 February 1776 Howe had an audience with George III and it was decided that Howe should have the whole American command and that Shuldham should be recalled.[56] To ease the blow to Shuldham he was promoted to vice admiral, made an Irish peer, and upon his return from America appointed commander in chief at Plymouth. Several days after the admiral's meeting with George III, a London newspaper reported that Howe would replace Shuldham as commander in chief of the squadron in America because a number of senior navy officials had represented to the king 'the impropriety of placing a junior to command older officers, and that in short it would be looked upon as an affront offered them.' On 5 February Howe kissed George III's hand and became commander in chief of the squadron in America.[57]

The price paid by the North government for validating Howe's self-esteem and lust for office over the affair of the lieutenant generalship of the marines was great. North, to reach a settlement suitable to Howe, was forced to disrupt the naval command arrangements by displacing Shuldham from the command in America. This was the immediate price the government had to pay for preventing Howe from resigning as a commissioner to negotiate with the Americans. There were also several largely unforeseen consequences of the affair of the lieutenant generalship of the marines. One of them was the promise to appoint Keppel to the command of the Channel squadron. This appointment would later haunt and almost destroy the North government. But of more immediate importance was that Howe's elevation to the command of the squadron in America would place in the sole hands of Richard and William Howe, at a distance of 3,000 miles from the seat of the government in London, the responsibility for the conduct of political and military affairs in America. This was a gamble for the North government. At the time, early in 1776, Howe's appointment was popular for he was considered to be an outstanding professional navy officer. Nevertheless, there were a number of minuses to this appointment which were not wholly perceived at the time. For instance, in all the years that Howe had been in the House of Commons, he had shown no outstanding skill as a politician. He was an independent in politics and not a hard and fast supporter of the North government. Howe also was not wholly trusted by Sandwich and Germain who were the two ministers responsible for the conduct of the war. More importantly Howe's knowledge of America was at best nebulous and the admiral had almost no expressed ideas on how to bring about an end to the rebellion in America other than the use of common sense and good will. Howe appeared to believe that his good will, common sense, and good officers alone could advance the cause of reconciliation and put an end to the civil war within the empire.

Formulating the terms of the instructions for the commission, under which Howe would negotiate with the Americans to end the conflict, forced the ministry, perhaps for the first time, to commit to paper specific conditions upon which it was prepared to settle the American rebellion. The original concept of the role of a commissioner as embodied in the king's speech on 26 October 1775 was to send a person to America to facilitate the end of hostilities by granting 'general and particular pardons' and 'to receive submission of any colony desiring to return to its allegiance'.[58] Most members of the government, and especially Germain, desired that Howe's powers as a peace commissioner be limited to ratifying the results obtained on the battlefield by a victorious British army. At first Germain attempted to enlarge the number of commissioners by suggesting that William Eden or William Knox, two under secretaries of state, be sent to America along with Howe as commissioners. Howe resisted this suggestion, but finally agreed to a joint commission with his brother William as an additional commissioner. Germain further demanded, as a *sine qua non* of any settlement, that the American colonies must acknowledge 'the supreme authority of the Legislature [parliament] to make laws binding on the Colonies in all cases whatsoever'.[59] The lawyers in the government would not permit any clauses in Howe's instructions which would 'delegate a power to qualify & diminish Parliamentary Power'.[60] Lord Suffolk, a secretary of state, would never agree 'upon anything derogatory to the authority of Parliament'. And Alexander Wedderburn, the attorney general, believed that 'this business of the Commission ... cannot proceed without some assurance to this country that its essential rights are not sacrificed.'[61] To the government a prerequisite for any negotiations was an American submission to royal authority and an acknowledgement of the supremacy of Parliament. Howe, when he first saw a draft of the proposed instructions to the commissioners, attempted to gain modifications believing that 'The Instructions of the Government were that he should be authorized upon his arrival, to hold forth to the Americans, in the mildest tho' firmest manner, the most favourable terms that the Government mean to grant. In order to induce them to lay down their Arms & return to their Duty'.[62] He again threatened to resign if the government did not modify the terms of the peace commission to permit negotiations with the Americans in the absence of complete submission to Parliamentary authority. However, the government absolutely refused to substantially alter the terms of the instructions to the commissioners. After much talk Howe was forced to accept terms for ending the conflict with the Americans for the admiral was in terms of his own prestige and self-esteem too committed to resign over what many would consider to be mere technicalities in his instructions. Germain was correct when he remarked that 'Lord Howe has many Difficulties about the Instructions; however at all Events he will not decline the Command of the Fleet.'[63]

On 4 May 1776 the Admiralty issued to Howe orders and instructions for the conduct of operations against the American rebels. Howe was directed to proceed to America and to take command of the king's ships stationed in American waters. Howe's instructions called for him to employ the ships and vessels under his command 'for preventing all Trade and Intercourse with the Colonies' and to quell 'the Rebellion which unhappily subsists in those Colonies and reducing His Majesty's Rebellious Subjects therein to a proper sense of the duty, co-operating with the Commander in chief of His Majesty's Land Force in North America in the most vigorous execution of such measures as shall be judged most advisable to be taken to attain these great and desirable Objects.' Howe was further ordered by the Lords of the Admiralty to select a port suitable as a fleet base for the support of operations during the winter months and when necessary to dispatch ships of his squadron requiring repairs either to the West Indies or England.[64]

Two days later, on 6 May 1776, the government issued to Howe 'Instructions to the Commissioners for Restoring Peace in North America.' Under the terms of these instructions Howe, in conjunction with his brother William, was authorised to issue proclamations offering to grant pardons to all Americans, within certain time limits and excepting certain leaders of the rebellion, 'who shall return to their allegiance'. The Howes were further ordered that before any colony could be declared at peace all revolutionary 'Congresses, Committees, Conventions, and other associations' must be dissolved, all armed forces acting under revolutionary authority must be disbanded, all American-held forts must be delivered up to the king's troops, and the legitimate colonial governments must be permitted to resume their functions. Then upon application the restrictions on the trade of the colonies would be removed. There then followed a long series of conditions and demands, with which the Americans had to comply for the reform of the governments of the colonies so as to prevent in the future any of the conditions which the British government believed might cause challenges to the authority of Parliament.[65] The instructions for commissioners for restoring the peace would prove to be totally unacceptable to the Americans for they called for the surrender of the Americans and were nothing more than a re-statement of the long-held British constitutional position and as such were the terms the North administration considered as just to be granted to defeated and chastised American rebels.

When Howe was appointed commander in chief in America HMS *Eagle*, a new 60-gun third rate, was assigned to be his flagship. At the time of his appointment to the command in America Howe requested that the Admiralty send to him a 'state of the ships' on the American station, abstracts of all orders issued to the squadron in America as well as copies of the dispatches of previous commanding officers of the squadron so that he could 'take in consequence the particulars [that] may be necessary for giving him insight into them.'[66] Howe quickly perceived that the ships of his command would be required to operate in shoal waters and requested that they be equipped with all the special steam and kedge anchors as well as the small craft required for 'warping and towing' of warships in shoal water. Further, the admiral also requested that the Admiralty assign to his squadron a number of heavily armed ships suitable for operations close to the shore in shoal water. No vessels of this type were available in England in the first months of 1776 and it was suggested that Howe take into the king's service suitable vessels and convert them into warships suitable for operations in shoal waters.[67] Later, when he arrived in America, Howe would follow this advice and commission into the navy a converted transport as a fire support ship to be employed in amphibious operations.[68] Indeed it was seen by both the Admiralty and Howe that amphibious operations would loom large among the tasks to be performed by the squadron in America and special emphasis was placed on obtaining flat-bottomed boats for the conduct of landing operations.[69] Howe's departure for America was delayed for several weeks owing mostly to problems of formulating the terms of the commission for restoring peace and it was not until 11 May 1776 that the admiral in HMS *Eagle* departed from Spithead for America.[70]

Notes

1. NA, ADM 1/1898, Howe to Clevland, 1 Feb. 1763.

2. Cf. Thomas Baily, *Annals of Nottinghamshire: Nottingham including the Borough* (London, 1853), vol. IV, p. 177.

3. J C Sainty, *Admiralty Officials, 1660–1870* (London, 1975), p. 133.

4. *The Parliamentary History of England from the earliest period to the Year 1803* (London, 1813), vol. XV, col. 1404.

5. NA, ADM 3/71–3, 20 April 1763 to 31 July 1765.

6. NA, PC 2/111, p. 302.

7. William James Smith, ed., *The Grenville Papers: Being the Correspondence of Richard Grenville Earl Temple, KG, and the Right Hon. George Grenville, Their Friends and Contemporaries…* (London 1852–3), vol III, p. 219.

8. Sainty, *Admiralty Officials*, p. 133.

9. BL, Add. MSS 33056, f. 76.

10. *Commissioners of Inquiry into the Fees and Emoluments received in Public Offices: Fourth Report. Treasurer of the Navy* (London, 1808), pp. 133–4, 138.

11. BL, Add. MSS 33065, ff. 204, 247.

12. E.g. Horace Walpole, *Memoirs of the Reign of King George the Third* (London, 1894), vol. I, p. 231n.

13. John Brewer, *Party Ideology and Popular Politics at the Accession of George III* (Cambridge, 1976), p. 84.

14. Ross J S Hoffman, *Marquis: A Study of Lord Rockingham* (New York, 1973), p. 123.

15. Horace Walpole, *Memoirs of the Reign of King George III*, Derek Jarrett, ed. (New Haven, Ct., 2000), vol. III, pp. 43, 60.

16. *A List of General Officers and Field Officers, As They Rank in the Army* (London, 1771), p. 171.

17. Walpole, *Memoirs of the Reign of King George III*, Jarrett, ed. vol. IV, p. 147.

18. John Wright, ed., *Sir Henry Cavendish's Debates of the House of Commons, during the Thirteenth Parliament of Great Britain, commonly called the Unreported Parliament (1768–1771) …* (London, 1841–3), vol. I, p. 535.

19. NA, ADM 1/4128, ff. 40, 77.

20. David Syrett and R L DiNardo, *The Commissioned Sea Officers of the Royal Navy, 1660–1815* (Aldershot, Hants 1994), p. 231.

21. W S Lewis, Warren Hunting Smith, and George Lam, eds, *Horace Walpole's Correspondence with Sir Horace Mann* (London, 1967), vol. VII, p. 250.

22. J Ralfe, *The Naval Biography of Great Britain* (London, 1828), vol. I, p. 94.

23. NA, ADM 1/587, Howe to Stephens, 17, 28 Dec. 1770.

24. NA, ADM 1/4128, ff. 104–5.

25. Sir John Fortescue, ed., *The Correspondence of King George III from 1760 to December 1782* (London, 1967 reprint), no. 901.

26. *Parliamentary History of England*, vol. XVII, cols. 705–17.

27. Fortescue, *Correspondence of King George*, no. 1193.

28. *Parliamentary History of England*, vol. XVII, cols. 721–2.

29. E.g., Peter Orlando Hutchinson, ed., *The Diary and Letters of His Excellency Thomas Hutchison Esq.* (Boston, 1883–6) vol. II, p. 33.

30. Peter D G Thomas, 'Check List of M.P.s Speaking in the House of Commons, 1768 to 1774', *Bulletin of the Institute of Historical Research* (Nov., 1962), vol. XXXV, p. 224.

31. P D G Thomas, ed., 'Parliamentary Diaries of Nathaniel Ryder, 1764–7', *Camden Miscellany* (London, 1969 fourth series), vol. 7, p. 278.

32. Henry B Wheatley, ed., *The Historical and Posthumous Memoirs of Sir Nathaniel William Wraxall, 1722–1784* (London, 1884.), vol. II, pp. 42–3.

33. Walpole, *Memoirs of the Reign of King George III*, Jarrett, ed., vol. III, p. 14.

34. Leonard W Labaree; William B Willcox; Claude A Lopez and Barbara B Oberg, eds, *The Papers of Benjamin Franklin* (New Haven, Ct., 1959–), vol. 21, p. 408.

35. Cf. J Heneage Jesse, *Memoirs of the Life and Reign of King George the Third* (London, 1867), vol. II, pp. 82–3.

36. Cf. Ira D Gruber, *The Howe Brothers and the American Revolution* (New York, 1972), p. 53–4.

37. E.g. Labaree et al eds, *Franklin Papers*, vol. 21, p. 571.

38. Ibid, vol. 21, pp. 565–7.

39. Ibid, vol. 21, pp 571–2.

40. Ibid, vol. 21, pp. 409–11, 573.

41. Ibid, vol. 21, pp. 499–503, 514–15, 588–9.

42. Fortescue, *Correspondence*, no. 1403.

43. *The Parliamentary Register* (London, 1775), vol. I, p. 291.

44. Piers Mackesy, *The War for America, 1775–83* (London, 1964), pp. 37–8, 57–60.

45. David Syrett, *Shipping and the American War, 1775–83: A Study in British Transport Organization* (London, 1970), p. 197.

46. Shute Barrington, *The Political Life of William Wildman, Viscount Barrington* (1814), pp. 140–50.

47. Bernard Donoughue, *British Politics and the American Revolution: The Path to War, 1773–5* (London, 1964), pp. 121–5, 130, 278–9.

48. Gruber, *Howe Brothers*, pp. 61–2.

49. Historical Mansucripts Commission, *Report on the Manuscripts of Mrs Stopford-Sackville, of Drayton House, Northamptonshire* (London, 1910), vol. II, pp. 10–11.

50. *History of Parliament*, vol. XVIII, col. 697.

51. William Bell Clark et al, eds, *Naval Documents of the American Revolution* (Washington DC, 1964–), vol. 3, p. 425.

52. E.g. Sir William Anson, ed., *Autobiography and Political Correspondence of Augustus Henry Third Duke of Grafton* (London, 1989), p. 276.

53. Gruber, *Howe Brothers*, pp. 63–4.

54. *Parliamentary Register* vol. III, p. 200.

55. Francis Steuart, ed., *The Last Journal of Horace Walpole during the Reign of George III from 1771 to 1783* (London, 1910), vol. I, pp. 521–3.

56. Fortescue, *Correspondence*, nos. 1816–1822.

57. Clark, *Naval Documents*, vol. 4, pp. 889, 892.

58. *History of Parliament*, vol. XVIII, col. 697.

59. Historical Manuscripts Commission, *Report on Manuscripts in Various Collections* (Dublin and Hereford, 1904–14), vol. IV, pp. 258–9.

60. BL, Add. MSS 34412, f. 369.

61. Historical Manuscripts Commission, *Stopford-Sackville*, vol. 24–5.

62. Clark, *Naval Documents*, vol. 4, p. 996.

63. Ibid, vol. 4, p. 998.

64. NA, ADM 2/1332, ff. 130–4.

65. K G, Davies, ed., *Documents of the American Revolution* (Dublin, 1972–1981), vol. XII, pp. 120–4.

66. NA, ADM 1/487, f. 4.

67. NA, ADM 1/487, ff. 7, 11; ADM 2/551, 360.

68. David Syrett, 'H.M. Armed Ship Vigilant, 1777–1780', *The Mariner's Mirror* (Feb. 1978), vol. 64, pp. 57–62.

69. NA, ADM 2/511, ff. 306, 361; Clark, *Naval Documents*, vol. 4, p. 1055.

70. NA, ADM 1/487, ff. 11, 22.

CHAPTER IV

America

On 12 July 1776 when Howe in HMS *Eagle* arrived off Sandy Hook at the entrance to New York Harbour[1] he was confronted with a political and military problem without precedent. The rebellion in America was a unique event, to which the strategic lessons of previous wars did not apply, for a conflict with an ideologically motivated and armed insurgent population was unknown to contemporary Britain. America in 1776, with a population of some two and a half million people living in thirteen different provinces located along the Atlantic coast of North America, was not an Ireland, which had been repeatedly terrorised into submission by relatively small military forces. Nor was America similar to Scotland, which had been blockaded by the Royal Navy, overrun by the king's army and then pacified by the construction of forts and military roads. Neither could guidance be drawn from the conquest of Canada in the Seven Years War. Then the British with one blow aimed at Quebec – the strategic centre of Canada – reduced the French forces to impotency in a manoeuvre similar to placing a cork in the top of a bottle. But America in 1776 was a vast, sprawling decentralised country without a strategic, economic or political centre. There was no Paris or Vienna, the capture of which would signal the defeat of the country. In the course of the war the British would occupy every urban area in America, only to find that the country was like China, in that the capture of a city, or even several cities, became a meaningless victory swallowed up by the vastness of the land itself. America – a continent in rebellion 3,000 miles from the focus of British power – presented Howe, and his brother General the Hon. William Howe, the commander of the British army in America, with a military problem without precedent.

Compounding the political and military problem presented by America was the fact that neither the Howes, nor most other members of the ruling elite in Britain, understood American society or the political dynamics of the American revolutionary movement. There was no society in Europe similar to that in America, so that the British in 1776 found it nearly impossible to rationally determine either the political or military potential of the American rebels. The rebellion in America was not caused, as many of the

49

British believed, by a fractious minority of the lower orders in American society, rather it was a powerful political movement led by the political and economic elite of America and drawing support from all elements of American society. Those British officials, with the possible exception of Lord Amherst, who had contact with Americans, loathed them, discounted the strength of the revolutionary movement in America, and underrated American military ability.

It was a widely-held belief among the ruling classes of Britain that the rebellion in America could be ended by the king's forces with one smart and decisive campaign. What was not seen by the British in 1776 was that the rebellion in America probably could not be ended by force of arms only. Royal authority in America since the times of the first settlements had always rested on the consent of the American population. When fighting broke out during 1775 in Massachusetts between the king's soldiers and American militia, royal authority collapsed and vanished throughout America. The problem confronting the Howes in 1776 was how to restore royal authority in America or to put it in other terms, the Howes, in order to end the rebellion in America on terms acceptable to the British government, using a combination of political and military means, had to obtain American submission to royal authority. And that could only, if at all, be obtained through a political settlement to which a majority of Americans would consent. The British government, however, when drawing up the instructions issued to the Howes for restoring peace in America, did not conceive of the process as one of negotiating a political settlement with the Americans, but rather as one in which those individual Americans who submitted to royal authority would receive pardons for past revolutionary acts. The reasoning behind this strategy was that the British forces would decisively defeat the American rebels and the Americans would then see the futility of further resistance and submit to royal authority. What the British in 1776 failed to see was the possibility, in the absence of a political settlement, that no matter how many military defeats were inflicted upon the Americans they might continue to refuse to submit to royal authority. The Howe brothers at New York in 1776 were confronted with a political and military problem which was not wholly comprehended and whose solution, if it existed at all, was at best elusive.

While only dimly perceiving the military and political difficulties posed by the revolution in America, the British government decided to crush the rebellion in one campaign by invading New York in the summer of 1776 with a massive force. The defeat of the rebel army at New York would not only demoralise the Americans, but the capture of the city would provide the British with a refuge for loyalists, an area from which to draw supplies, and a military base from which future operations could be undertaken. It would also open to British amphibious forces the Hudson river, which is navigable for more than a hundred miles along the western flank of

New England.[2] By the middle of August 1776 therefore, the British had amassed an army on Staten Island at the entrance of New York Harbour consisting of some 25,000 soldiers supported by thirty warships,[3] scores of transports, and all the special equipment required to conduct amphibious operations. As the final preparations for the British offensive at New York were being completed Admiral Howe attempted to open negotiations with the Americans with the aim of seeing if there was any possibility of reconciliation before the beginning of the campaign.

During the voyage to America Howe had written a declaration announcing the appointment of himself and his brother to the commission to restore peace to the American colonies. At the same time Howe drew up a covering letter to accompany this declaration addressed to the royal governors or the chief magistrates of all the American colonies. It was not Howe's 'expectation' that this declaration and the covering letter would actually be received by the royal governors, who had all been deposed from office, but rather the admiral was employing this as a device to obtain the greatest possible readership among the American population. The declaration and the letters to various royal officials were dated 20 June 1776 'off the coast of the Province of Massachusetts Bay' and it was probably Howe's intention to employ intercepted merchant ships to dispatch documents to various colonies. However, no opportunity was offered to send the declarations and letters ashore before Howe arrived at Staten Island. On 12 July, when HMS *Eagle* anchored off Staten Island, her first lieutenant was sent to Perth Amboy, New Jersey with a number of letters and copies of the declarations 'intended for the colonies to the southward of New York directing him to deliver them to any person who might appear in authority and desire they might be forwarded by the post'. Those declarations and letters intended for the New England colonies were sent to Rhode Island by HMS *Merlin*.[4]

When Howe arrived at Staten Island on 12 July it was discovered that political circumstances in America had been greatly altered by the American Declaration of Independence. On 4 July 1776 the American Congress had proclaimed that America was now an independent nation and that the American colonies were no longer, in any way whatsoever, subject to the British crown. Ambrose Serle, one of Howe's secretaries, upon learning of the American Declaration of Independence, probably spoke for a majority of the British when he noted in his diary that 'A more impudent, false and atrocious Proclamation was never fabricated by the Hands of Man.'[5] What was not perceived by Serle, and probably not by Howe, as well as many others among the British at New York, was that the American Declaration of Independence, if not totally foreclosing any possibility of reconciliation, greatly reduced any chances of restoring royal authority in America. Howe's declaration, as well as all the accompanying documents, which had been sent ashore at Perth Amboy were dispatched by the American military authorities to Philadelphia for consideration by the Continental Congress. When the American leaders read Howe's declaration they discovered that the document only contained the statement that Howe and his brother, under the terms of the peace commission, were empowered to remove restrictions on American trade when a colony or any other region in America was 'at peace with His Majesty' and to grant pardons to those Americans who returned to their allegiance to the crown.[6] The Continental Congress quickly concluded that Howe's declaration was at best irrelevant. Samuel Adams upon reading Howe's declaration observed that 'it is now too late for that insidious Court to play such Tricks with any reasonable Hopes of Success. The American States have declared themselves no longer the Subjects of the British King.'[7] On 19 July the Congress resolved to publish Howe's declaration so that:

> The good people of these United States may be informed of what nature are the Commissioners, and what terms, with the expectation of which, the insidious court of Britain has endeavored to amuse and disarm them, and that the few, who still remain suspended by a hope founded either in justice or moderation of their late King, may now, at length, be convinced, that the valor alone of their country is to save its liberties.[8]

No further action was taken by the Continental Congress and Howe's declaration was ignored by the American authorities.

Accompanying Howe's declaration was a personal letter from the admiral addressed to Benjamin Franklin. In this short letter Howe assured Franklin that he wished 'to see our differences accommodated' and that he desired to promote 'the reestablishment of lasting Peace and Union with the Colonies'.[9] Franklin, after receiving permission from the Continental Congress to correspond with the enemy, answered Howe's letter in the most uncompromising of terms. Franklin informed Howe that his declaration concerning the peace commission contained 'nothing more than we had seen in the Act of the parliament' and that Britain was now waging a war of 'wanton Barbarity and Cruelty' against the Americans by means of destroying 'defenceless Towns in the midst of Winter', inciting massacres and murders by rebellious slaves and marauding Indians, and 'bringing foreign Mercenaries to deluge our Settlements with Blood'. These 'atrocious Injuries have extinguished every remaining Spark of Affection for the Parent Country we once held so dear'. Franklin then went on to point out that he had worked long and hard:

> to preserve from breaking that fine & noble China Vase the British Empire: for I knew that being broken, the separate Parts could not retain ever their Share of the Strength or Value that existed in the whole, and that a perfect Re-Union of those Parts could scarce even be hoped for.

The letter ended with Franklin saying that he believed that Howe desired reconciliation between Britain and America, but it would be 'impossible on any Terms given to you to propose' and that the best course of action that the admiral could adopt would be to resign from his command and return to private life.[10] If there were ever any doubts in Howe's mind as to American determination not to submit again to royal authority, Franklin's letter should have removed them.

On 13 July, the day after he had arrived at Staten Island, Howe attempted to arrange a meeting with General George Washington, the commander in chief of the American army. The British admiral wrote a letter to Washington which was addressed 'To George Washington Esq &c. &c. &c.' in which he proposed that the two men meet on a frigate off New York City to discuss the peace commission which 'May be a means of preventing the further Effusion of Blood, and become productive of Peace and lasting Union between Great Britain and America.'[11] This letter, under a flag of truce, was carried in a ship's boat by Lieutenant Philip Brown of HMS *Eagle* into Upper New York Bay. Off Governor's Island the boat carrying Brown was met by three American boats who demanded to know the British officer's business. When Brown informed the Americans that he had a letter from Howe to their commanding officer he was ordered to lay to while one of the American boats returned to New York City. Shortly afterwards the American boat returned carrying Colonels Joseph Reed, Samuel Blachely Webb and Henry Knox. The American officers, who 'would not touch' Howe's letter, asked Brown to whom it was addressed. When Brown replied 'To George Washington Esq &c. &c. &c.' one of the Americans said 'there was no such Person among them and therefore would not receive it.' Brown then asked how should the letter be addressed? One of the American officers then replied that 'all the World knew who Genl. Washington was since the transactions last summer'.[12] When Brown's boat with a flag of truce was sighted from New York City, Washington decided that he should not receive any letter or other communication from the British which did not address him in his official capacity and include his official title and position. This was not a matter of mere 'Punctilio' to Washington, but rather an effort to force recognition by the British of the belligerent status of American forces. Over the next several days both of the Howes would continue, without success, to attempt to communicate with Washington without officially recognising his rank or position.[13] The Continental Congress on 17 July approved Washington's refusal to accept what he considered to be improperly addressed communications from the enemy and directed that all American commanders should receive no letter or message from the British, but those that 'shall be directed to them in the characters they respectively sustain'.[14] From Washington's refusal to communicate with Howe, and especially from Franklin's letter, it was increasingly clear that the Americans were unmoved by the terms of the peace commission and that the only recourse now open to the British was military action.[15]

The British at New York in August 1776 had the best opportunity of the entire war for inflicting upon the Americans a decisive defeat. The American forces, some 19,000 ill-trained, poorly led and badly supplied troops without naval support, were stationed in exposed and weak positions, for New York City was indefensible. Guns mounted on Brooklyn Heights commanded the city. To defend New York City, Washington had to divide his army and occupy Brooklyn which in itself was indefensible. The Americans could not prevent the British from landing on Long Island in overpowering force, while units of the Royal Navy entered the East river to block the retreat of the garrison at Brooklyn. Furthermore, if the British boldly exploited their amphibious mobility, not only the American garrison at Brooklyn, but the entire American army at New York could possibly be enveloped and destroyed. The effects of the capture or destruction of Washington's army at New York in August of 1776 would be beyond calculation. Since the Americans had only one army, the Declaration of Independence had been issued only a few weeks before, and loyalism was still a political power, the rebellion in America might not have been able to withstand military ruin at New York.

As early as 12 July the strategic weakness of the American position at New York was revealed when HMS *Phoenix*, HMS *Rose* and HMS *Trial* ran the American batteries at Forts Lee and Washington on the Hudson river and broke into the Tappan Zee, threatening American east–west communications south of the Hudson Highlands and demonstrating the vulnerability of the western flank of the American forces at New York.[16] However, with the exception of Major General Henry Clinton, the second in command of the British army, who later at Charleston in 1780 would envelop and trap an entire American army, no one among the British appears to have seen the importance of forcing the Hudson river as a prelude to enveloping the entire American army at New York. Of the top British commanders, Clinton alone saw that the strategic key to New York City was Kingsbridge in the Bronx. If a British force could occupy Kingsbridge and Fordham Heights before Washington could escape from Brooklyn and lower Manhattan, the American army would be trapped. Following this line of reasoning, Clinton proposed that British naval power and amphibious capabilities be exploited by passing troops up the Hudson river, landing at Spuyten Duyvil at the western end of the Harlem river and seizing Kingsbridge and Fordham Heights.[17] Although General Howe at first seemed quite taken with Clinton's scheme to destroy the American army, in the end it was discarded, for as early as 7 June the commander in chief of the British army had decided to attack New York City by way of Gravesend and Brooklyn.[18]

The British campaign at New York opened on 22 July 1776, when under the guns of warships British infantry from Staten Island, in a superbly executed shore-to-shore amphibious assault, landed at Gravesend. As was the case with all the amphibious operations of the campaign, General Howe picked the site for the landing and then Admiral Lord Howe planned the operation in which the troops would be conducted to the shore and landed. The landing at Gravesend was carried out under the command of Lord Howe, when hundreds of seamen from the fleet manned some seventy-five flat-bottomed boats as well as other small craft to land the king's troops on Long Island.[19] Then, on the night of 26 August, the British army went on the offensive. In a masterly series of manoeuvres the American forces in Brooklyn were outflanked, surprised, beaten on the field of battle and driven in panic into the weak fortifications at Brooklyn Heights. The only thing that saved the American army from being destroyed was that General Howe ordered, though there were several hours of daylight left, that the attack be broken off and that the American position at Brooklyn Heights be reduced by regular siege operations. In an attempt to distract the attention of the Americans during the battle for Brooklyn Lord Howe had ordered five warships[20] to proceed 'higher up the Channel towards the Town of New York' as the army advanced on Brooklyn Heights. In the face of a north wind, the effort was only half-heartedly carried out, and only HMS *Roebuck* got near enough to the Americans to exchange a 'few random' shots with an enemy battery at Red Hook. Shortly thereafter, with the onset of the ebb tide, Lord Howe called off the operation. As a result, on the night of 29–30 August, as the British army was still preparing for the 'siege' of Brooklyn Heights, Washington evacuated Brooklyn under cover of bad weather without any hindrance from the Royal Navy.[21]

With the American evacuation of Brooklyn Heights, New York City became the next British objective. The American army on Manhattan was in a desperate situation and the British believed that Washington was already withdrawing from New York City.[22] Clinton, however, thought that the opportunity still existed to trap the entire American army on the island of Manhattan if the British moved quickly and exploited their amphibious mobility to seize Fordham Heights and Kingsbridge. Clinton advocated launching an amphibious attack from Astoria in Queens, and seizing Wards Island, Randalls Island, and the South Bronx, and then advancing north-west to the Kingsbridge region, thus cutting off the American escape route from Manhattan. Clinton believed that the destruction of Washington's army should be the objective of the campaign at New York while General Howe apparently was thinking in terms of occupying and controlling strategic locations such as New York City. Although Clinton argued at length for seizing the line of the Harlem river, General Howe would have none of it. Finally, in response to Clinton's demands for an attack on the Americans' rear, General Howe proposed that the British land simultaneously at Kipps Bay and in Harlem opposite Randalls and Wards Islands.[23] On 10 September ten British light infantry companies supported by units of the Royal Navy seized Randalls and Wards Islands, and for a time it appeared that an attack would be undertaken towards Harlem or the South Bronx. In the end, however, caution prevailed; citing the difficulties of making a landing near the turbulent waters of Hell Gate, General Howe accepted a plan put forward by Captain John Montressor of the engineers for a concentrated attack at Kipps Bay on the east side of Manhattan.[24]

As General Howe was preparing the attack on Manhattan and New York City, Admiral Howe was again seeking to open a dialogue with the Americans. Among the American prisoners taken in the Battle of Long Island was Major General John Sullivan of New Hampshire. Howe, with the concurrence of his brother the general, decided to use Sullivan to convey a message to the Americans. According to Howe's account in a dispatch written to Lord George Germain, the secretary of state for America, Sullivan was told by the admiral that while most Americans believed that the peace commission was

> Restricted to granting Pardons and declaring the Colonies at Peace ... that the Object of His Majesty's paternal Desire was to make His American Subjects happy, as well as to relieve them from the Calamities of War; that the Commissioners were willing to consult and confer, with any Persons of Influence upon the means of attaining those Ends; and the Reconciliation, Union, and Redress of Grievances might be the happy consequences.[25]

Sullivan was then sent into New York City with a verbal message for the Americans. Washington, who had no authority to negotiate with the British, sent Sullivan on to the Continental Congress at Philadelphia.[26] When Sullivan arrived at Philadelphia the Continental Congress had the American general convert Howe's verbal message to writing. According to Sullivan's written version Howe, while not permitted by the terms of his instructions to 'treat with Congress as such', nevertheless wanted to meet with several members of the Congress 'as private Gentlemen' and, in conjunction with General Howe, 'had full powers to compromise the Dispute between Great Britain and America, upon terms advantageous to both'.[27] Obviously, in the message conveyed by Sullivan, Howe had played down the restrictive nature of his instructions as a peace commissioner in order to gain a meeting with the members of the Continental Congress.

The arrival of Howe's message at Philadelphia placed the Continental Congress in a dilemma. According to Josiah Bartlett of New Hampshire, the members of the Congress were certain that Lord Howe had 'no power to grant any terms we can possibly accept' and if unofficial talks were entered into, Congress would be perceived as 'catching hold of so slender a thread to bring about a settlement'. On the other hand, if the Americans refused to enter into talks with Howe, then 'the Tories and moderate men, so called, will try to represent the Congress as obstinate'.[28] After several days of debate the Congress decided to send a committee to meet with Howe. This would be an official committee of the Continental Congress for it was decided that members of the Congress could not meet with the admiral 'in their private characters'. Further, the committee would be charged with the task of discovering 'whether he [Howe] has any authority to treat with persons authorized by Congress … and what that authority is and to hear such proposition as he shall think fit to make respecting the same'.[29] Sullivan was sent back to Howe with a copy of the congressional resolution and after an exchange of letters it was agreed that Howe would meet the committee from the American congress on Staten Island opposite Perth Amboy, New Jersey.[30]

The meeting between Howe and the American congressional committee, consisting of Benjamin Franklin of Pennsylvania, John Adams of Massachusetts and John Rutledge of South Carolina, took place on 11 September on Staten Island. It was the only meeting during the entire war prior to the peace negotiations in 1782 between the legally constituted representatives of the British and American governments. Howe opened the meeting by informing the Americans that he believed that the differences between Great Britain and America 'might be accommodated to the satisfaction of both'. Then Howe explained the background of the peace commission and said 'That he had not, nor did expect ever to have, powers to consider the colonies in the light of independent States.' The admiral then proceeded to say that he was conferring with the Americans as private individuals and not as an official committee of the Continental Congress for he did not have the authority to recognise that body. At this point Franklin interjected saying that the admiral

> might consider the gentlemen present in any view he thought proper, that they were also at liberty to consider themselves in their real Character ... and that the conversation might be held as amongst friends.

Howe then said that it was 'absolutely impossible' for him to 'treat, or confer' upon the basis of American independence, but that

> he flattered himself if That were given up, there was still room for him to effect the King's Purpose. That His Majesty's most earnest desire was to make his American subjects happy, to cause a Reform in what affected their Freedom of their Legislation, and to concur with his Parliament in the Redress of any real Grievances. That his Powers were, generally, to restore Peace and grant Pardons, to attend to Complaints and Representations, and to confer upon means of establishing a Re Union upon terms honorable and advantageous to the Colonies as well as Great Britain.

Howe then concluded by saying that he had explained the 'general purport of the commission' and that he now wished to hear what the Americans proposed.

The American answer to Howe was uncompromising and unyielding. Franklin, who spoke first, said that the Americans

> could not expect happiness now under the *Domination* of Great Britain, that all former attachment was *obliterated*, and that America could not return again to the Domination of Great Britain.

Adams then followed, saying that all the American colonies had agreed to independence and that it was not in the power of Congress to 'treat' in any other way but as 'independent states' and, that he would 'not depart from the Idea of Independency'. Rutledge agreed with Franklin and Adams saying that 'it was impossible the People should consent to come again under the English Government' and that South Carolina 'would not (even if they, the Congress could desire it) return to the King's government'. At this point Howe, seeing the futility of further discussions, concluded the meeting by saying that he had no authority, and never expected to have, to negotiate with the American colonies as independent states. Further, 'That if the colonies would not give up the system of Independency, it was impossible for him to enter into any negotiation'. On this note the discussions ended, having floundered on the issue of American independence. The Americans returned to Philadelphia and submitted a report of the meeting with Howe to the Continental Congress which was published several days later.[31]

Howe's attempt to end the American rebellion through negotiation collapsed with the meeting with Franklin, Adams and Rutledge on 11 September at Staten Island. The Howes, in an attempt to appeal to the American people over the heads of the Continental Congress, published a declaration asking the Americans to return to their allegiance to the Crown and to 'accept the Blessings of Peace, and be secured in the Free Enjoyment of their LIBERTY AND PROPERTIES, upon the true Principles of the Constitution'. The next day, 20 September, Howe wrote a dispatch to Germain giving an account of the meeting with the three-man American Congressional committee and the issuing of the 19 September declaration to the Americans. At the same time both of the Howe brothers wrote a joint dispatch to Germain saying:

> We do not yet perceive any symptom of that Disposition to Allegiance and Submission to legal Government, which would justify us in expecting to see public Tranquillity soon restored.[32]

In the talks with Franklin in London during December 1775, Howe did not discuss any of the great constitutional questions, which if settled might have averted the American Declaration of Independence. Then after 4 July 1776, in the absence of a totally catastrophic American defeat on the battle-field, Howe apparently expected the Americans to disregard and ignore the Declaration of Independence and simply return to their allegiance to the crown. One of the striking things about all of the negotiations, and attempts at negotiations, with the Americans, is that nowhere in the record is there the slightest hint of Howe's personal views of what should be the proper and correct constitutional relations between Britain and America. From the opening of the talks with Franklin in London at the end of 1774 to the meeting with the American congressional committee in September of 1776 at Staten Island, Howe showed an uncanny ability not to under-stand the realities of the politics of the American Revolution.

The British renewed the offensive fifteen days after the American evacu-ation of Brooklyn Heights and four days after the talks between Howe and the Americans at Staten Island. On 15 September British troops landed at Kipps Bay on the east side of the island of Manhattan. The battle for New York began on the morning of 15 September when four British war-ships,[33] in a diversion, proceeded about six miles up the Hudson river. The actual attack began at 10am when flat-bottomed boats carrying British and German infantry emerged from the shelter of Newtown Creek on the Long Island shore and began to form into assault formations in the East river. About an hour later five frigates,[34] which had anchored under cover of darkness in a line broadside to the shore, opened a heavy bombardment at the site of the intended landing. This violent bombardment forced the American defenders from the landing site; and at about noon the first wave of king's troops landed at Kipps Bay without opposition. The British then advanced as far inland as Murray Hill (now about 38th Street and Park Avenue), cutting the Post Road but then halted for several hours until the rest of the army had landed and the position was consolidated before resuming the advance. The failure of the British to attack imme-diately to the west across Manhattan Island to the Hudson river, cutting both the Bloomingdale Road and the Post Road, gave several thousand American troops the opportunity of escaping from New York City. The British resumed the offensive in the late afternoon and by the end of the day had cleared Manhattan of American troops south of MacGown's Pass (roughly the present 96th Street). At this point the British offensive halted for nearly a month while a way was discovered to manoeuvre the Americans out of their strong positions in northern Manhattan.[35] A slow-ness and ponderousness of decision and movement marked the British effort before New York City in 1776.

After the capture of New York City and Lower Manhattan Island the British military actions and movements were further slowed when General Howe concluded that it would take at least another year of campaigning to defeat the Americans and crush the rebellion.[36] Therefore, the British army spent the next several weeks consolidating their hold on Lower Manhattan and figuring out how to force the Americans from their strongholds in northern Manhattan, Kingsbridge and Westchester. Finally, after almost a month of inaction, a series of amphibious movements, beginning on the night of 11 October, were undertaken to land troops at Pell's Point near New Rochelle on Long Island Sound. After another short delay, the British army then marched northwards towards White Plains in an attempt to trap the American forces between the Bronx and Hudson rivers before they could retreat from northern Manhattan and Kingsbridge. Washington, however, quickly perceived General Howe's intentions, evacuated northern Manhattan and Kingsbridge (with the unwise exception of the garrison of Fort Washington), and with the bulk of the Continental Army marched to White Plains, reaching that area before the British, and in time to take up a strong defensive position. Here on 28 October the Americans fought an indecisive defensive battle after which they withdrew northward beyond the Croton river into another strong defensive position.[37]

After the Battle of White Plains General Howe withdrew southward towards the Bronx in order to attack the isolated American stronghold at Fort Washington and to then land on the west bank of the Hudson river and drive the American army from New Jersey. On 16 November Fort Washington was stormed and captured by the king's troops taking over two thousand American prisoners. Two days later the Royal Navy landed British troops on the western shore of the Hudson river, about eight miles north of Fort Lee, forcing the Americans to withdraw into central New Jersey.[38]

While British and German troops were landing in New Jersey and capturing Fort Lee, Clinton and Commodore Sir Peter Parker at New York City were preparing an expeditionary force to seize Newport, Rhode Island which was to be used as a base by the Royal Navy. New York City was not deemed a proper base for the Royal Navy because of the navigational difficulties in entering the place and lack of suitable areas, owing to ice and no holding ground, to anchor warships during the winter. However, Clinton objected to the entire project as a strategic blunder. He still thought that enveloping and destroying the American army was the best way to victory. With the American army in New Jersey rapidly retreating towards the Delaware river and being pursued by the king's troops, Clinton put forward a number of schemes to have the force intended for Rhode Island transported instead to the Delaware river, Chesapeake Bay, or the coast of New Jersey to be landed ahead of the retreating American army to trap them.[39] However, Clinton's strategic advice was rejected once more, and the expedition to Rhode Island sailed. On 9 December 7,000 British troops, supported by fifteen warships,[40] landed on the island of Rhode Island and occupied Newport without opposition.[41]

The British effort to crush the rebellion in America with one campaign at New York in 1776 ended in December with the occupation of Newport and the flight of an apparently disintegrating American army across New Jersey into Pennsylvania. The British had swept all before them: with the exception of a skirmish at Harlem Heights, the British had been victorious in every battle of the campaign and the Americans had been driven from every position they had occupied. At the end of the campaign General Howe's soldiers controlled Staten Island, the western end of Long Island, Manhattan Island, a large area of New Jersey, and Newport, Rhode Island. But the campaign at New York in 1776 had not been a decisive victory for the British as American resistance had not been broken. All the efforts at negotiation with the Americans had failed and the Continental Army had not been destroyed. The war in America would continue and most importantly Washington, during the fighting around New York in 1776, had learned that the key to American victory was not winning battles, but rather keeping the Continental Army intact as a fighting force. After New York, Washington resolved:

> We should on all occasions avoid a general action, or put anything to risk, unless compelled by a necessity into which we ought never be drawn.[42]

This doctrine became the keystone of Washington's strategy.

Military strategy in America for the most part had been formulated by General Howe and it fell to his brother Admiral Howe to provide the requisite ships, small craft and seamen to support the operations of the army. What is now called the New York Metropolitan Area is laced with waterways, and during the 1776 campaign the British army carried out five major amphibious assaults. According to Admiral Howe the 1776 campaign at New York consisted of 'repeated Embarkations and Landings often of considerable corps of troops for near four months'.[43] Further, it was quickly discovered that the army was dependent on naval resources to provide the water transport for all the supplies and materials required for military operations. In fact even before the campaign began, General Howe believed that it would be logistically impossible for the army to operate far from a navigable waterway in America.[44] The provision of all the small craft and naval manpower required to support the army's operations cut deeply into the resources of the squadron in America and Admiral Howe found that he did not have the ships to both blockade the American coast and at the same time support the operations of the army in America.[45]

The need to support military operations in America required the employment of a large number of warships as well as the use of huge amounts of other naval resources. As one navy officer explained:

> You have no idea of the number of men it takes to attend upon such an army as this; with all the ships we have (which is two thirds of those

employed in America) when all the flat boats, galleys, gondolas, horse stages &c. &c. are mann'd there is scarce men enough left on board many of the ships to move them so that we really want six or eight lines of battle ships; not so much perhaps for the use of the ships, as for their large complements of men for the purposes before mentioned.[46]

During the campaign of 1776 the strength of Howe's squadron averaged some seventy ships, of which only two were ships of the line. On 13 August 1776 twenty-seven warships (with an additional six expected to arrive) of Howe's squadron were deployed at New York supporting the army, twelve more were supporting land operations in Canada; only twenty-four warships, mostly small ones, were scattered along the coast of North America from Prince Edward Island to St Augustine in what amounted to a token blockade of America. By 18 September no ships of the Royal Navy were blockading the entrances of Chesapeake and Delaware Bays while thirty-three ships were at New York and nine more were in the St Lawrence river supporting the army; only forty-two ships were left to blockade the entire coast of America. The situation did not change as the campaign of 1776 drew to a close. On 24 November, only twenty ships were on blockade duty while the remaining fifty-four were deployed in support of the army.[47]

With the end of offensive land operations in December 1776, a number of ships were released from the task of supporting the army. However, because of the lack of repair facilities in America and the need to defend British bases at New York, Newport, R.I., and Halifax, Nova Scotia, the blockade of the American coast did not markedly improve in effectiveness. New York, after its capture in the autumn of 1776, became not only the centre of British operations, but also the main logistical base for the British forces in America. To defend New York, a number of warships had to be stationed there permanently. Newport, R.I. and Halifax, Nova Scotia also required warships for their defence. The number of warships available for blockade duty was further reduced during the winter of 1776–7 by the need to send vessels for careening either to Halifax, Antigua or Jamaica and, if a major dockyard repair was required, to England.[48] The need to send ships either to the West Indies or Nova Scotia for minor repairs was somewhat mitigated by undertaking some of the work at New York. Howe recruited civilian workmen at New York and also employed seamen and ships' carpenters drawn from HMS *Eagle* as well as from transports to repair ships. During the period from September 1776 to March 1777 some sixty ships and vessels of Howe's squadron, as well as some eighty flat-bottomed boats, were repaired at New York.[49] Nevertheless, at any given time during the winter of 1776–7 a substantial number of the ships of Howe's squadron were either undergoing repairs or deployed in static defence of British bases in America.

On 5 January 1777, out of eighty ships under the command of Howe, twenty-four were stationed in the New York area though three were under orders to proceed to the West Indies for repairs. Another eleven were either en route or about to depart for England. Six were in the St Lawrence river. Another twenty-four ships based at Halifax and Rhode Island were deployed to blockade the coasts of New England or to protect Newport and Halifax. The remaining fifteen ships (of which five were under orders to refit in the West Indies and one was unfit for further service) were assigned to the impossible task of attempting to blockade the American coast southward from New York to St Augustine. By 1 March 1777 there were seventy-two ships under Howe's command and still no effective blockade of the American coast. Twenty-three warships (six of which were refitting) were stationed in the New York region. Two were en route to England. Twenty-four others (of which one was ordered to the West Indies for refitting) were blockading the coasts of New England and protecting Newport and Halifax. Seven other ships were in the St Lawrence. South of New York the coast of America was virtually unblockaded and only sixteen warships were stationed there, of which eleven were either about to depart or had already left for the West Indies.[50] Hence the failure of the blockade of the American coast during the winter of 1776–7 was largely due to a shortage of ships. The need to protect places such as New York, Newport and Halifax, when combined with the necessity of sending ships for repairs to the West Indies, Nova Scotia or England owing to a lack of careening wharfs and dockyards in America, reduced the force actually available to Howe to a mere rump of the squadron stationed in America.

The blockade, even with all its shortcomings, during the winter of 1776–7 did adversely affect the American economy. American seaborne trade decreased and the prices of foreign goods rose in American markets.[51] Nevertheless, the economic dislocation caused by Howe's blockading ships was not sufficient to alter the course of the war. The inability of Howe's ships to effectively blockade the American coast had a huge effect on the conduct of the war in America. Even if one measures the success or failure of the British effort simply in terms of ships taken or lost, the blockade was a failure. While none of the new frigates of the Continental Navy got to sea in 1776 due to the blockade,[52] the Royal Navy could not prevent the Americans from sending cruisers to European seas to attack British shipping. The first American cruiser to appear in European waters was perhaps the *Rover* of Salem, which was reported on 31 August 1776 to have captured four British merchant ships off Cádiz.[53] The *Rover* was quickly followed to European seas by a number of other American warships and privateers.[54] During 1776 American warships and privateers captured or destroyed at least 347 British vessels, including several loaded ordnance storeships and six troop transports,[55] while Howe's squadron recaptured twenty-six British ships and took at least 140 American ships.[56] However, the real failure of the Royal Navy's blockade can best be measured by the degree to which the British were able to cut off, or at least retard, the flow of munitions and other warlike stores to America from Europe and the West Indies. During the first two years of the war American armies were sustained by foreign munitions, and the failure of the blockade gave the Americans the opportunity to obtain the necessary materials with which to continue the war.[57] Howe was severely criticised for his conduct of the blockade of America.[58] One of his many contemporary critics was Germain who called the admiral 'the most disinterested man I know ... when he might avail himself of some rich prizes'.[59] There are also those who believed that the inability of the British to effectively blockade the American coast during the winter of 1776–7 can be in part traced to a reluctance in Howe to deal harshly with the Americans.[60] The admiral's instructions of 15 January 1777 to Commodore William Hotham, the commander of a detachment of ships blockading the southern American coast, are usually cited as evidence of Howe's unwillingness to conduct ruthlessly the blockade of America. Hotham was ordered not only to enforce the Capture Act by seizing or destroying all American ocean-going vessels, but,

> To grant, and it is advisable to take all suitable opportunities to allow, the Inhabitants dwelling upon the Coast adjacent to the Stations of the Ships under your Orders, to use their ordinary Fishing-Craft, as other means providing for their daily subsistence and support; where the same does not seem liable to any material abuse.[61]

These instructions, which by the standards of modern total war are conciliatory and moderate in tone, can be interpreted in several different ways. When the text of Howe's instructions for the conduct of the blockade of America was seen in England many people thought 'that these kind of indulgences are more likely to protract than hasten the conclusion of this unnatural contest'.[62] On the other hand it can be argued that attacking small fishing craft would be counter-productive because it would force, by economic necessity, a large section of the American maritime population to seek employment as privateersmen. Probably Howe issued these instructions to Hotham simply because he was not an ideologically inflamed Loyalist, nor a practitioner of total war. Howe, as a product of the *ancien régime*, probably did not think in terms of total destruction as a means of obtaining a military objective. While Howe's instructions to Hotham do raise questions about his conduct of the war in America, many of the criticisms of his conduct of the blockade are unfair and overlook the great difficulties in blockading America: the shortage of ships, the great length of the American coast, and the need to support the army.

The policy of stationing ships on blockade duty singly or in small groups up and down the American coast was potentially one of considerable risk. There was always the possibility that a superior American force might, without warning, put to sea, and overpower the blockading ships before they could be effectively concentrated to oppose the American force. On 21 May 1777 the strategic weakness of the British naval deployments in America became apparent when an American squadron commanded by Captain John Manley of the Continental Navy escaped from Boston. The American squadron consisted of the Continental frigates *Boston* and *Hancock* along with nine privateers. This American squadron appeared to be extremely powerful and dangerous, but in fact owing to the weakness of the American command arrangements, all but disintegrated as a fighting force several days after leaving Boston.[63] Manley's departure from Boston greatly alarmed the British, for the American force appeared to be capable of destroying piecemeal the ships of the British blockade.

When news of the American squadron sailing from Boston reached Howe at New York, there were no effective counter-measures that the admiral could take. Howe had twenty-nine warships in the New York area,[64] but they were assigned to support pending military operations in New Jersey. Howe explained his helplessness:

> The attendance of the ships of war which might otherwise be spared from occasional service within the limits of this port, being necessary to co-operate in the expected movements of the army, I am not able, in this case, to make any detachments from the number to proceed in pursuit of the enemy, which under the circumstances would be proper.[65]

The blockade of New England had to be abandoned while the blockading ships were concentrated and began searching for the American squadron.

Manley, after a brush with the escort of a British military convoy, proceeded to the Grand Banks of Newfoundland, and on 7 June the *Boston* and *Hancock* captured the 28-gun frigate HMS *Fox* of the Newfoundland squadron.[66] News of the loss of HMS *Fox* and the appearance of the American squadron on the Grand Banks threw the British into a panic, and the ship of the line HMS *Bienfaisant* was sent from England to reinforce the Newfoundland squadron.[67] After cruising for several weeks on the Grand Banks, Manley with the *Boston*, *Hancock* and their prize proceeded towards the coast of New England. But on 7 July off Cape Sable the American force was intercepted by HMS *Flora*, HMS *Rainbow* and HM Brig *Victor*. A running battle ensued, lasting thirty-nine hours, during which the British captured the *Hancock* and Manley retook HMS *Fox*.[68] While resulting in little material damage, Manley's raid demonstrated the strategic weakness of the British blockade of America. Coupled with other failures of the blockade, Manley's sortie showed that Howe's squadron did not consist of the required number of ships for the simultaneous tasks of blockading the American coast while at the same time supporting the operations of the British army.

One way to increase the effectiveness of the blockade while at the same time maintaining the capability of supporting military operations was to reinforce the squadron in America. However, the British simply did not have the required number of ships to simultaneously conduct operations in America and maintain a two power standard in Europe. It was believed at the Admiralty that France and Spain posed a greater danger to Britain in the long run than the rebellion in America. It was Sandwich's maxim 'that England ought for her own security to have a superior force in readiness on her side'.[69] Hence, because of the possibility of French and Spanish intervention against Britain in the war, there were limits to the number of ships that could be deployed in America. Germain on the other hand believed that it would be unnecessary to send additional ships to America, for if harsh measures were adopted by the British forces in America 'a salutary check will unavoidably be put on the success of the rebel privateers'. Therefore, on 3 March 1777 the American secretary directed that Howe consider attacking and destroying or occupying major seaports in New England as a means of destroying the bases of American naval forces and immobilising the manpower of New England in local defensive measures.[70] However, both of the Howes rejected schemes for attacking and destroying New England seaports on the grounds that they did not have the necessary ships and troops to undertake such projects 'without interfering materially with more important operations of the campaign'.[71]

The Howe brothers believed that the best way to end the rebellion was by means of regular military operations aimed at the occupation of American cities and the maintenance of an effective blockade. They had concluded at the end of 1776 that the American rebels could be decisively defeated in the campaign of 1777 if the British forces were reinforced with 15,000 additional troops and ten ships of the line manned by a number of 'supernumerary seamen for manning boats'.[72] The brothers intended to use the additional ships of the line to supply the naval manpower required to support military operations and thus end the necessity of having to lift the blockade of the American coast in order for the army to be able to undertake amphibious operations. However, the Howes would not receive the reinforcements they desired for the Admiralty would only release five ships of the line for service in America.[73] On 1 May 1777 Howe appointed Captain Henry Duncan, the commander of HMS *Eagle* to be 'adjutant general' of the squadron in America. At the same time Captain Roger Curtis, commander of HMS *Senegal* was promoted to post captain and appointed to command HMS *Eagle*. Howe invented the position and title of adjutant general. Sandwich, who did not approve of the title and thought the position to be 'a novel institution', nevertheless saw the need for the appointment and agreed to find the money to pay Duncan.[74] Later Rodney would appoint Captain Sir Charles Douglas to a similar position. Duncan's new duties would be the same as those of a first captain or captain of the fleet. That is to say that Duncan would become Howe's chief-of-staff and the appointment was designed to relieve Howe from the crushing load of paperwork involved in commanding and administering a squadron which by 1778 would consist of some eighty ships scattered up and down the length of the American coast. In previous command assignments, such as those during the Seven Years War, Howe's task for the most part was one of putting into effect policies and carrying out orders formulated by others. Now in command of the squadron in America, Howe had ceased to be a doer or a follower of orders. Rather, he was increasingly required to conceptualise and formulate policy and strategy which then had to be transformed into the orders and instructions required by his subordinates to carry his intentions into effect. Duncan's role was to release Howe from routine paperwork in order to free up time for the admiral to engage in more important responsibilities of the exercise of command.

The 1777 campaign in America is one of the most appalling examples of strategic planning in British military history. During the campaign one British army would move southward from Canada towards Albany on the Hudson river, while another British army would proceed by sea to capture Philadelphia. The disaster at Saratoga was the result of the British failure to co-ordinate the movements of the armies of Generals Howe and Burgoyne who would engage in two mutually exclusive campaigns during 1777 in America. Admiral Howe appears to have played little part in the strategic planning: one of the two most important decisions of the British effort – to permit Burgoyne to attack upstate New York from Canada via Lakes Champlain and George – was made in London and General Howe in New York made the decision to mount a sea-borne invasion of Pennsylvania to capture Philadelphia. Admiral Howe's and the Royal Navy's contribution to the campaign was to provide naval support for the expedition to capture Philadelphia.[75]

From the autumn of 1776 to the spring of 1777 General Howe drew up plans for the campaign of 1777. His first scheme called for British forces in America to be reinforced by 15,000 men and 'eight or ten' ships of the line and for simultaneous offensives to be undertaken in New England, New Jersey and the Hudson river valley. But with the failure of the government to send reinforcements, General Howe's plan for the 1777 campaign began to turn away from New England and the Hudson river and to evolve into a fixation on the capture of Philadelphia. At the beginning of 1777 the general proposed that the main British army should move across New Jersey towards Philadelphia while a corps went by sea to the Delaware river. Then in the spring of 1777 General Howe's plan underwent another drastic change. On 2 April the general wrote to London that he was going to leave a garrison at New York City and transport the bulk of his army by sea to Philadelphia.[76]

After weeks of delays the invasion of Pennsylvania got under way on 23 July, when under the command of Admiral Howe, a force of 267 ships carrying 14,000 rank and file escorted by twenty-two warships, sailed from Sandy Hook.[77] Beset by calms and in the face of prevailing south-westerly winds, the fleet crawled southward along the coast of New Jersey towards the entrance of Delaware Bay.[78] On 30 July the invasion force was off Cape Henlopen and was joined by Captain Andrew Snape Hamond, the commander of the squadron blockading Delaware Bay. Hamond had precise knowledge of the navigation of Delaware Bay and the lower reaches of the Delaware river and had for several weeks, on the orders of Admiral Howe, been making preparations for landing the British army on the banks of the Delaware. But General Howe had not yet settled on a landing site; he was waiting to see what the American army would do. On 16 July before leaving New York the general wrote to Germain explaining that he:

> Proposed going up the Delaware in order to be nearer this place [New York City] than I should be by taking the course of the Chesapeake Bay which I once intended and preferred to that of the Delaware provided the enemy had discovered a disposition to defend Pennsylvania.[79]

That is, if Washington and the American army crossed the Delaware and moved south of Philadelphia, General Howe would invade Pennsylvania by way of Chesapeake Bay; but if Washington remained in New Jersey, the British would go up the Delaware river.

On the morning of 30 July Hamond went on board HMS *Eagle* and conferred at some length with the Howes. The meeting began with Hamond stating erroneously that Washington's army had crossed the Delaware river and was marching on Wilmington, Delaware, when in fact the Continental Army was just crossing the Delaware north of Philadelphia. Hamond and the Howes then discussed the relative merits of conducting a landing either in Chesapeake Bay or Delaware Bay. According to Hamond's account of the meeting, General Howe opposed landing on the shores of Delaware Bay for the following reasons:

> As General Washington, by the long passage of the Fleet from New York, had got his army over the Delaware before the fleet arrived, great opposition was expected to be given the troops at landing at Newcastle or Wilmington the place intended. That the Enemy expecting the Fleet to come into the River had made uncommon preparations to the men of War & Transports with Fire Ships, fire rafts, and had besides a considerable number of Row Galley, Xebecks, & Floating Battery's, which in the narrow navigation & rapid tides of the River might do great damage among the transports.

Hamond went on to report that the general was in favour of proceeding to the head of Chesapeake Bay where

> The troops would be put ashore without any molestation, have time to recover the Horses after the fatigue of the Voyage before they entered service, and where the Transports could remain in perfect security.

The discussion ended when the two Howes stepped out on the stern galley of HMS *Eagle* for a short private talk. When they returned to the cabin, Hamond was informed by General Howe that: 'Since there was no doubt that the enemy was apprised of the plan of the Expedition ... it confirmed him to his design of landing his army at the Head of the Elk in the Chesapeake rather than the Delaware.' Hamond was surprised by this decision and attempted to persuade the Howes to land the army on the shores of Delaware Bay. General Howe refused to reconsider, and on the afternoon of 30 July the fleet sailed southward from Cape Henlopen. General Howe seems to have decided to land at the head of the Elk river in Chesapeake Bay instead of in Delaware Bay because he thought that the American army was approaching Wilmington.[80]

For the next fifteen days, during the hottest season of the year, the ships carrying General Howe's army crept slowly southward along the coast of America towards the entrance of Chesapeake Bay. They encountered nothing but calms and south-westerly winds; water ran short and all but a few of the army's horses died. It was not until 15 August that the fleet entered Chesapeake Bay. With Hamond in HMS *Roebuck* leading the way and acting as a guide, the force proceeded slowly up the bay to Turkey Point, Maryland. Finally, on 25 August the British army landed without opposition on the eastern side of the Elk river near Cecil Court House.[81] Thirty days in all had been consumed reaching the Head of the Elk river, a point almost as far from Philadelphia as the port of embarkation – New York City. After landing, the British army marched on Philadelphia. An indecisive action was fought with the Americans at Brandywine Creek and then on 26 September General Howe's troops occupied Philadelphia without opposition. At this point, all offensive operations in Pennsylvania halted while the ships of the Royal Navy, supported by troops, fought a bitter prolonged battle to open the Delaware river to British shipping.

The American forces had to be cleared from the maritime approaches to Philadelphia if the British army in the city was to be supplied. This task proved to be extremely difficult, for the Americans had placed six lines of underwater obstacles, or *chevaux-de-frise*, in the Delaware river effectively blocking navigation before the city of Philadelphia.[82] The American *chevaux-de-frise* were defended by a number of gunboats, fire-rafts and galleys. In addition, the American obstacles were covered by the guns of a

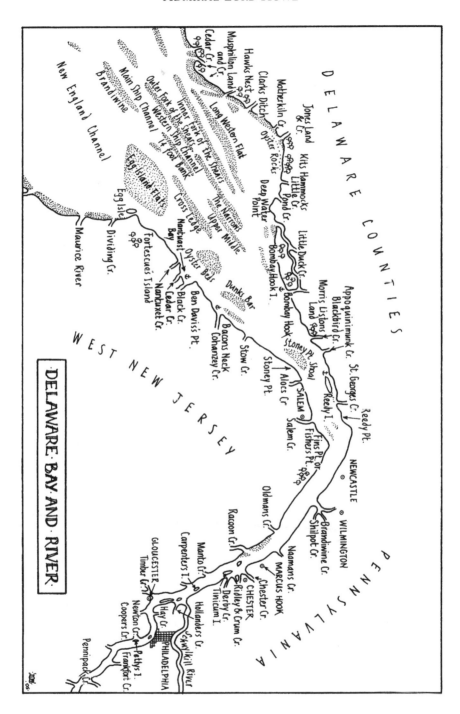

number of forts and batteries that were difficult to approach because they were protected by shoal water and swamps. The American underwater obstacles, small craft and forts formed an extremely strong defensive system that, at considerable cost in men and material, would take the king's forces almost two months to reduce.

The forcing of the Delaware began on 2 October when two regiments of infantry, supported by a small squadron[83] under the command of Hamond, seized without resistance the American fort at Billingsport, New Jersey, which defended the first two lines of *chevaux-de-frise*. On 4 October Hamond's seamen began clearing a passage through the obstacles at Billingsport. It was not an easy task. The working parties were hampered and harassed by long-range fire from Fort Mifflin on Ford Island, and the British warships were forced almost daily to withdraw temporarily down river by frequent American sorties with galleys and fire-rafts. On 15 October Hamond had at last managed to clear a passage to the *chevaux-de-frise* at Billingsport.[84]

Admiral Howe had arrived in the Delaware river on 6 October and soon perceived, even before Hamond succeeded in breaching the first two lines of American underwater obstacles, that the remaining four lines of *chevaux-de-frise* could not be cleared until Fort Mifflin had been seized.[85] But as General Howe confessed in a letter to Germain, simply getting near enough to attack Fort Mifflin was a 'tedious operation', for it was thought that the only way to do so was to gain control of both banks of the Delaware opposite the American fort.[86]

On the night of 8 October British army engineers began constructing batteries on Carpenter's and Province Islands on the Pennsylvania side of the river. The work was retarded by rain and by the Americans, who not only attacked the British, but also attempted to flood the low-lying islands by destroying dykes. Nevertheless, on 15 October four weak batteries were completed and began to bombard Fort Mifflin.[87]

While the army engineers worked on the Pennsylvania side of the Delaware, the Howes devised a plan for attacking and capturing the New Jersey side of the river. They decided to undertake a combined ground and naval attack against Fort Mifflin and Fort Mercer at Red Bank on the New Jersey shore opposite Fort Island. The plan called for 1,600 Hessian infantry, led by Colonel Carl Emil Kurt von Donop, a brave but impetuous officer, to storm Fort Mercer. Meanwhile HMS *Vigilant* was to proceed up the river through a narrow and shallow channel lying between Hog Island and the Pennsylvania shore and arrive at the rear of Fort Mifflin. As the Hessians and HMS *Vigilant* advanced, a diversion was to be created by HMS *Augusta*, a new 64-gun ship of the line, HMS *Roebuck*, HMS *Liverpool*, HMS *Pearl* and HMS *Merlin* advancing directly up the main channel of the Delaware river towards Fort Mifflin and the lines of *chevaux-de-frise*.[88]

The attacks on Forts Mifflin and Mercer were disasters. In the late afternoon of 22 October the Hessians, led by von Donop, assaulted Fort Mercer without scaling ladders or adequate artillery support. The attack failed and the Hessians were repulsed, with a loss of 371 men including von Donop, who was mortally wounded and captured.[89] As the Hessians attacked Fort Mercer, the Royal Navy attempted to move simultaneously against Fort Mifflin. However, because of adverse winds, HMS *Vigilant* could not proceed up the channel between Hog Island and the Pennsylvania shore as planned. Nevertheless, on the flood tide and against a northerly wind HMS *Augusta*, HMS *Roebuck*, HMS *Liverpool*, HMS *Merlin* and HMS *Pearl* managed to proceed up the main channel towards the *chevaux-de-frise* off Fort Mifflin in an attempt to divert American attention from the Hessian assault. Anchoring off the *chevaux-de-frise* the five warships were engaged by Fort Mifflin and a number of American galleys for several hours. With the failure of the Hessian attack on Fort Mercer and the coming of darkness and the ebb tide, the British warships began to withdraw down the river. But in the darkness and because the current, obstructed by the *chevaux-de-frise*, had changed the course of the river's channel, *Augusta* and *Merlin* ran aground. Attempts to refloat the ships were frustrated by the northerly wind, and early the next morning the Americans discovered the plight of the British vessels. A fierce action ensued as the Americans attacked the grounded British warships with galleys, floating batteries and fire rafts. Then, at about 11am as the British were preparing to lighten HMS *Augusta* to refloat her, the ship 'by some accident, not otherwise connected with the circumstances of the action but as it was probably caused by the wads of her guns ... took fire abaft'. She was rapidly engulfed in flames and had to be abandoned by her crew. To prevent the other ships from being damaged when HMS *Augusta*'s magazines exploded, Howe ordered that HMS *Merlin* be evacuated and destroyed and that HMS *Roebuck*, HMS *Liverpool* and HMS *Pearl* should withdraw down the river. At noon the first British attempt to gain control of the Delaware river ended when HMS *Augusta* blew up with such force that the shock 'felt like an earthquake in Philadelphia'.[90]

After the failure of the attack on Fort Mercer and the loss of HMS *Augusta* and HMS *Merlin* the British concentrated their efforts on reducing Fort Mifflin. Ten heavy naval guns were emplaced on Province Island to fire on the fort from the Pennsylvania shore and, on 10 November, the British began to bombard heavily. At the same time, navy officers were preparing to attack the fort with warships and were reconnoitring and buoying the approaches. On the morning of 15 November, with a favourable wind and a flood tide, the British attack began. While HMS *Vigilant* and a hulk mounting three heavy guns inched their way through the narrow channel between Hog and Carpenter's Islands towards the rear of Fort Mifflin, HMS *Somerset* and HMS *Isis* proceeded up the main channel and attacked the front of the American fortification. Simultaneously,

HMS *Roebuck*, HMS *Pearl* and HMS *Liverpool* vigorously bombarded and silenced a newly-constructed American battery at Manit Creek in order to prevent it from firing on the ships attacking the front of Fort Mifflin. By 9am HMS *Vigilant* and the hulk began to bombard the rear of Fort Mifflin, while *Somerset* and *Isis* continued to heavily engage the front of the American fort. By nightfall the American fire from the rear of Fort Mifflin was silenced and HMS *Vigilant* had moved to within 300 feet of the fortification, ready to support with naval gunfire an amphibious assault planned for the morning. However, during the night the American forces escaped to New Jersey, so when the British troops landed on Fort Island in the morning, they occupied Fort Mifflin without opposition.[91]

With the loss of Fort Mifflin, the Americans gave up the fight for the Delaware river. Fort Mercer was abandoned and blown up, and most of the American galleys, gunboats and floating batteries were either captured or destroyed while attempting to escape up river past the British forces at Philadelphia. On 23 November the first British ships arrived at the city.[92] Fifty-nine days had elapsed between the time when the first British troops and the first British ship arrived at Philadelphia. For two months the British forces in Pennsylvania had been strategically immobilised, while a protracted, costly and difficult battle was fought to secure the maritime supply lines of the British army at Philadelphia. The opening of the Delaware to British navigation marked the end of the campaign of 1777.

The blockade of the American coast, owing to a shortage of ships, was for the most part suspended during the British offensive against Philadelphia. Except for a strong squadron off the coasts of northern New England and Nova Scotia, during the summer of 1777 most of the ships of Howe's fleet were tied down in supporting the operations of the army in New York and Pennsylvania, thereby as the admiral himself admitted, making it impossible to effectively blockade the American coast.[93] Even with a rump of a blockade the Royal Navy in America did inflict some hard blows on the Americans during 1777. Between 27 May and 24 October, during the height of the army's campaigning season, Howe's ships captured 131 enemy ships,[94] and all of the thirteen large new frigates of the Continental Navy had either been captured, destroyed, or bottled up in port, while HMS *Fox*, the only British warship to be captured by the Americans in 1777, was quickly retaken.[95] However, capturing American ships and crippling the striking power of the Continental Navy would not bring about the defeat of the Americans.

On 31 October 1777, at the height of the battle to open the Delaware river to navigation, news of Burgoyne's surrender reached the British in Pennsylvania.[96] The disaster at Saratoga had a shattering effect on the British in America for the defeat unmasked the futility of the British effort and the realities of the war. Lord Cornwallis, with classic understatement, summed up the feelings of a majority of the British when he wrote:

'Burgoyne's disaster has greatly changed the face of affairs in this country. God only knows how this business will end.'[97] After learning of Saratoga, General Howe informed Whitehall that nothing could be done in America without more troops and ships, and yet he did not foresee 'a successful termination to the war'.[98]

Admiral Howe, in a dispatch to the Admiralty from the Delaware river dated 10 December, declared flatly that owing to the shortage of ships and the need to support the army, the blockade of America was and would continue to be a failure. The admiral wrote that the British army had not been able to subdue the Americans and was penned up in three small bridgeheads – Philadelphia, New York City and Newport, R.I. – which were indefensible without large-scale naval support. He further stated that he understood 'the first object of my instructions to be, cooperating with the army in services the general is to undertake'. He was carrying out these instructions at the beginning of 1778 by stationing twenty-six warships at Rhode Island, twenty-five at New York, in the Delaware river, and twelve cruising in the Gulf of Maine or stationed at Halifax, five in the entrance of Chesapeake Bay, four at Quebec and six off the coasts of the Carolinas and Georgia. In this dispatch Howe also pointed out that the number and effectiveness of the ships on blockade duty was reduced because of the shortage of seamen; the disrepair of the ships; a lack of proper repair facilities; the need to withdraw ships, without replacement, from cruising stations in order to obtain water and provisions; and the great strain placed on officers and men by serving constantly, even while in port, under combat conditions. As a result, until he received more ships and was freed from the need to support the army the bulk of the ships of the Royal Navy in America would be absorbed in defensive operations instead of blockade duty. Howe in this dispatch failed, as did most other British officers in America at the beginning of 1778, to perceive that the war was no longer a matter of quelling a rebellion in America: Britain was being propelled into a world war by the disaster at Saratoga.[99]

Both of the Howes by the end of the campaign of 1777 had become disillusioned with the war in America. On receiving the news of Burgoyne's surrender at Saratoga they requested to be relieved of their commands and to be granted permission to return to England. General Howe gave as his reasons that the government had not listened to his recommendations nor had it supported him properly.[100] Admiral Howe, who thought that it was impossible to win the war, hinted that his health was failing, and his wife wrote to Lord North requesting that he be permitted to quit the command in America. Both of the Howes probably had unstated motives for desiring to give up their commands in America.[101] No doubt they believed – and correctly so – that they would be blamed for the failure of the British effort and wanted to hurry to London to seek vindication for their conduct in America.

Admiral Howe, while awaiting permission to return to England, spent the winter of 1777–8 at Newport, R.I. The ships under Howe's command continued to be deployed in defence of the British enclaves – Philadelphia, New York and Newport, R.I. – while at the same time continuing to blockade the coast of America in an attempt to suppress American seaborne trade and to prevent the sailing of enemy warships and privateers. With more than ninety ships of all classes under his command, Howe nevertheless found his force inadequate to blockade effectively the American coast from the Gulf of Maine to Florida while at the same time supporting the British army in America. On 9 March 1778 fifty-one out of ninety-two warships of Howe's command were deployed supporting and defending those British enclaves in America. The remaining forty-one ships in his command were spread along the American coast from Canso to St Augustine on blockade duty.[102]

At times, especially in terms of the number of vessels captured, the British blockade appeared to be working. For example, the ten ships stationed at the entrance of Chesapeake Bay and off the coasts of the Carolinas captured more than eighty enemy vessels during the winter of 1777–8.[103] Nevertheless, Howe reported to the Admiralty that while a considerable number of American ships had been captured off the southern colonies, the blockade of the northern colonies was ineffective during that winter owing to bad weather, which had damaged a number of warships, as well as an insufficient number of ships for the task.[104] Thus, as was the case in previous years, the need to support the army and to protect British enclaves from American attack, the great length of the American coast, bad weather, and a general lack of warships all conspired to render the British blockade of America ineffective.

On 23 March 1778 Howe in HMS *Eagle* sailed from Newport, R.I, and after a stopover at New York City, arrived in Delaware Bay on 21 April.[105] Just over a fortnight later, on 8 May, HMS *Porcupine* arrived in the Delaware river from England with dispatches telling of the Franco–American alliance. At the same time, owing to the threat of French intervention, orders were received from the government to evacuate Philadelphia, and if necessary New York and Newport.[106] In addition Howe received permission to give up his command for reasons of health and to return to England, upon the arrival of Vice Admiral the Hon. John Byron in America.[107] It was now Howe's task to carry out the government's instructions to evacuate Philadelphia while awaiting the arrival in America of Byron before returning to England.

On 25 May General Howe, who had been replaced as commander- in-chief of the army in America by Lieutenant General Sir Henry Clinton, sailed for England. Even before the departure of General Howe, the preparations were begun to evacuate Philadelphia. All through the month of May orders were issued for the collection and embarkation of army baggage, equipment and munitions[108] while at the same time warships and transports were being amassed and fitted in order to withdraw the army by sea from Philadelphia.[109] Admiral Howe and Clinton at first intended to move the army by sea to New York City, but this was soon abandoned when it was discovered that there were not enough transports available to carry the army, all its horses and equipment, and those Loyalists who wished to flee Philadelphia with the British.[110] Therefore, Clinton decided to march the army overland to New York through New Jersey, while the heavy equipment, stores and the Loyalists were to be withdrawn by sea. This was perhaps an extremely lucky decision for although neither Howe nor Clinton knew it, the transports carrying the troops to New York City might have been at sea when d'Estaing's squadron of French warships arrived on the American coast.

On the morning of 18 June the British army evacuated Philadelphia and crossed the Delaware river into New Jersey on their way to New York. At the same time, Howe's warships, escorting transports crowded with military equipment and Loyalists, dropped down the Delaware. Owing to the lack of wind, the fleet did not clear Delaware Bay until 28 June, and the next morning off the New Jersey coast Howe met the *Grantham* packet carrying an Admiralty dispatch of 3 May alerting him to the expected arrival in America both of d'Estaing's French squadron of eleven ships of the line, one 50-gun ship, and five frigates, and of reinforcements from England under the command of Byron. In fact the commander of the packet informed Howe that he had encountered the French squadron on 6 June at 30°N 48°W and had been chased by the French for three days.[111]

The news that a powerful and hostile French squadron was about to appear on the American coast placed Howe in a difficult situation. The British army was in central New Jersey marching towards New York City and the ships of Howe's squadron were strung out along the American coast either on blockade duty or supporting military operations. The squadron in America mostly consisted of small warships and Howe had only eight ships of the line and four 50-gun ships with which to confront d'Estaing's squadron of eleven ships of the line and one 50-gun ship.[112] The British position at New York might possibly be simultaneously attacked by the American army and d'Estaing's squadron after Howe's squadron had been overpowered by sheer weight of numbers and superior firepower. However, the officers and men of the British ships stationed in America had three years' war experience, and Howe, unlike so many other British commanders in America, would prove not only lucky, but also skilful, determined and capable of acting quickly and effectively in adverse circumstances. Thus, luck, French and American ineptitude, and the skill and experience of Howe and the British might possibly parry the unexpected Franco–American attack until the arrival of Byron's reinforcements.

On 29 June Howe arrived at Sandy Hook at the entrance of New York Harbour. The next day the British army, after fighting a sharp rearguard action at Monmouth Court House, reached Navesink and then on a bridge of flat-bottomed boats crossed over to Sandy Hook whence the troops were conveyed to New York City and Long Island by the Royal Navy. Immediately upon reaching New York, Howe and Clinton began defensive preparations against a Franco–American attack.[113] Howe resolved to remain in America until the crisis passed and a suitable officer appeared to take command of the squadron.[114] Rear Admiral James Gambier, who had been sent out to America by Sandwich and was considered by everybody to be incompetent, was shoved aside and made into a port captain at New York.[115] A dispatch was sent to Halifax, Novia Scotia, the supposed destination of the expected reinforcements from England under Byron, with the latest intelligence of the movements of d'Estaing's squadron.[116] However, Howe soon found that he had limited forces with which to defend the maritime approaches of New York. There were only fifteen warships at New York: seven ships of the line, two 50-gun ships, two 44-gun frigates, three frigates and an armed vessel.[117] Further, the crews of these ships were sickly, and about 900 men were ashore in the naval hospital.[118]

Howe, nevertheless, deployed the ships of his command with great skill to meet the expected French attack. A string of cruisers were stationed along the American coast between New York and Chesapeake Bay to warn of the approach of d'Estaing's squadron.[119] On 5 July the French squadron was intercepted by Howe's cruisers off the entrance of Chesapeake Bay, and as d'Estaing proceeded northward along the coast he was constantly shadowed by British cruisers who reported his every movement to Howe. At 6am on 8 July Howe learned of the arrival of the French off Virginia and later that same day the admiral determined that the French objective was New York City.[120] But on 10 July Howe also learned that units of the Continental Army were crossing the Hudson river north of New York City and heading towards New England, which pointed towards an attack being made on the British base at Newport, R.I. Howe then planned to hold the French at Sandy Hook and to reinforce the garrison at Rhode Island before Long Island Sound could be closed by the enemy. And on the morning of 11 July Howe received intelligence that d'Estaing was approaching Sandy Hook.[121]

As the French approached the seaward side of Sandy Hook, Howe anchored the ships of his command in a line broadside to the channel just inside the Hook. If the French attempted to enter Lower New York Bay, each of their ships would be raked by cannon fire as they passed up the channel along the line of anchored British ships. Howe had picked an extremely strong position: the French could only enter Lower New York Bay on a flood tide and with an east or south-easterly wind, and the British ships could cripple the French ships in the rigging as the enemy passed up the channel. Those French ships that were disabled would then drift into

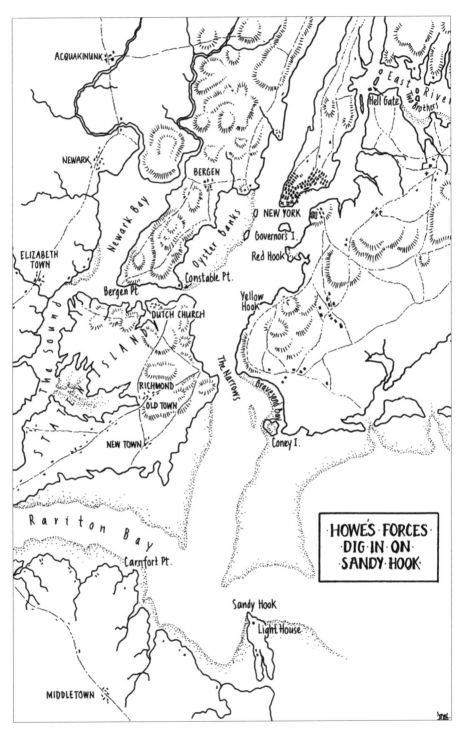

ACQUAKINUNK

East River

Hell Gate

The Brothers

NEWARK

BERGEN

Newark Bay

NEW YORK

Oyster banks

Governor's I.

Red Hook

ELIZABETH TOWN

Bergen Pt.

Constable Pt.

Yellow Hook

DUTCH CHURCH

The Sound

STATEN ISLAND

RICHMOND

OLD TOWN

The Narrows

Gravesend Bay

NEW TOWN

Coney I.

Raariton Bay

HOWE'S · FORCES ·
· DIG · IN · ON ·
· SANDY · HOOK ·

Carnfort Pt.

Sandy Hook

Light House

MIDDLETOWN

Lower New York Bay and fetch up on the shores of either Staten Island or Brooklyn or be overpowered by British small craft. However, there were two weaknesses to the British position. According to Howe's flag captain, Henry Duncan, the British ships 'in general were but very indifferently manned, owing to sickness and their being short of complement'. The second weakness in the British position was the defenceless state of Sandy Hook. If when the French first appeared off Sandy Hook, which was then an unoccupied island, they or the Americans seized the place and mounted heavy guns there, the British ships could have easily been forced from their anchorage. But Howe quickly perceived this weakness, and on 11 July the 15th and 44th Regiments were sent to occupy and dig in on Sandy Hook.[122]

On the evening of 11 July the British and French squadrons were only a mile or two apart and separated from each other by the dunes of Sandy Hook. Some of the British, such as Hamond, 'fully expected an attack',[123] but d'Estaing hesitated. Although on 12 July the French began to take soundings off Sandy Hook,[124] they still did not attempt to force an entry into Lower New York Bay. What deterred d'Estaing from attacking the British was a lack of information about the tides, bar and channel at Sandy Hook. D'Estaing had at hand the greatest strategic prize in America, but having already had one of his ships of the line run aground at the entrance of the Delaware, he feared that he might lose his squadron if he attempted to force his way past the British at Sandy Hook without adequate pilots. So while the French waited for pilots, the British defensive position grew stronger. By 19 July the garrison of Sandy Hook had increased to 1,800 men, and at the request of Howe a number of cannon and howitzers were emplaced there as well.[125] HMS *Leviathan*, formerly a ship of the line that had been converted into a navy storeship, joined the squadron at Sandy Hook after being armed with cannon drawn from the army's siege train, and a number of transports were converted into fireships. The shortage of seamen was also overcome by embarking soldiers as marines, and at the request of Howe over 1,000 seamen from the transports volunteered to serve in the king's ships on the condition that they be discharged from the Royal Navy when the admiral gave up his command.[126] As the British forces grew stronger, d'Estaing's desire to attack them grew weaker. One British officer, Commodore William Hotham, thought the mere sight of the British 'weighed as much with the Count as the pretended difficulty of passing over the bar with his long-legged ships might do'.[127] After eleven days of inactivity, and receiving pessimistic reports on the navigational difficulties of crossing the bar into Lower New York Bay, d'Estaing sailed from Sandy Hook on the morning of 22 July, headed south into the Atlantic, and disappeared.[128]

The sudden departure of the French squadron from Sandy Hook placed Howe in a strategic quandary. It seemed unlikely that the French would

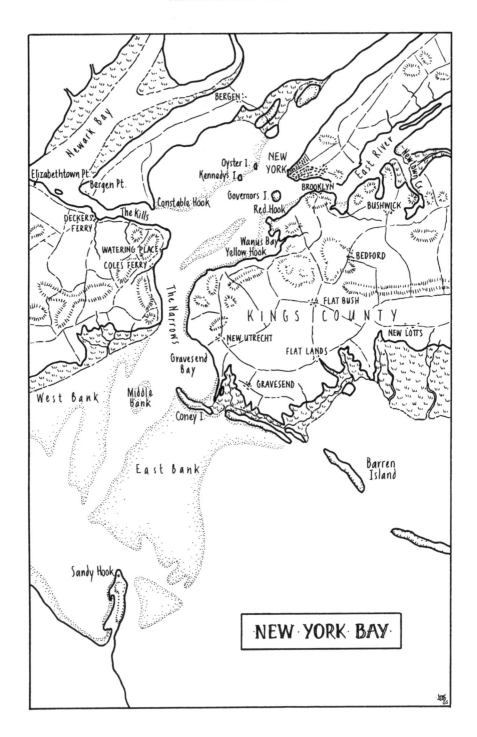

NEW·YORK·BAY·

either return to Europe after such a brief appearance off New York or head for the West Indies so near the beginning of the hurricane season. On 26 July Howe received information that d'Estaing had been sighted thirty leagues off Delaware Bay and was steering south-south-east but the British admiral could not determine the objective of the French squadron.[129] Because of the build-up of American forces in New England, Clinton concluded by 27 July that Newport, R.I. was going to be attacked.[130] This was little more than an educated guess, however, for the French squadron could have been going to Chesapeake Bay or some other place in the American South, or d'Estaing could double back and attack either New York, or Newport, or possibly Halifax, which was not very well defended. The garrison of Newport was weak and the place probably could easily be captured by the French squadron in conjunction with the American army. Another danger to the British in America was the shortage of provisions at New York, combined with the possibility that d'Estaing's squadron would return to Sandy Hook and intercept the British army victuallers as they arrived, and thereby starve the British at New York into capitulation.[131] Effectively, no matter what d'Estaing's squadron did, its mere existence in American waters posed a great threat to the British until the arrival of the expected reinforcements under Byron.

The speculation ended on 28 July when Howe, aided by intelligence from his cruisers, determined that d'Estaing had in fact doubled back and was heading for Newport and would arrive at that place at the beginning of August. Howe decided to sail to Rhode Island at once with what ships he could muster in order to attempt to relieve Newport.[132] But unless Byron arrived with reinforcements or the Americans and French were incredibly inept and unlucky, Howe's effort could not be much more than a valiant gesture, for while the British ships were more numerous, the eleven French ships of the line were greatly superior in firepower. Before Howe could sail from New York, the badly damaged HMS *Cornwall*, one of the ships of Vice Admiral the Hon. John Byron's squadron, arrived on 30 July at Sandy Hook with the first news to reach Howe of the fate of the reinforcements from England.[133] From what little information the captain of HMS *Cornwall* could supply, it was clear that Byron's squadron would not be of immediate assistance in the relief of Newport. Byron, known throughout the service as 'Foul-Weather Jack' because of his tendency to encounter bad weather, had sailed from England on 9 June. On 30 June at 40°51′N 31°16′W the admiral encountered a storm that heavily damaged and scattered the ships of his command. HMS *Russell* was forced back to England. HMS *Guadeloupe* and HMS *Invincible* made it into St John's, Newfoundland, though badly damaged. HMS *Albion* reached New York in October after being refitted at Lisbon. By the end of August eight more of Byron's ships[134] had managed to stagger into New York with sick crews and with extensive damage to their masts and rigging. After sighting d'Estaing's squadron off the coast of New York, Byron headed in HMS *Princess Royal* for Halifax where he was joined by HMS *Culloden*. The two ships did not sail for America until 2 September.[135] Despite the tardy departure of Byron's squadron from England, the British possibly could have concentrated an overpowering naval force against d'Estaing at Rhode Island but for the ill luck suffered by the squadron from England. However, the arrival of HMS *Cornwall* made it clear to Howe at New York that he would have to counter the expected Franco–American attack on Rhode Island without any hope of being sufficiently reinforced.

Ever since the British had seized Newport in 1776, Rhode Island had been a tempting target for the Americans, but as long as the Royal Navy controlled Narragansett Bay, the Americans could do little. Before the arrival of d'Estaing's squadron in America, the British restricted their main defence effort to mounting amphibious 'spoiling' attacks against concentrations of American small craft and supply depots at various points along the shore of Narragansett Bay.[136] However, with the arrival of d'Estaing off New York and the build-up of American forces in the region of Narragansett Bay, the British began to fear that their position at Rhode Island might be jointly attacked by the Americans and the French. Just before the French squadron arrived off Sandy Hook, fifteen transports full of troops were dispatched on 9 July from New York down Long Island Sound to reinforce the garrison at Newport.[137] But sending additional troops to Rhode Island would not make that place secure, for the key to the defence of Newport was naval control of Narragansett Bay. Even if the Americans managed to gain a foothold on Rhode Island, the British ships could cut their supply lines to the mainland. But if d'Estaing's squadron entered the bay and overpowered the British ships there while the American army attacked Newport, the British garrison would find itself in a situation similar to that which would confront Cornwallis at Yorktown in 1781.

At 10am on 29 July d'Estaing's squadron appeared off Newport, and the next morning two French ships of the line pushed up Narragansett Channel and anchored between the mainland and Conanicut Island, which the British then evacuated. At the same time, French frigates entered Sekonnet Passage between the mainland and the island of Rhode Island. Just over a week later on 9 August several thousand American troops crossed over from the mainland to the northern end of the island of Rhode Island and began to slowly envelop the British positions at Newport.[138] By withdrawing into defensive positions around Newport, the British forces were preparing for a siege in order to buy time because the only thing that could save them was the prompt arrival of Howe from New York with sufficient ships either to destroy or drive the French squadron from Narragansett Bay.

Howe was prevented from sailing from Sandy Hook by adverse winds and tides for several days after he had received intelligence that d'Estaing's squadron was proceeding to Rhode Island. But finally on 6

August the admiral sailed for Rhode Island with a squadron of thirty-five warships including seven ships of the line, five 50-gun ships and two 44-gun frigates. The rest of the ships of his command were regular frigates, bomb ketches, galleys, tenders and fireships.[139] According to his dispatch to the Admiralty dated 17 August, Howe believed that d'Estaing's squadron was divided into three detachments stationed in the three entrances of Narragansett Bay – Narragansett Passage, the Middle Channel and Seckonnet Passage – for the purpose of attacking Newport. Howe intended, if possible, to attack one or more of these French detachments piecemeal, in order to employ to maximum advantage the small warships, such as bombs fireships, and galleys, under his command.[140]

At noon on 9 August, as American troops were closing in on Newport, British lookouts saw far to the south the sails of Howe's squadron approaching Rhode Island, and at 7pm the British ships anchored off Point Judith. But with the arrival of Howe's squadron the situation was far from saved, for if the French did not lose their nerve or make a major mistake they could with a force of eleven ships of the line, a 50-gun ship, and four frigates easily block the entrance to Narragansett Bay in much the same way that Howe had blocked the channel at Sandy Hook. Or the French could barricade themselves against Conanicut Island, as Barrington would later do at St Lucia. With a little thought and skill aided by the American army, there is no reason why the French could not subject the British garrison at Newport to the same fate as Cornwallis would suffer at Yorktown. Despite the arrival of Howe, on the evening of 9 August, the British garrison at Newport appeared doomed. The Americans outnumbered the king's troops, and Howe's squadron, if not shot to bits, could be very roughly handled by the French while attempting to relieve Newport. All the French and the Americans had to do was maintain their present positions in the face of inferior British forces, and eventually the British at Newport would be forced to surrender.

But d'Estaing did not desire to fight a defensive battle in the confined waters of Narragansett Bay: if any of his ships were damaged, he feared they would be forced by the prevailing southerly winds on to the shore of British-held Rhode Island.[141] Therefore, on the morning of 10 August when a north-easterly wind developed, d'Estaing sailed from Narragansett Bay with the apparent intention of either fighting a decisive battle with Howe's squadron, or at the least driving the British naval force away from Rhode Island. When Howe saw the French leaving Narragansett Bay, he detached HMS *Sphinx* to escort to New York the squadron's tenders, bomb ketches and galleys. With his main force, including three fireships, formed into a line of battle, Howe retreated before the wind on a southerly course with the French in pursuit. Howe was in a difficult situation, for his squadron did not have the fire power to stand up to the French ships of the line in a regular ship to ship engagement. And as long as the wind remained northerly, which was unusual for the coast of New England during the summer, d'Estaing had the weather gauge and could, if he overtook the British, force Howe to fight at a disadvantage. Howe nevertheless hoped that the wind would swing around to a prevailing south or south-westerly direction later in the day, so that he would then have the weather gauge and could turn on the French and attack them with his frigates and fireships.[142]

The wind did not shift around to the south. On the morning of 11 August it was east-north-east and the French squadron was hull down and directly to windward of the British. Howe then began a series of manoeuvres in order to gain the weather gauge, so that he could engage d'Estaing's ships. Both the British and the French squadrons assumed line astern formations sailing before the wind, with the leading French ships following the rearmost British ships. At 8am Howe began gradually to alter the course of the British line towards a westerly heading and then towards a more northerly one. These changes in course were performed by the British line in succession from the van; that is, the lead British ship would change its course and the manoeuvre would be repeated, in turn, by each of the British ships. The French squadron followed in the wake of the British as d'Estaing failed to counter Howe's actions, and only adjusted his course to match the British change in direction. The result of these manoeuvres was that by 1:30pm Howe's squadron, still in line ahead formation, had made almost a complete about-face and was steering north-east with the line of French ships still astern on the same course.

In the middle of the afternoon Howe shifted his flag to the frigate HMS *Apollo* so that he would be in a position to supervise the movements of the ships. By 4pm the French squadron had been manoeuvred into a position so far to leeward of the British that, had he attacked, Howe could have weathered d'Estaing's squadron and gained the weather gauge. But before Howe could execute this manoeuvre, the French squadron, which was now south of the British, turned away to the southward because of the lateness of the day and the increasingly foul weather.[143]

On the evening of 11 August the weather turned bad with heavy seas and gale force winds. Both Howe's and d'Estaing's squadrons were scattered and suffered heavy damage in the masts and rigging before the storm blew itself out on 13 August.[144] Because of the inclement weather, Howe could not return to his flagship from HMS *Apollo*, which had been reduced by the storm to little more than a wreck, until the afternoon of 13 August. By then the only ships that still remained in company with Howe were one 50-gun ship, four frigates and an armed ship.[145] The remainder of the British squadron was limping back to Sandy Hook with broken masts and shattered rigging. The French ships of the line *Languedoc* and *Marseillais* lost all their masts, except for the latter's mainmast, in the storm and during the evening of 13 August these two disabled French ships were attacked by HMS *Renown* and HMS *Preston*. But because of the heavy seas and darkness, the captains of the two British ships did not press home their attacks during the night, and the British ships were driven away from the *Languedoc* and *Marseillais* the next morning when six enemy ships appeared. Three days later, on 16 August, HMS *Isis*, some twenty leagues from Sandy Hook, engaged the 70-gun *César* in an hour and a half-long running battle, during which the rigging of both ships was badly shot up. But despite such chance engagements, both the French and British squadrons were for some time virtually disbanded as organised, fighting formations by the storm.

After shifting his flag to HMS *Centurion*, Howe, with the remnants of his squadron, proceeded south along the American coast in quest of d'Estaing. On the morning of 15 August, after hearing gunfire in the distance, Howe located a number of French warships laying at anchor about twenty leagues east of Cape May. Leaving a ship to shadow the French force, the British admiral sailed for Sandy Hook where he arrived on 18 August to find most of the missing ships of his squadron anchored with varying degrees of damage in their masts and rigging.[146]

The danger to the British garrison at Rhode Island had not diminished with the departure of d'Estaing's squadron. The American army, in the absence of the French ships, had been laying siege to Newport, and if the French returned, the situation at Newport would be exactly the same as it was before 10 August when d'Estaing had sailed forth in pursuit of Howe's squadron. The threat seemed imminent when, on 22 August, Howe learned from HMS *Galatea*, which had sighted nine French ships of the line off Block Island, that d'Estaing was returning to Rhode Island, apparently with the intention of renewing the siege of Newport in conjunction with the American army.[147] During the next two days Howe learned from other frigates that all of d'Estaing's ships, including the dismasted *Languedoc* and *Marseillais* had returned to Rhode Island. On 24 August, after having passed through the French squadron at night in a small boat, Lieutenant John Stanhope, RN, arrived at Sandy Hook from Newport with information that the British garrison at Rhode Island was still capable of continued resistance. Howe thereupon planned to sail as soon as possible from Sandy Hook for Rhode Island with what ships he could muster in order to either drive or again draw d'Estaing's force away from Rhode Island. Meanwhile Clinton would ready transports and troops at the western end of Long Island Sound in order to reinforce Newport quickly as soon as the French squadron left the region.[148]

On 25 August Howe, whose ships had been quickly repaired, sailed from Sandy Hook for Rhode Island. Just after departing, however, the British admiral received intelligence that d'Estaing's entire squadron had left Rhode Island before daylight on 22 August and was apparently proceeding to Boston.[149] The departure of d'Estaing for Boston enraged the Americans at Rhode Island, for they believed that if the French squadron had remained a short time longer off Newport, the British garrison there would have been forced to surrender. But the French ships had been greatly damaged in the storm of 11 August; Howe at New York was obviously preparing to return to Rhode Island to attack the French squadron; and the brief encounter with Byron's flagship HMS *Princess Royal* on 18 August, off the coast of Long Island, indicated to the French that the British in America were being reinforced.[150]

Upon learning that d'Estaing had left Rhode Island, Howe decided to attempt to intercept the French before they could reach the safety of Boston Harbour. Howe believed that the French squadron, because of the dismasted condition of the *Languedoc* and *Marseillais*, would have to pass to the eastward of George's Bank; if he acted quickly and proceeded directly towards Boston through the Muskeget Channel between Martha's Vineyard and Nantucket, passing to the westward of George's Bank, he had a good chance of intercepting d'Estaing either off Cape Cod or in Massachusetts Bay.[151] Arguably Howe should not have pursued d'Estaing's squadron, but rather sailed directly for Rhode Island, then proceeded up Narragansett Bay as far as Bristol Ferry in order to trap the American army besieging Newport.[152] Clinton intended to send a 4,000-man reinforcement down Long Island Sound and land the force at Bristol Neck before the Americans could get off Rhode Island. But because of calms and other delays, the Americans were warned of the approach of the transports carrying the troops from New York and evacuated Rhode Island on 30 August just as the British reinforcements reached Newport.[153] If Howe had gone directly to Rhode Island instead of Massachusetts Bay, he could have cut off the American army on that island, for his squadron would have approached Newport without warning by a route that was out of sight of land. There had been ample time, for on 30 August, the day the Americans evacuated Rhode Island, Howe was already off Boston. The possibility, however, of trapping and destroying an American army at Rhode Island apparently never entered Howe's head: the British admiral considered d'Estaing's squadron his major objective.

Howe, after intercepting and capturing while en route for Boston the Continental Armed Brig *Resistance*, entered Boston Bay on 30 August and found that d'Estaing had already reached the safety of Boston Harbour. Hamond in HMS *Roebuck* stood in near to the shore to reconnoitre the French position, and reported to Howe that d'Estaing's squadron could be successfully attacked if it was done at once. However, it was almost dark and Howe decided to withdraw from the entrance of Boston Harbour and reconnoitre the French position further the next day. But during the night of 30–31 August HMS *St Albans* ran aground near the end of Cape Cod and by the time the ship had been refloated and the British squadron had recrossed Massachusetts Bay, it was the evening of 1 September, and in the meantime the French had moved their ships deeper into Boston Harbour and fortified the approaches to that port. Howe then concluded that the French position was too strong to attack and that d'Estaing intended to remain there for some time, so on 2 September the British sailed for Rhode Island.[154]

Howe's squadron arrived off Rhode Island on 4 September and remained there for the next five days while British amphibious forces raided New Bedford, the shores of Buzzard's Bay, and Martha's Vineyard, seizing provisions and cattle and destroying ships and buildings. During this period Clinton urged over and over again that the admiral return to Boston accompanied by 6,000 troops under his command to attack and destroy d'Estaing's squadron in port before it could be refitted for further service. But this scheme received a cool reception from Howe, who according to Clinton, was determined now that d'Estaing was safely in Boston and the naval crisis in America had passed, to give up his command to Byron and return to England as soon as possible.[155] Whether or not Clinton's plan for destroying the French squadron at Boston by an amphibious attack would have been successful will never be known. But Howe's failure to seriously consider the general's scheme was one of the many opportunities to strike a heavy blow at their enemies in America that the British passed lightly over.

On 9 September the wind swung around to the eastward signalling the onset of bad weather. Thereupon, Howe withdrew from the coast of southern New England and sailed for New York where he arrived on 11 September to find at anchor six of Byron's squadron under the command of Rear Admiral Hyde Parker, Sr, which had reached Sandy Hook on 28 August.[156] Howe then informed Clinton that he was turning over the command of the ships at New York to Gambier and would leave for England as soon as possible.[157] Howe was not only disillusioned with the war in America, but most likely had come to the conclusion that the government in London would use him as a scapegoat for the failure of its American policy. There were also signs that he had fallen out of favour with the North government. For instance, North had passed Howe over when appointing a treasurer of the navy.[158] On the very day that Howe had told Clinton that he was leaving America, the admiral wrote a letter to the secretary of the Admiralty complaining that his promotion to vice admiral of the red squadron, dated 1 July 1778,[159] had been delayed, probably for political reasons, with the result that he had been separated 'from the class of flag officers with whom I was first advanced to that rank'.[160] It must have been obvious to Howe that he should return to London as soon as possible to justify himself and to seek vindication for his actions in America.

On 24 September, in HMS *Eagle*, Howe left New York to go to Rhode Island in order to transfer command of the squadron in America to Byron, who was now at Newport. Two days later Howe sailed from Newport for England, and after being chased by two French ships of the line off the Scilly Islands, arrived at St Helens on 25 October. Five days later Howe received from the Admiralty permission to strike his flag.[161]

Notes

1. NA, ADM 1/487, f. 24.

2. NA, CO 5/92, ff. 290–1; William Bell Clark et al, *Naval Documents of the American Revolution* (Washington, DC, 1964–), vol. 2, pp. 11, 703; Historical Manuscripts Commission, *Report on the Manuscripts of Mrs Stopford-Sackville, of Drayton House, Northamptonshire* (London and Hereford, 1904–10) vol. I, pp. 135–7; vol. II, pp. 1, 3, 6.

3. On 13 August 1776 there were at New York the *Eagle, Asia, Chatham, Preston, Centurion, Renown, Rainbow, Emerald, Repulse, Flora, Greyhound, Solebay, Swan, Tamar, Strombolo, Thunder, Carcass, St Lawrence, Niger, Kingfisher, Halifax, Phoenix, Rose, Trial*. In American waters en route to New York were *Bristol, Experiment, Siren, Roebuck, Fowey, Otter*. NA, 1/487, ff. 55–6.

4. NA, CO 5/177, ff. 14–15.

5. Edward H Tatum, Jr, *The American Journal of Ambrose Serle* (San Marino, Calif., 1940), p. 31.

6. NA, CO 5/177, f. 19.

7. Paul H Smith, ed., *Letters of the Delegates to Congress, 1774–1789* (Washington, DC, 1979–), vol. 4, p. 485.

8. Worthington Chauncey Ford, Gaillard Hunt, John C Fitzpatrick, and Roscoe R Hill, eds, *Journals of the Continental Congress, 1774–1789* (Washington, DC 1904–37) vol. V, pp. 592–3.

9. Leonard W Labaree, William B Willcox, Claude A Lopez, and Barbara B Oberg, eds, *The Papers of Benjamin Franklin* (New Haven, Ct., 1959–), vol. 2 pp. 483–4.

10. Smith, ed., *Letters of the Delegates to Congress*, vol. 4, pp. 498–500.

11. W W Abbot, Dorothy Twohig, Frank E Grizzard, Philander D Chase, and Edward Lengels, eds, *The Papers of George Washington: Revolutionary War Series* (Charlottesville, Va., 1985–),vol. 5, p. 297.

12. Tatum Jr, *American Journal of Ambrose Serle*, pp. 32–3.

13. Abbot et al, eds, *Papers of George Washington*, vol. 5, pp. 207, 305–6.

14. Ford et al, eds, *Journals of the Continental Congress*, vol. 5, p. 567.

15. NA, CO 5/177, f. 23.

16. G R Barnes and J H Owen, *The Private Papers of John, Earl of Sandwich, First Lord of the Admiralty, 1772–1782* (London, 1932–8), vol. I, pp. 149–54.

17. William B Willcox, *Portrait of a General: Sir Henry Clinton in the War of Independence* (New York, 1964), pp. 95, 104.

18. Historical Manuscripts Commission, *Stopford-Sackville MSS*, vol. II, p. 33.

19. NA, ADM 1/487, f. 60.

20. *Asia, Renown, Preston, Roebuck, Repulse*.

21. NA, ADM 1/487, ff. 60–1.

22. Tatum Jr, *American Journal of Ambrose Serle*, p. 88.

23. Willcox, *Portrait of a General*, pp. 108–9, 117.

24. New York Historical Society Collections, *The Montressor Journals* (New York 1881), p. 121.

25. NA, CO 5/177, f. 38.

26. Otis G Hammond, ed., *Letters and Papers of Major General John Sullivan, Continental Army* (Concord, N.H., 1930–9) vol. I, pp. 299–300.

27. Ford, ed., *Journals of the Continental Congress*, vol. V, pp. 730–1.

28. Smith, ed., *Letters of the Delegates to Congress*, vol. 5, pp. 94–5.

29. Ford et al, eds, *Journals of the Continental Congress*, vol. V, p. 737.

30. Labaree et al, eds, *Papers of Benjamin Franklin*, vol. 22, pp. 593–597.

31.Ibid, pp. 598–608.

32. NA, CO 5/177, ff. 35–40.

33. *Renown, Repulse, Pearl, Trial*.

34. *Rose, Roebuck, Phoenix, Orpheus, Carysfort*.

35. NA, ADM 1/487, ff. 85–6; Willcox, *Portrait of a General*, pp. 110–12.

36. William L Clements Library, Sackville-Germain Papers, vol. 5, 25 September 1776.

37. NA, ADM 1/487, ff. 118–19; CO 5/236, pp. 2–3; Willcox, *Portrait of a General*, pp. 112–13.

38. NA, ADM 1/487, ff. 119–20; Willcox, *Portrait of a General*, pp. 121–3.

39. Willcox, *Portrait of a General*, pp. 115–16.

40. *Sphinx, Kingfisher, Ambuscade, Mercury, Chatham, Preston, Renown, Centurion, Asia, Experiment, Emerald, Brune, Cerberus, Carysfort, Diamond.* NA, ADM 1/487, f. 151.

41. NA, ADM 1/487, ff. 149–50; CO 5/236, pp. 23–4.

42. Quoted in D S Freeman, *George Washington* (New York, 1948–57), vol. IV, p. 217.

43. NA, ADM 1/487, f. 148.

44. Cf. HMC, *Stopford-Sackville MSS.*, vol. II, p. 30.

45. NA, ADM 1/487,ff. 24, 86–7.

46. University of Virginia, Hamond Papers, Hamond to Stanley, 24 Sept. 1776.

47. NA, ADM 1/487, ff. 55–6, 89–90, 135–6.

48. NA, ADM 1/487, f. 87.

49. NA, ADM 1/487, ff. 325, 339–45.

50. NA, ADM 1/487, ff. 178–9, 350–3.

51. Richard Buel Jr, *In Irons: Britain's Naval Supremacy and the American Revolutionary Economy* (New Haven, Ct., 1998), p. 43.

52. Gardner W Allen, *A Naval History of the American Revolution* (New York, 1962 reprint), vol. I, p. 158.

53. NA, ADM 1/386, Extract of a letter from the consul at Faro, dated Faro 31 Aug. 1776.

54. For an account of the beginnings of the American cruiser offensive in European waters, see David Syrett, *The Royal Navy in European Seas during the American Revolutionary War* (Columbia, S.C., 1998), pp. 63–9.

55. Allen, *A Naval History*, vol. I, pp. 181–2.

56. NA, ADM 1/487, ff. 334–8.

57. O W Stephenson, 'The Supply of Gunpowder in 1776', *American Historical Review* (Jan. 1925), vol. 30, pp. 177–281.

58. E.g [Joseph Galloway], *A Letter of the Right Honourable Lord Viscount H---e* (London, 1779).

59. Historical Manuscripts Commission, *Report on the Manuscripts in Various Collections* (London, Dublin, and Hereford, 1901–14), vol. IV, pp. 131, 137.

60. E.g, Ira D Gruber, *The Howe Brothers and the American Revolution* (New York, 1972), pp. 150–2; Troyer Steele Anderson, *The Command of the Howe Brothers during the American Revolution* (New York, 1936), pp. 223–4; Don Higginbotham, *The War of American Independence: Military Attitudes, Politics, and Practices, 1763–1783* (New York. 1971), p. 171.

61. NA, ADM 1/487, ff. 172–6.

62. Barnes and Owen, eds, *Sandwich Papers*, vol. II, p. 288.

63. Allen, *Naval History*, vol. I, pp. 202–3.

64. NA, ADM 1/487, ff. 388–9.

65. NA, ADM 1/487, ff. 401–2; ADM 2/104, p. 427.

66. Allen, *Naval History*, vol. I, pp. 204–6.

67. NA, ADM 2/103, pp. 168–70; William L Clements Library, Sackville-Germain Papers, vol. 6, Montagu to Germain, 11 June 1777; Barnes and Owen, eds, Sandwich Papers, vol. I, p. 234.

68. Allen, Naval History, vol. I, pp. 206–15; Barnes and Owen, eds, Sandwich Papers, vol. I, pp. 296–301.

69. Barnes and Owen, eds , *Sandwich Papers*, vol. I, pp. 234–8, 250.

70. William L Clements Library, Sackville-Germain Papers, vol. 5, Germain to W Howe, 5 March 1777.

71. NA, CO 5/236, p. 81.

72. William L Clements Library, Sackville-Germain Papers, vol. 5, W Howe to Germain, 25 Sept. 1776; Historical

Manuscripts Commission, *Stopford-Sackville MSS*, vol. II, p. 50.

73. *Augusta, Nonsuch, St Albans, Raisonable, Somerset*. Barnes and Owen, eds, *Sandwich Papers*, vol. I, pp. 279–80, 285.

74. Barnes and Owen, eds, *Sandwich Papers*, vol. II, pp. 294–5.

75. The origins and evolution of the strategy followed by the British in America during 1777 is a subject clouded by polemics. Perhaps the best modern treatment is William B Willcox, 'Too Many Cooks: British Planning before Saratoga', *Journal of British Studies* (Nov., 1962), vol. II, pp. 56–90.

76. Willcox, *Portrait of a General*, pp. 147–68.

77. *Eagle, Nonsuch, Augusta, Somerset, Sphinx, Dispatch, Swift, Strombolo, Vigilant, Haerlem, York, Cornwallis, Stanley, Adventure, Richmond, Apollo, Raisonable, Isis, Emerald, Solebay, Otter, Senegal*. NA, ADM 1/487, ff. 480, 483.

78. *Roebuck, Pearl, Camilla, Merlin*. NA, ADM 1/478, ff. 480, 483.

79. NA, CO 5/94, f. 432.

80. H W Moomaw, 'The Denouement of General Howe's Campaign of 1777', *English Historical Review* (July, 1964), vol. 79, pp. 498–512. The quotes are from page 504.

81. NA, ADM 1/487, ff. 480–2; CO 5/236, pp. 121–2.

82. For an account of the American river obstructions, see C R Harte, 'The River Obstructions of the Revolutionary War', *Annual Report of the Connecticut Society of Civil Engineers* (1946), vol. 62, pp. 135–186a.

83. *Merlin, Roebuck, Liverpool, Carysfort, Pearl, Camilla*.

84. William Hugh Moomaw, *The Naval Career of Captain Hamond, 1775–1779* (Unpublished University of Virginia PhD dissertation, 1955), pp. 355–60.

85. NA, ADM 1/488, f. 74.

86. NA, CO 5/236, p. 159.

87. New York Historical Society Collections, *The Montressor Journals*, pp. 463–6.

88. NA, ADM 1/488, ff. 112–14.

89. NA, CO 5/236, pp. 116–67; Edward L Lowell, *The Hessians and other German Auxiliaries of Britain in the Revolutionary War* (New York, 1884), pp. 204–8.

90. NA, ADM 1/488, ff. 75–6; Moomaw, *Naval Career of Captain Hamond*, pp. 153–4; John Knox Laughton, ed., *The Naval Miscellany* (London, 1901), vol. I, pp. 153–4.

91. NA, ADM 1/488, ff. 79–80; CO 5/236, pp. 185–6; Moomaw, *The Naval Career of Captain Hamond*, pp. 369–73; New York Historical Society Collections, *Montressor Journals*, pp. 470–4.

92. NA, ADM 1/488, f. 81.

93. NA, ADM 1/487, ff. 388–9; 483–4; ADM 1/488, ff. 112–14.

94. NA, ADM 1/488, ff. 65–70.

95. Allen, *Naval History*, vol. I, pp. 286–7, 289–90.

96. Laughton, ed., *Naval Miscellany*, vol. I, p. 154.

97. Historical Manuscripts Commission, *Various Collections*, vol.VI, p. 316.

98. William L Clements Library, Sackville-Germain Papers, vol. 6, Howe to Germain, 30 Nov. 1777.

99. NA, ADM 1/488, ff. 118, 123, 128–9.

100. Maldwyn A Jones, 'Sir William Howe: Conventional Strategist', *George Washington's Opponents*, George Athan Billas, ed. (New York, 1969), p. 61.

101. NA, ADM 1/488, ff. 82–3, 176–9; Barnes and Owen, eds, *Sandwich Papers*, vol. II, p. 292.

102. NA, ADM 1/488, ff. 190–1.

103. NA, ADM 1/488, ff. 239–41.

104. NA, ADM 1/488, ff. 207–9.

105. NA, ADM 1/488, f. 209.

106. NA, ADM 1/488, ff. 250–1. See also William L Clements Library, Sackville-Germain Papers, Military Dispatches, 1775–1782, Precis of Letters and Instructions for Vice Admiral Howe and notes thereon, 10 March

to July 1778.

107. NA, ADM 2/557, f. 93.

108. New York Historical Society Collections, *Kemble Papers* (New York, 1884–5), vol. I, pp. 581, 584, 586.

109. NA, ADM 1/488, ff. 277–8.

110. NA, CO 5/96, ff. 22–3.

111. NA, ADM 1/488, ff. 292, 294.

112. Ships of the line: *Eagle, Nonsuch, Somerset, Raisonable, Preston, St Albans, Ardent, Trident.* 50-gun ships: *Renown, Centurion, Isis, Experiment.* NA, ADM 1/488, ff. 190–1.

113. William L Clements Library, Clinton Papers, Howe to Clinton, 1 July 1778.

114. NA, ADM 1/488, f. 293.

115. David Syrett, '"This Penurious Old Reptile": Rear-Admiral James Gambier and the American War', *Historical Research* (Feb. 2001), vol. 74, p. 68.

116. NA, ADM 1/488, ff. 294–5.

117. Ships of the line: *Eagle, Ardent, Trident, St Albans, Somerset, Nonsuch, Preston.* 50-gun ships: *Experiment, Isis:* 44-gun frigates: *Phoenix, Roebuck, Pearl, Venus, Richmond:* armed vessel: *Vigilant.* NA, ADM 1/488, f. 293.

118. NA, ADM 1/488, f. 292.

119. Barnes and Owen, eds, *Sandwich Papers*, vol. II, p. 285n.

120. William L Clements Library, Clinton Papers, Howe to Clinton, 1 July [1778]; NA, ADM 1/488, f. 299; The French squadron under d'Estaing consisted of sixteen ships. Ships of the line: *Languedoc, Tonnant, César, Zélé, Hector, Guerrier, Marseillais, Protecteur, Vaillant, Provence, Fantasque.* 50-gun ship: *Sagittaire.* Frigates: *Chimère, Engageante, Aimable, Almène.* Barnes and Owen, eds, *Sandwich Papers*, vol. II, p. 286.

121. William L Clements Library, Clinton Papers, Howe to Clinton, 10 July [1778]; Howe to Clinton, Friday [July 1778].

122. Laughton ed., The Naval Miscellany, vol. I, p. 160; New York Historical Society Collections, *The Montressor Journals*, p. 504.

123. Quote from Moomaw, *Naval Career of Captain Hamond*, p. 505.

124. New York Historical Society Collections, *The Montressor Journals*, p. 505.

125. William L Clements Library, Clinton Papers, Howe to Clinton, Monday 13 [July 1778].

126. Laughton ed., *The Naval Miscellany*, vol. I, p. 160; Barnes and Owen, eds, *Sandwich Papers,* vol. II, pp. 304, 307; New York Historical Society Collections, *The Montressor Journals*, pp. 504–6.

127. Quoted in Willcox, *A Portrait of a General*, p. 239.

128. NA, ADM 1/488, f. 304. For d'Estaing's explanation of why he did not attempt to cross the bar at Sandy Hook see Henri Doniol ed., *Histoire de la participation de la France à l'établissement des États-Unis d'Amérique* (Paris, 1886–92), vol. III, pp. 448–9.

129. William L Clements Library, Clinton Papers, Howe to Clinton, 28 July 1778.

130. Historical Manuscripts Commission, *Stopford-Sackville MSS.* vol. II, pp. 116–17.

131. Willcox, *Portrait of a General*, pp. 239–40.

132. William L Clements Library, Clinton Papers, Howe to Clinton, 28 July 1778.

133. For an account of Byron's voyage see David Syrett, 'Home Waters or America? The Dilemma of British Navy Strategy in 1778', *The Mariner's Mirror* (Nov. 1991), vol. 77, pp. 365–77.

134. *Cornwall, Monmouth, Royal Oak, Conqueror, Fame, Sultan, Bedford, Grafton.* Barnes and Owen, eds, *Sandwich Papers*, vol. II, p. 287.

135. NA, ADM 1/488, ff. 115–19, 126, 128; ADM 1/489, ff. 19–22.

136. NA, ADM 1/488, ff. 288–9.

137. New York Historical Society Collections, *Montressor Journals*, pp. 504–6.

138. NA, ADM 1/488, ff. 123–38.

139. Ships of the line: *Eagle, Trident, Cornwall, Nonsuch, Raisonnable, Somerset, St Albans, Ardent;* 50-gun ships: *Experiment, Isis, Renown;* 44-gun frigates: *Phoenix, Roebuck;* frigates: *Venus, Richmond, Pearl, Apollo, Sphinx;* armed

vessels: *Vigilant*; sloop: *Nautilus*; fireships: *Strombolo, Sulphur, Volcano*; bomb ketches: *Thunder, Carcass*; galleys: *Philadelphia, Hussar, Ferret, Cornwallis*; plus two tenders. NA, ADM 1/488, 319.

140. NA, ADM 1/488, f. 314.

141. Doniol, *Histoire de la participation*, vol. III, p 452.

142. Howe in his dispatch to the Admiralty does not mention his intention of attacking the French with fireships, but only that he had kept three of them with him. NA, ADM 1/488, ff. 314–15. But Duncan believed that Howe kept the fireships with the squadron in order to attack the French with them when the wind changed direction. Laughton, ed., *The Naval Miscellany*, vol. I, p. 161. See also [Thomas O'Beirne], *Candid and Impartial Narrative of the Transactions of the Fleet under the Command of Lord Howe* (London, 2nd ed., nd), p. 30.

143. NA, ADM 1/488, f. 315–16; Laughton, ed., *The Naval Miscellany*, vol. I, pp. 161–2.

144. For an account of the condition of HMS *Apollo* after the storm and Howe's difficulty in leaving the ship see Moomaw, *Naval Career of Captain Hamond*, pp. 409–11.

145. *Centurion, Apollo, Richmond, Roebuck, Phoenix, Vigilant*. NA, ADM 1/488, ff. 315–17, 332–3.

146. NA, ADM 1/488, f. 316.

147. William L Clements Library, Clinton Papers, Howe to Clinton, 22 Aug. 1778.

148. Ibid, 22, 24 Aug. 1778 and Clinton to Howe, 24 Aug. 1778; NA, ADM 1/488, f. 336.

149. NA, ADM 1/488, f. 338.

150. Hamond, ed., *Letters and Papers of ... Sullivan*, vol. 11, pp. 237–8.

151. William L Clements Library, Clinton Papers, Howe to Clinton, 25 Aug. 1778.

152. Willcox, *Portrait of a General*, p. 250.

153. William B Willcox, ed., *The American Rebellion: Sir Henry Clinton's Narrative of His Campaigns, 1775–1782, with an Appendix of Original Documents* (New Haven, Ct., 1954), pp. 102–5.

154. NA, ADM 1/488, ff. 340–1; Moomaw, *Naval Career of Captain Hamond*, p. 412.

155. Willcox, ed., *American Rebellion: Sir Henry Clinton's Narrative*, p. 104.

156. *Royal Oak, Fame, Grafton, Bedford, Sultan, Conqueror*. William L Clements Library, Clinton Papers, Howe to Clinton, 11 Sept. 1778; NA, ADM 1/489, f. 21.

157. William L Clements Library, Clinton Papers, Howe to Clinton, 12 Sept. 1778.

158. Gruber, *The Howe Brothers in the American Revolution*, pp. 212–13.

159. NA, ADM 118/26, 1 July 1778.

160. NA, ADM 1/488, f. 343.

161. NA, ADM 1/488, ff. 372–3, 475.

CHAPTER V
Vindication of a Kind

When Admiral Lord Howe arrived from America at St Helens on 25 October, he was one of several defeated and discredited admirals and generals who had returned to England to salvage their reputations and to seek vindication on the floors of Parliament. Many believed that the next session of Parliament would be marked by 'disputes between Generals, Admirals, Ministers and Commissioners'.[1] It was not unusual for disgruntled army and navy officers to voice their opinions at Westminster.[2] In normal times these outbursts were usually personality conflicts or disputes over patronage. But the year 1778 was not a normal political time. Defeat and the ideological nature of the war in America had deeply divided the ruling classes in Britain. Since the beginning of the war in America, a number of navy officers had opposed the government's American policy. For instance, Captain the Hon. Robert Walsingham, RN, a Member of Parliament for Knaresborough, voted against the government on three major divisions concerning American policy during the years 1775–8.[3]

The first years of the American War had been frustrating ones for officers of the Royal Navy. There was little in the way of glory or prize money, and the Royal Navy, with its tradition of victory, appeared to be humiliated by its inability to deal effectively with a handful of American cruisers and blockade runners.[4] This discontent was aggravated among the senior officers by the fact that before the French entered the war in 1778 there were very few commands available to flag officers. Lord Sandwich, the First Lord of the Admiralty, had compounded the problem by tending to surround himself at the Admiralty with comparatively junior officers like Vice Admiral Sir Hugh Palliser and Captain Lord Mulgrave. This produced a sense of neglect and unease among senior officers, who suspected him of trying to create his own political following among the officer corps. Political differences, personality conflicts, and professional frustrations ran high within the officer corps of the Royal Navy during the autumn of 1778. Throughout the summer of 1778, the government's conduct of the war had been subjected to vociferous but ineffective attacks in the Houses of Parliament by the opposition aided by dissident army and navy officers. At the beginning of December 1778 the political opposition, aided by discredited generals and flag officers as well as dissident elements in the office of the Royal Navy, seized upon a dispute between Admiral the Hon. Augustus Keppel and Vice Admiral Sir Hugh Palliser, the commander and third in command of the Channel Fleet respectively, as a means not only to attack Sandwich, but also perhaps to bring down the government.

General Sir William Howe immediately after his return to England assured the king: 'nothing shall make either His Brother or Him to join the opposition.'[5] Nevertheless, General Howe believed that he and his brother, the admiral, must be 'allowed some means to justify' themselves because Lord George Germain and other officials in the secretary of state for America's office were blaming the Howe brothers for the failure of British arms in America.[6] It was not only members of the government who sought to blame the Howe brothers for the British defeat in America. For instance, in May of 1778 the American Tory Israel Mauduit published the first in a series of pamphlets attacking the Howes[7] and the erratic Commodore George Johnstone, RN, blamed Admiral Howe for the failure of the naval war in American waters and wanted Parliament 'to impeach the Howes'.[8] Admiral Howe upon his return from America quickly discovered that he could not expect the assistance or support of the Parliamentary opposition if he defended himself on narrow military grounds. Instead he had to join with the opposition in a broad-based attack designed not simply to save his reputation but rather to overthrow the government by placing the entire blame for the failure of the war in America on the administration.[9]

Amongst the sea of emotion and rhetoric that was the Keppel-Palliser affair the strategy and objectives of the Howes, the opposition, and the government began to emerge. The Howes would seek vindication for their actions through a Parliamentary enquiry into the conduct of the war in America. The Parliamentary opposition would seek to discredit, and perhaps even haul down, the government using the vehicle of an enquiry into the war in America to attack Germain and Sandwich. And the government would attempt to weather the crisis by detaching the Howes from the opposition. Lord Howe in a series of speeches in the House of Commons made it clear to everyone that he welcomed an enquiry into his conduct in America and that he was in league with the Parliamentary opposition. On 4 December 1778 Howe told the House of Commons that 'he should be glad that an enquiry should take place upon himself, his brother, and the noble Lord [Germain], that all three might have a fair opportunity of vindicating their characters'.[10] Then on 14 December in a speech during the debate on the army estimates Howe accused Germain of 'acting sometimes on his own account, independent of every other member of the administration' and having reduced the combat effectiveness of the Royal Navy in America by 'authorizing' the fitting out of privateers at New York City.[11] And two days later, on 16 December, Howe seconded the motion on a bill in the House of Commons to permit the court martial of Keppel to be held ashore.[12] Howe had allied himself with those who opposed the North government.

On 12 December, as the debates in the House of Commons on the conflict between Keppel and Palliser rocked the political world of London, the king suggested that perhaps the best way to end the crisis was for Howe to replace Sandwich as First Lord of the Admiralty. This appointment would have several advantages for the government. It would prevent Howe and his brother, the general, from pressing further with demands for a Parliamentary enquiry into the conduct of the war in America while simultaneously blunting the attacks by navy officers on the government's management of the Admiralty. The king knew that Howe was a popular officer, and the appointment might heal the divisions in the officer corps of the Royal Navy. There were several disadvantages to Howe becoming First Lord of the Admiralty. It would be viewed both as a condemnation of Sandwich's and Germain's conduct of the war and as a bribe to the Howes. Further, if Howe became First Lord, Sandwich would have to be made a secretary of state. Germain would then surely resign and would have to be pacified with a peerage or some other reward. This, in turn, would enrage those such as the Attorney General who thought that they deserved peerages more than the secretary of state for America. All in all the king's plan would be a large price to pay for buying off attacks on the government's handling of naval affairs. North thought it would be unnecessary for he believed that the government could survive without including Howe.[13]

Still, the negotiations with Howe mostly at the insistence of the king, were begun at the end of 1778. The effort failed because of Howe's conditions for becoming First Lord of the Admiralty: these were the removal of both Germain and Sandwich from office, an official government statement approving the conduct of the Howe brothers in America, and rewards for both Howes in the form of sinecures, promotions, or peerages. This seemed too much to pay for heading off a Parliamentary enquiry into the conduct of the war in America and ending the criticism by navy officers of government naval policy. With the breakdown of negotiations with Howe it became the government's policy to accept the possibility of the Howes joining the ranks of the Parliamentary opposition and to ride out the controversy.[14]

As the negotiations with the government over Howe becoming First Lord of the Admiralty broke down, the admiral increasingly joined with the Parliamentary opposition in debates over the conduct of the American War. On 17 February 1779 General Howe moved in the House of Commons that the government lay before Parliament all the papers concerning the conduct of the war so that members of the House of Commons could discover 'whether the fault lay with the commanders of His Majesty's fleets and armies, or in the ministers of state'. Speaking in support of his brother's motion Lord Howe stated that he wished to retire from public life with honour. Therefore, he desired that the House of Commons make an enquiry into the American War 'to show whether it was the fault of the commanders, or of the administration'.[15] Several days later during the debate on Colonel Isaac Barré's motion calling for the dismissal of Palliser from the navy, Howe said that it was 'impossible' that Palliser should continue to serve in the navy, but if the vice admiral was to be court-martialled then he would not support the motion.[16] On 3 March Howe in the House of Commons spoke in favour of Charles James Fox's motion to censure the Admiralty for sending Keppel's fleet to sea with a force inferior to that of the French.[17] And then on 8 March, during the debate on Fox's motion 'respecting the State of the Navy upon the breaking out of the War with the French', Howe told the House of Commons that not sending a fleet to the Mediterranean was a strategic error. Howe then went on to inform the House that he had been 'deceived' by the government into accepting the command of the squadron in America and 'that he was deceived while he retained it; that tired and disgusted he desired permission to resign'. This is why he had resigned his command in America and as long as the present government remained in power he could 'render no essential service to his country'.[18] Fox's motion was defeated by a vote of 246 to 174, and the next day the king, after learning of the admiral's speech, concluded that 'Lord Howe may now be ranked in the opposition'.[19]

The enquiry demanded by the Howes into the conduct of the war in America began on 22 April when the House of Commons resolved itself into establishing a committee for the whole enquiry. In the course of these proceedings the Howes, and especially General Howe, would seek vindication for their actions in America while attempting to place the whole of the blame for the failure of the British effort on the North government. The administration's strategy would be one of not conceding anything to the Howes while solidifying their majority in the House of Commons. Admiral Howe would in the course of the Parlimentary enquiry play a subsidiary role to that of his brother because most of the controversial events and decisions of the campaigns in America were military and the Royal Navy for the most part was deployed in support of the army. The enquiry began with a long speech by General Howe which was a detailed narrative and justification of his actions in America.[20]

Admiral Howe did not address the House of Commons until 29 April. On that day the admiral justified the need for an enquiry by telling the House of Commons that the administration was subjecting both him and his brother to underhand character assassinations. According to Howe the criticism of them had not been confined to 'newspaper attacks, conversations without doors, to coffee-house runner and emissaries of the administration', but also consisted of 'pamphlets written by persons in high credit and confidence with the ministry'. Commodore George Johnstone was specifically mentioned by Howe, 'but the admiral probably also had in mind the American Loyalist Israel Mauduit, who was supported by Germain, and had published several pamphlets attacking the Howes' conduct of the war in America.[21] An enquiry into the conduct of the war was required, according to Howe, because the 'Ministers, though their dispatches were filled with the fullest testimony of approbation of their conduct, remained silent when the general censures were passed upon him and his brother in their absence.' Howe believed that if there was not a public enquiry by the House of Commons then his brother and he 'must continue under a load of public obloquy, without a possibility of ever clearing themselves from the various imputations made against them'.[22] What the Howes desired was for the government publicly to censure their critics while at the same time expressing satisfaction with their own conduct in America.

The enquiry rambled on for weeks. There were endless speeches by ministers, navy officers, generals, government supporters and opposition politicians. The Howes called five witnesses – Major General Earl Cornwallis, Major John Montressor, Major General Charles Grey, Captain Sir Andrew Snape Hamond and Sir George Osborn – to support their version of events. All five of these men were either dependants, political supporters, or friends of the Howes and could be depended upon to be discreet while supporting the two brothers.[23] For instance, Hamond, who commanded the frigate HMS *Roebuck* in America and owed his knighthood to Admiral Howe, would tell less than the whole truth to the House of Commons when testifying about the July 1777 decision to approach Philadelphia by way of the Chesapeake.[24]

Admiral Howe, after his initial speech of 29 April, took the floor of the House of Commons only four more times to address the enquiry. On 13 May Admiral Howe, in answer to a speech by Germain, said that he and his brother were not the 'accusers' and were only defending their 'own honour and characters'. On 18 May the admiral informed the House that Commodore George Johnstone, RN was mistaken when he said that the expedition to Philadelphia in 1777 had been delayed in the Delaware river for the ships of Howe's command never entered that river when en route to Chesapeake Bay. Later on 8 June Admiral Howe declared that the American Loyalist Joseph Galloway, a government witness, was a man without honour 'because it appeared from his evidence, that he had divulged a matter in America, which had in fullness of confidence been imparted to him'. The enquiry drew to an inconclusive end on 30 June when Admiral Howe called upon Lord George Germain

> to declare his reasons, if he had any, why his Majesty's ministers had withdrawn their confidence from himself and his brother; if they had done anything that rendered them incapable of serving their country; or if he intended any future charge against them, he desired

it might be declared; or if not, that all imputations might be wiped away by his avowal that he had no accusation against them.

Germain remained seated. 'Not one of the ministers said a word; and the enquiry was put to an end without coming to a single Resolution upon any part of the business'.[25]

The enquiry into the conduct of the war in America made great Parliamentary theatre but it did not provide the Howes with the vindication they were seeking. It should have been apparent to the Howes, or any other observer for that matter, that because of the political nature of the enquiry the type of vindication they sought would be impossible to obtain. Debates and speeches in the House of Commons could not alter the fact that the British effort in America had failed. It was naive of the Howes to have expected that the government would commit political suicide by publicly absolving them of responsibility for the failure of British arms in America. Politically, a debacle of the scale of the British failure in America required atonement. To the North government the Howes, as failed military and naval commanders, were expendable. It was in the political interest of the administration to permit the Howes to carry the major portion of the blame for the British failure in America. In the wake of such a defeat the responsible military and naval commanders were obviously expendable to a government with a solid majority in the House of Commons. At no time during the enquiry into the American war did the North government come close to losing a vote in the House of Commons[26] or even near to being driven from office.

The opposition failed to bring down the North government during the enquiry into the conduct of the war in America for a number of reasons. Most significant was the make-up of the membership of the Parliament and the composition of the opposition party. The backbone of the Parliamentary opposition in the spring of 1779 consisted of three small and inter-connected groups. First there were members of Parliament such as Burke, Fox, Grafton, Barré, Shelburne, Richmond and Rockingham, who opposed the government on political and ideological grounds. Another faction included disgruntled generals and admirals, such as the Howes, who were attempting to protect their reputations on the floor of Parliament. A third group comprised navy officers who were opposed to the government, and especially to the First Lord of the Admiralty, on a wide range of naval affairs. Even combined these three groups lacked the numbers and strength to overthrow the government without the support of those members of Parliament who were independent country gentlemen. These men owed their seats to neither political patronage nor the crown. They were independent in their political judgements and, except in times of extreme political crisis tended to support the king's government.[27] Vindication for the Howes during the course of the enquiry into the conduct of the war in America would in all probability force the North government from office and this was a step most of the independent country gentlemen in the House of Commons were not prepared to take in the spring of 1779.

The controversy over Admiral Howe's period of command in America did not end with the conclusion of the Parliamentary enquiry into the conduct of the war, for the pamphlet conflict went on. In the weeks and months after the conclusion of the Parliamentary enquiry, a number of pamphlets were published in London attacking the Howes' actions during the war in America.[28] Admiral Howe for the most part ignored these hostile pamphlets with the exception of one[29] which appeared in November of 1779 and is thought to have been written by the American Loyalist Joseph Galloway. In this pamphlet Howe is accused of mismanaging the peace commission and of not waging the war at sea against the Americans in a sufficiently aggressive manner. Howe wrote a response to this pamphlet refuting the attacks, but did not publish his rebuttal.[30]

Perhaps the reason why Howe did not join the pamphlet wars was that it was soon apparent with the end of the enquiry into the conduct of the war in America that he had survived the controversy with his professional reputation as a navy officer largely intact. Howe's professional survival was due to the fact that not only had the Royal Navy played a secondary role in the war against the Americans, but also during the 1778 campaign against d'Estaing's squadron, the admiral had shown great skill in defending the British position in America when under attack by superior French forces. In fact Howe, along with Keppel, emerged from the political conflicts of 1779 as one of the major naval figures in the ranks of the Parliamentary opposition. It was widely assumed among opposition politicians that if the North government fell from power Howe would be placed in command of the Channel Fleet.[31]

During the period between the conclusion of the enquiry into the conduct of the war in America and the fall of the North government in March of 1782, Howe was a member of the Parliamentary opposition. In the House of Commons Howe spoke mainly on naval affairs. While supporting, in February of 1780, North's motion for a vote of thanks to Admiral Rodney for his victory over the Spanish in the Moonlight Battle,[32] Howe's speeches were for the most part attacks on the government's mismanagement of the Royal Navy and the conduct of the war at sea.[33] For instance, Howe bitterly attacked the government over the appointment of Palliser to the governorship of Greenwich Hospital.[34] In the general election of 1780, due mainly to local interest as well as the issue of the American War, the Howe family's political power base in Nottingham was destroyed and General Sir William Howe lost his seat in the House of Commons.[35] In contrast, Admiral Howe went to his constituency at Dartmouth, campaigned and won re-election.[36] Although Howe's re-election in the usually government-controlled

Dartmouth was due to the support of Arthur Holdsworth, who managed the borough for the government and who broke with the government over the election, the admiral would maintain that his victory was due to the 'virtue' of the voters.[37] Howe during this time not only engaged in opposition politics, but also indulged in his long-held interest in improving the Royal Navy's system of signalling.[38] Nevertheless, Howe was in many respects just treading water while waiting for the North administration to fall in order to resume his career as a navy officer.

On 1 April 1782 the government of Lord North fell to be replaced by a new administration headed by the Marquess of Rockingham and the Earl of Shelburne. Admiral the Hon. Augustus Keppel, created Viscount Keppel, was appointed First Lord of the Admiralty. Immediately upon assuming office Keppel, supported by a new board of the Admiralty, removed from positions of high command all those officers who were thought to be followers of the Earl of Sandwich and political supporters of the North government. Howe was slated to command the Channel Fleet.[39] But in a display of 'obstinacy', Howe would not accept the appointment as commander of the Channel Fleet until he and his brother, the general, had been vindicated and rewarded by a display of royal favour. It fell to Keppel to negotiate a settlement with Howe whose price for serving was high.[40] On 20 April 1782 Howe was created Viscount Howe of the Kingdom of England[41] and his brother was appointed lieutenant general of the ordnance. Learning of the royal rehabilitation of the Howes, that hardened observer of Westminster politics Horace Walpole wondered 'why honours and profit were showered on two such men, who with the most constitutional intrepidity had no other merit of head or heart, is utterly inconceivable. No party owed gratitude to them.'[42] Admiral Howe's advancement from a discredited admiral and backbench politician to an English peerage and command of the Channel Fleet was in some respects an astonishing act of political adroitness.

When Howe on 20 April hoisted his flag on board HMS *Victory* and took command of the Channel Fleet[43] the American War was almost at an end. Nevertheless, Howe and the Channel Fleet confronted a difficult strategic situation for Britain in 1782 was at war not only with America and France but also with Spain and the Netherlands. Intelligence reports arriving in London told of enemy naval preparations and activities.[44] Not only were there reports of French and Spanish preparations, but also rumours that the Dutch were assembling ships for a sortie into the North Sea from the Texel.[45] From this information the First Lord of the Admiralty concluded that the French would have at least fourteen ships of the line at Brest; that the combined Franco-Spanish fleets would number some sixty-two ships of the line; and that the Dutch fleet, including 50-gun ships 'may amount to twenty or twenty-five ships'. To oppose this force the Admiralty calculated that there were 'a normal twenty ships many of them short of men' in the Channel Fleet; that the North Sea squadron fitting at the Medway and Thames would number about 'six or seven' capital ships; and that in the course of the next several months a total of twenty-two ships of the line could be made available.[46] With an inferior force Howe as commander of the Channel Fleet would not only have to guard the western approaches to the English Channel against the French and Spanish, but also the North Sea against the possibility of a Dutch attack.

On 8 May Howe received orders to put to sea and proceed east 'to watch the motions of the Dutch fleet which anchored without the Texel'.[47] Intelligence of Dutch preparations for the sortie from the Texel raised the possibility that the Dutch might raid the east coast coal trade or attack a Baltic convoy.[48] There were just not enough British ships of the line in England to cover simultaneously both the North Sea and the western approaches to the English Channel.

As Keppel put it in a letter to Howe 'these quick movements with our little fleet seem to be our only recourse circumstanced as we are in point of numbers'.[49] On 10 May Howe sailed for the North Sea with nine ships of the line[50] and several smaller warships.[51]

Not long after the Channel Fleet arrived off the Dutch coast on 16 May, Howe received reports that the Dutch force consisted of thirteen ships of the line, of which nine were operational, and a number of smaller vessels. Further the Dutch apparently had no intentions of leaving the Texel.[52] In the light of the apparent Dutch passivity and Keppel's fears for the safety of the largest British ships in a north-west gale, the government issued orders on 25 May for Howe to return to Spithead.[53] To continue the blockade of the Texel, Howe left a force of nine ships of the line[54] commanded by Rear Admiral Sir John Lockhart Ross.[55] Keppel complained that the 'Dutch war is a millstone around our necks' and informed Howe that if necessary, Ross's squadron could be used to reinforce the Channel Fleet.[56] On 8 June Howe with three ships of the line arrived at Spithead.[57]

At the beginning of June the French and Spanish began a series of movements which would result in the assembling of a powerful fleet in the western approaches to the English Channel. On 4 June thirty-two enemy ships of the line sailed from Cádiz. This force would later be joined off the Ile d'Ouessant on 8 July by eight French ships of the line from Brest. Heading north towards Ushant, the enemy encountered a British convoy proceeding to Newfoundland and Quebec and captured nineteen of its merchant ships.[58] The British thought that the French and Spanish fleets would probably conduct operations in the Western Approaches as they had done in 1781, but when the enemy ships sailed from Cádiz, London possessed little hard information about their intentions and movements. When asked by the government what he believed enemy intentions to be, Howe replied on 24 May that he lacked enough information to make 'conjectures' about the movements of the Bourbon fleets.[59] On the day that the enemy fleet sailed from Cádiz, intelligence reached the Admiralty that there were twenty-seven French and Spanish ships of the line at that port.[60] By 17 June the British knew that the Franco–Spanish fleet had sailed from Cádiz, and Keppel concluded that with the addition of the ships from Brest, the enemy would have a force of more than thirty ships of the line.[61]

To counter the threat posed by the Franco–Spanish fleet, the government reinforced the Channel Fleet to twenty ships of the line by detaching four ships from the squadron off the Dutch coast.[62] The government realised that the British squadron off the Dutch coast had to be reinforced if it was to be able to contain the Dutch[63] for there was a possibility that the squadron at the Texel might sortie in support of the Franco–Spanish combined fleet when that force entered the Western Approaches.[64]

As the Channel Fleet sailed west from St Helens, Howe encountered a neutral ship that informed him that the French and Spanish fleets might have put into Brest. Howe notified the Admiralty that he would continue to proceed down the Channel but warned that he would return to Spithead if the intelligence proved true. On 5 July Howe learned that the Combined Fleet had been sighted off Ushant.[65]

South-east of the Isles of Scilly on 11 July, the Channel Fleet met HMS *Cormorant*, whose captain informed Howe that a large West India convoy was approaching from the west, expecting to make its first landfall on the southern Irish coast. In the early morning of the next day, the Channel Fleet, twenty-five ships[66] of the line strong, was fifteen leagues south-south-east of the Isles of Scilly when it sighted the Franco–Spanish fleet to westward. The enemy fleet consisted of thirty-six ships of the line 'besides frigates'. The wind was north-west and the Franco–Spanish fleet was to windward. This meant that Howe would have to deal with a superior enemy force that lay between his ships and the approaching West India convoy, which he had to protect. As the enemy ships formed a line of battle, the Channel Fleet stood to the northward, passing between Land's End and the Isles of Scilly. This manoeuvre required nerve and considerable seamanship. Its purpose was 'to get the westward of the enemy, both for the protection of the Jamaica convoy; and to gain the advantage of the situation for bringing them to action which the difference in our numbers renders desirable'. At the same time, Howe sent HMS *Cormorant* west to warn the West India convoy of the enemy's presence and to order the merchant ships into southern Irish ports.[67] The next morning the Channel Fleet was to the northward and west of the Isles of Scilly and the Franco–Spanish fleet was nowhere in sight. The Channel Fleet then stood to the westward to intercept the West India convoy.

After eluding the Franco–Spanish fleet by passing to the north, the Channel Fleet waited in the track of the expected convoy from the West Indies. Howe used this opportunity to drill the ships of his command in battle tactics. On 27 June, failing to obtain any information on the movements of the West India convoy and forced off station by a northerly gale, Howe decided 'to return to the eastward ... to go in quest of the enemy' in hope of 'attempting to draw them from their station off Scilly'. Arriving off the Isles of Scilly on 2 August, Howe discovered that the Franco–Spanish fleet had left and that the West India convoy had entered the English Channel. The Channel Fleet anchored in Torbay on 9 August and returned to Spithead ten days later.[68]

Howe, while skilfully manoeuvring the Channel Fleet by passing to the northwards between Land's End and the Isles of Scilly, had failed to bring the Franco–Spanish fleet to a battle. After the British fleet passed to the northward of the Isles of Scilly, the Bourbon ships maintained station west of Scilly until driven south by the same northerly gale that had forced Howe off station. After the combined fleet left the region of the Isles of Scilly, the British convoy from the West Indies entered the English Channel. At the beginning of August the Spanish ships of the enemy force received orders to return to Spain to prepare to oppose an expected British attempt to resupply Gibraltar.[69] The Franco–Spanish fleet's parade in the western approaches of the English Channel during the summer of 1782 was embarrassing for the British, but it achieved nothing of importance. While the French and Spanish had amassed a superior fleet at the western end of the English Channel, they had failed to intercept a major convoy and had been outmanoeuvred by Howe and the Channel Fleet.

The British attention now turned southward. Everyone knew that the British would have to resupply the besieged fortress of Gibraltar. On 30 July Keppel had informed Howe that 'the object at present is how & when to relieve Gibraltar' and that the government had to choose between two courses: immediately mount a small relief expedition with a weak escort that might be blocked by an enemy or wait until September when the resupply could be supported by the whole Channel Fleet.[70]

All the ships of the Channel Fleet could not be employed to support the relief of Gibraltar because a force of ships of the line had to be sent into the North Sea to meet a new Dutch naval threat. Keppel and other officials in the Admiralty considered it absolutely imperative that the Baltic trade return to Britain safely and, with the possibility of a Dutch sortie from the Texel, this required a detachment from the Channel Fleet.[71]

On 16 August the Admiralty ordered Howe to detach the ships of the line from the Channel Fleet for possible service in the North Sea.[72] At a cabinet meeting on 9 August, Howe was directed to return immediately to Spithead and prepare the Channel Fleet for further service. At the same time it was decided to dispatch ten ships of the line to the North Sea. Howe was to stay at Spithead with a force of twenty-three ships of the line, to prepare either to sail into the North Sea or to undertake the resupply of Gibraltar.[73] As Keppel explained the plan to Howe, ten ships of the line were to sail into the North Sea to protect the Baltic trade from attack by a Dutch squadron thought to be off the Naze of Norway. If the ten ships could not deal with this Dutch squadron, Howe was to enter the North Sea with reinforcements. When the Dutch threat was removed, Howe was to return to Spithead to undertake the resupply of Gibraltar employing the entire Channel Fleet.[74] On 14 August the cabinet decided that as soon as the ships of the Channel Fleet were ready for sea, Howe was to go with 'twenty or thirty ships of the line in quest of the Dutch Squadron'. Howe was to seek out the Dutch, first at the Texel and then, if necessary, off the Naze of Norway. He was further directed to return to Spithead by the beginning of September to undertake the Gibraltar operation.[75]

The strategic problem confronting the British in the summer of 1782 was simple. If Gibraltar was not quickly resupplied, the fortress would fall to the Spanish. But if the Dutch threat was not contained, the British might lose naval control of the North Sea. This would cut off Britain's supplies of naval stores from the Baltic and enable the Dutch to blockade London and 'every other port on the northern coast, and put an end to our coastal trade and every other branch of commerce'. On 24 August Keppel clearly stated the dilemma when he wrote to Howe:

> If we fail getting the ships safe from the Baltick our next years equipping the Fleet must also fail, if our relief does not get soon to Gibraltar that garrison must fall.

There seemed to be no way to resupply Gibraltar until the ships of the Channel Fleet returned from the North Sea.[76]

On 25 August the North Sea threat disappeared when intelligence arrived in England that the Dutch fleet had returned to the Texel. Nevertheless, ten ships of the line were detached from the Channel Fleet and sent east into the North Sea. The squadron had orders to look into the Texel. If the Dutch fleet was in port and did not appear likely to put to sea, the ships were to return immediately to Spithead.[77] It was soon apparent that the Dutch had once again sunk into inactivity. The ships of the Channel Fleet which had been sent to the coast of the Netherlands returned to Spithead on 6 September.[78]

On 30 August the Admiralty began to issue Howe's instructions for the resupply of Gibraltar. Troops of the 29th and 59th Regiments were to embark on warships for conveyance to Gibraltar. Howe was to use the Channel Fleet to escort not only merchant ships carrying provisions, ordnance, stores and fuel to Gibraltar, but also the trade proceeding to the East and West Indies and a convoy to Portugal. If the Franco–Spanish fleet was encountered during the operation to resupply Gibraltar, it was left to Howe's judgement and direction to determine what measures to pursue upon such an event. After unloading the troops and supplies at Gibraltar, Howe was to return to England.[79]

The Channel Fleet, consisting of thirty-five ships of the line,[80] sailed from Spithead with the supply ships bound for Gibraltar and the three trade convoys. 'Contrary winds & unfavourable weather' delayed the fleet's arrival off Cape St Vincent until 9 October. Howe had intelligence that the Franco–Spanish fleet, thought to consist of fifty ships of the line, was in Gibraltar Bay. During the evening of 10 October a gale scattered the enemy fleet, forcing many ships out of Gibraltar Bay, damaging some vessels, and forcing four ashore, including the ship of the line *San Miguel*, which was captured by the British.

Early in the morning of 11 October, the Channel Fleet and the relief convoy entered the Straits of Gibraltar. The fleet was off Gibraltar by the evening giving the storeships 'a favourable opportunity' to enter the anchorage without being attacked; but a 'want of timely attention to the circumstances of navigation' by the merchant ships' masters meant that only four of these vessels entered Gibraltar. The merchant ships as well as the warships of the Channel Fleet passed by Gibraltar and entered the Mediterranean. On 13 October the Channel Fleet was off the Spanish coast some fifty miles east of Gibraltar. Howe sent the storeships, escorted by HMS *Buffalo*, to an anchorage off the African coast to await events.

The enemy fleet 'standing to the southward' was sighted during the evening of 13 October. The next morning, the Franco–Spanish force was six or seven leagues north of the Channel Fleet. Later in the day the wind came to the east, giving the Channel Fleet the opportunity to make for Gibraltar and to enter Rosa Bay. The storeships anchored off the African coast were sent for later and also anchored in Rosa Bay. Troops, stores, provisions, and fifteen hundred barrels of gunpowder from the ships of the fleet were quickly sent ashore. Gibraltar had been successfully resupplied.

On the morning of 19 October, with the wind out of the east, Howe and the Channel Fleet put to sea for the return voyage to England. As the fleet left Gibraltar Bay, the Franco–Spanish fleet was sighted to the north-east. There was no room between Europa Point and Ceuta to manoeuvre or to form a line of battle, so Howe and the Channel Fleet passed through the Straits into the Atlantic, followed by the enemy. The next morning the Channel Fleet was to leeward of the Franco-Spanish fleet of forty-five or forty-six ships, giving the enemy the opportunity to force an engagement on the British. Both fleets were in line ahead formations, but it was sunset before the French and Spanish ships were close enough to the Channel Fleet 'at a considerable distance to cannonade' the British. The fire was returned by the Channel Fleet and dilatory gunfire continued until 10pm, when both fleets drew apart. The British lost sixty-eight men killed and 208 wounded in this action. The next morning the 'reduced state' of water in the ships of the Channel Fleet persuaded Howe not to chase and renew the action with the enemy, but rather to return to England. The Channel Fleet arrived at St Helens on 14 November, and the next day Howe received permission to come ashore and go to London.[81] This was the last naval operation conducted by Howe during the American War for the conflict was virtually over. On 15 February 1783 orders were issued ending hostilities.[82]

Most observers thought that Howe had skilfully conducted the relief of Gibraltar. However, Captain Lord Hervey, the eccentric oldest son of the Earl of Bristol, believed that the relief of Gibraltar had been 'mismanaged' and published in the newspapers an abusive attack on Howe for not engaging the Franco–Spanish fleet. Thereupon Howe challenged Hervey to a duel claiming that his honour had been insulted. When the two men met on a field of honour Hervey explained that his article in the newspaper was about 'mismanagement of the fleet and not an accusation of his Lordship's want of courage and veracity'. With this Howe withdrew his challenge and there was no duel.[83] For Howe the American War, from beginning to end, was filled with pitfalls and difficulties.

Notes

1. A Francis Steuart, ed., *The Last Journal of Horace Walpole during the Reign of George III from 1771 to 1783* (London, 1910), vol. 2, pp. 208–9.

2. Sir Lewis Namier and John Brooke, *The History of Parliament* (London, 1964), vol. I, pp. 138–45.

3. Namier and Brooke, *History of Parliament*, vol. III, p. 604.

4. Cf. David Syrett, *The Royal Navy in American Waters, 1775–1783* (Aldershot, Hants., 1989), pp. 1–91.

5. Sir John Fortescue, ed., *The Correspondence of King George III from 1760 to December 1782* (London, 1927–8), no. 2387.

6. Historical Manuscripts Commission, *Report on Manuscripts in Various Collections* (London, Dublin, and Hereford, 1901–14), vol. VI, p. 153.

7. Israel Mauduit, *Remarks upon Gen. Howe's Account on Long Island in the Extraordinary Gazette of October 10, 1776* (London, 1778).

8. John A Woods, ed., *The Correspondence of Edmund Burke* (Cambridge, 1963), vol. IV, p. 29.

9. Peter Orlando Hutchinson, ed., *Diary and Letters of His Excellency Thomas Hutchinson* (London, 1883), vol. 2, p. 210.

10. *Parliamentary History of England from the earliest period to the Year 1803* (London, 1814), vol. XIX, col. 1398.

11. *Parliamentary History*, vol. XX, col. 79.

12. *Parliamentary Register; or History of the Proceedings and Debates of the House of Commons* (London, 1779), vol. 11, p. 181.

13. Fortescue, *Correspondence*, nos. 2470, 2485, 2486.

14. For an account of the negotiations to make Howe First Lord of the Admiralty, see Ira Gruber, *The Howe Brothers and the American Revolution* (New York, 1972), pp. 330–6.

15. *Parliamentary History*, vol. XX, col. 139.

16. Ibid, col. 147.

17. Fortescue, *Correspondence*, no. 2567.

18. *Parliamentary History*, vol. XX, cols. 204, 217–18, 227–8.

19. Fortescue, *Correspondence*, nos. 2574, 2575.

20. *Parliamentary History*, vol. XX, cols. 677–706.

21. Worthington C Ford, 'Parliament and the Howes', *Proceedings of the Massachusetts Historical Society* (1910), vol. 44, p. 130.

22. *Parliamentary History*, vol. XX, cols. 720–1.

23. Gruber, *The Howe Brothers*, pp. 342–3.

24. W H Moomaw, 'The denouement of General Howe's Campaign of 1777', *English Historical Review* (July 1964), vol. 79, pp. 509–11.

25. *Parliamentary History*, vol. XX, cols. 765–6, 807–8, 816–18.

26. Fortescue, *Correspondence*, nos 2621, 2658.

27. For the cult of the independent country gentlemen, see Namier and Brooke, *History of Parliament*, vol. I, pp. 145–9.

28. In Gruber, *Howe Brothers*, pp. 366–70 there is a list of pamphlets attacking the Howes' conduct of the war in America.

29. *A Letter to the Right Hon. Ld. Howe on his Naval Conduct in the American War* (London, 1779).

30. Gerald Saxon Brown, ed., *Reflections of a Pamphlet Intitled 'a Letter to the Right Hon. Lord Vist. H--e'* (Ann Arbor, Mich., 1959).

31. E.g. Woods, ed., *Correspondence of Edmund Burke*, vol. IV, pp. 144, 154.

32. *Parliamentary History*, vol. XXI, cols. 138–9.

33. Namier and Brooke, *History of Parliament*, vol. II, p. 648.

34. *Parliamentary History*, vol. XXI, cols. 947–8.

35. I R Christie, *End of North's Ministry, 1780–1782* (London, 1958), pp. 144–8.

36. HL, Howe to Curtis, 6 Sept. 1780.

37. HL, Howe to Curtis, 2 Oct. 1780.

38. E.g. HL, Howe to Curtis, 10, 21 Sept. 1779.

39. Cf. Historical Manuscripts Commission, *Report on Manuscripts of the Late Reginald Hastings, Esq., of the Manor House, Ashby de la Zouche* (London, 1928–47), vol. III, pp. 198–9.

40. Fortescue, *Correspondence*, nos. 3606, 3623, 3624.

41. *The Complete Peerage* (Gloucester, 1987 reprint), vol. 2, no. 600.

42. Steuart, ed., *The Last Journal of Horace Walpole*, vol. II, p. 429.

43. NA, ADM 1/97, f. 5.

44. NA, ADM 1/4147, ff. 50, 70, 79, 88.

45. NA, ADM 1/4147, f. 10.

46. Ipswich and East Suffolk Record Office, Keppel Papers, Keppel to Shelburne, 18 April 1782.

47. NA, ADM 1/97, ff. 18–19, 22.

48. Fortescue, *Correspondence*, nos 3720, 3721, 3722.

49. Ipswich and East Suffolk Record Office, Keppel Papers, Keppel to Howe, 31 May 1782.

50. *Victory, Britannia, Edgar, Ocean, Cambridge, Dublin, Alexander, Raisonable, Panther.*

51. NA, ADM 1/97, 21.

52. NA, ADM 1/97, ff. 30–41.

53. Ipswich and East Suffolk Record Office, Keppel Papers, Keppel to Shelburne, 26 May 1782.

54. *Ocean, Cambridge, Princess Amelia, Dublin, Panther, Buffalo, Ripon, Bienfaisant, Raisonable.*

55. NA, ADM 1/97, ff. 42–5.

56. Ipswich and East Suffolk Record Office, Keppel Papers, Keppel to Howe, 30 May 1782.

57. *Victory, Britannia, Edgar*. NA, ADM 1/97, f. 56.

58. Jonathan R Dull, *The French Navy and American Independence: A Study in Arms and Diplomacy, 1774–1787* (Princeton, N.J., 1975), p. 290.

59. NA, ADM 1/97, f. 36.

60. NA, ADM 3/95, 4 June 1782.

61. Ipswich and East Suffolk Record Office, Keppel Papers, Keppel to Ross, 17 June 1783.

62. Fortescue, *Correspondence*, no. 3817.

63. Ipswich and East Suffolk Record Office, Keppel Papers, Keppel to Milbank, 28 June 1782.

64. Fortescue, *Correspondence*, no. 3829.

65. NA, ADM 1/97, ff. 82–3, 91.

66. There is no list of the ships of the Channel Fleet during this operation in Howe's dispatches to the Admiralty.

67. NA, ADM 1/97, ff. 93–4.

68. NA, ADM 1/97, ff. 95–100, 106.

69. Dull, *French Navy*, pp. 290–1.

70. Ipswich and East Suffolk Record Office, Keppel Papers, Keppel to Howe, 30 July 1782.

71. Fortescue, *Correspondence*, no. 3877.

72. NA, ADM 3/96, 6 Aug. 1782.

73. Bedford Record Office, Grantham MSS. L.29/661, Cabinet Minutes, 9 Aug. 1782.

74. Ipswich and East Suffolk Record Office, Keppel Papers, Keppel to Howe, 10 Aug. 1782.

75. Fortescue, *Correspondence*, no. 3880.

76. Ipswich and East Suffolk Record Office, Keppel Papers, Keppel to Howe, 24 Aug. 1782; Keppel to Shelburne, 24 Aug. 1782.

77. NA, ADM 1/97, ff. 115–17.

78. NA, ADM 1/97, f. 135.

79. NA, ADM 2/1341, ff. 154–64.

80. *Ganges, Royal William, Britannia, Atlas, Ruby, Panther, Edgar, Foudroyant, Polyphemus, Suffolk, Vigilant, Courageux, Crown, Alexander, Sampson, Princess Royal, Victory, Blenheim, Asia, Egmont, Queen, Bellona, Raisonable, Fortitude, Princess Amelia, Berwick, Bienfaisant, Dublin, Cambridge, Ocean, Buffalo, Vengeance, Goliath, Union* and *Tésiphone*.

81. NA, ADM 1/97, ff. 141–58.

82. NA, 3/97, 15 Feb. 1783.

83. *Whitehall Evening Post*, 9–11 Oct. 1783.

CHAPTER VI

At the Admiralty and the
Command and Control of Fleets

The resignation of Lord North, because of the British defeat at Yorktown, ushered in a period of political instability and crisis in Britain during which a succession of governments firstly sought to end and then grapple with the aftermath of the American War. The Rockingham–Shelburne government, which had replaced the North administration, disappeared with the death of the Marquess of Rockingham and by the end of 1782, the new government headed by the Earl of Shelburne was collapsing owing to the political pressures and conflicts generated by negotiating an end to the American War. One of the first members of the Shelburne government to drop by the wayside was Lord Keppel, the First Lord of the Admiralty, who resigned from office over the terms of the peace treaty with the Americans. In his place Lord Shelburne appointed Howe who assumed office on 30 January 1783.[1] Howe had supported Shelburne in the House of Lords during the debates on the peace treaties declaring that 'the peace was necessary, as our Fleets were in wretched decayed condition'.[2] However, Howe's appointment was not for political reasons, but clearly a stopgap measure, for the Shelburne government was on its last legs and the admiral was still the commander in chief of the Channel Fleet. Howe was probably appointed to the office of First Lord of the Admiralty because a senior navy personage was required to oversee the beginning of the demobilisation of the Royal Navy from a war footing to a peacetime establishment.

On 4 February 1783 reports arrived in London telling of disturbances among the seamen, marines and soldiers serving on warships in the Portsmouth area who were demanding their pay and discharge from the service.[3] Howe, who believed that the complaints of the men were to some extent justified, went to Portsmouth to calm the situation by seeing 'that proper attention is had to the just representation of the Claimants and that due order is preserved'.[4] He was apparently successful in this endeavour for he returned to London by 8 February to oversee the beginning of the demobilisation of the fleet. On 10 February the Admiralty directed that the Navy Board submit plans showing what number of vessels should be employed as guardships at various English ports[5] and then over the next several days orders were issued for the paying off and decommissioning of ships.[6] Nevertheless, protests again broke out among the seamen and Howe had to return to Portsmouth a second time to restore order.[7] As a result not only of disturbances among the seamen of the fleet, but also a desire by the government to save money by reducing the cost of the naval establishment,[8] the flow of instructions calling for the demobilisation of the Royal Navy increased over the next few weeks. For example, on 10 March the commander in chief at the Leeward Islands was directed to return to England to pay off all the ships of his command except for one 50-gun ship, one 44-gun ship, two frigates and two sloops.[9] However, before the demobilisation process could be completed, Howe was replaced at the Admiralty by Keppel who again became First Lord on 10 April 1783 when the North-Fox coalition assumed power. Howe, nevertheless, would soon return to the office of First Lord of the Admiralty.

On 26 December 1783 William Pitt the Younger became First Lord of the Treasury and formed a government with Howe as First Lord of the Admiralty.[10] Howe's appointment was apparently again a stopgap measure and not the first choice of either the king or Pitt.[11] At first sight his appointment to the Admiralty was somewhat incongruous for the admiral was not a close political ally of Pitt and was without a Parliamentary following and thus did not add political weight to the new government. Howe was old enough to be Pitt's father and in fact had been a supporter of the first Earl of Chatham before the American War. Howe was nonetheless a distinguished admiral who had broken with the North administration in the late 1770s and who had also opposed the North-Fox coalition, and had been selected to be a member of the new government not because of his skills or abilities, but rather because of his reputation and respectability. Yet Howe would discover, as First Lord, that he could never gain the confidence of Pitt and that on many important matters concerning the Royal Navy, the First Lord of the Treasury would simply bypass the First Lord of the Admiralty.[12]

Howe's years at the Admiralty must have been frustrating for the post of First Lord in the government of the Younger Pitt became a position without real authority over the central issues of policy concerning the Royal Navy. The major themes of the Pitt administration during the years before the French Revolutionary War were financial retrenchment and reform of the British government. Nevertheless, great sums of money were expended on the Royal Navy during the 1780s for Pitt, unlike many peacetime First Lords of the Treasury, saw the importance of a strong Royal Navy in the violent environment of European power politics.[13] During the years that Howe was First Lord of the Admiralty eight new ships of the line were constructed and a further forty-eight were repaired or rebuilt in the king's dockyards. Great stocks of naval stores, ship's furniture, and other equipment and fittings required for the building and repair of warships were also amassed at various dockyards and naval bases in the British Isles. Parliament voted huge amounts of money during the years 1783–8 for the support of the Royal Navy. For instance in 1786 an unprecedented £1,492,326 was spent on the Royal Navy which had a peacetime establishment of only 18,000 seamen and marines.[14] Yet Howe had comparatively little to do with this peacetime naval build-up for Pitt dealt directly with Captain Sir Charles Middleton, the Controller of the Navy.[15] According to one observer:

> It was not an uncommon thing for Mr. Pitt to visit the Navy Office to discuss naval matters with the Comptroller, and to see the returns made from the yards of the progress in building and repairing the ships of the line; he also desired to have a periodical statement from the Comptroller of the state of the fleet, wisely holding that officer responsible personally to him, without any regard to the Board.[16]

This arrangement between Pitt and Middleton rendered the higher reaches of the civil administration of the Royal Navy dysfunctional.[17] Howe was placed on the sidelines and conflict was generated between the First Lord of the Admiralty and the Controller of the Navy.

That Howe and Middleton would fall into conflict when the admiral became First Lord was all but inevitable. Both men were headstrong and obsessed with rank, position and their own self-importance. But here the similarities ended. Howe was an aristocrat and a successful commander of men, ships and fleets, but not an administrator and was basically unskilled in the ways of bureaucratic in-fighting. Middleton, on the other hand, the son of a Scots customs collector and a relation of the Dundases (a distinguished legal and political family), was neither a great seaman nor leader of fighting men, but an obscure post captain before being unexpectedly appointed controller of the navy in 1778. But upon taking up this appointment Middleton found his element, becoming a hard-nosed bureaucrat who, by the end of the American War, dominated the civil establishment of the Royal Navy. It was natural that Pitt and Middleton would become close allies in the 1780s for not only were they distant relations by marriage,[18] but both were also men of business who understood public finances and administration, and shared a vision of the importance of British naval power.

Howe fought back against marginalisation by periodically invading the domain of Middleton. At the end of 1784 Howe successfully, over the objections of Middleton, altered the make up of the Navy Board by ordering the discharge of two extra commissioners – Sir Richard Temple and Captain Samuel Wallis – and insisting on the appointment of John Henslow to succeed Sir John Williams as one of the two surveyors.[19] This was a direct assault on Middleton's area of responsibility for extra commissioners and surveyors were members of the Navy Board. Middleton retaliated by claiming that the pressures of work at the Navy Office required the services of the two extra commissioners while a second surveyor was not necessary. However, the dismissal of Temple and Wallis and the appointment of Henslow stood, for Pitt would not in 1784 cause a crisis within his cabinet by overriding decisions which were clearly within the authority of the First Lord of the Admiralty.[20] Another area of Middleton's domain, where Howe asserted the authority of the office of the First Lord of the Admiralty, was the Royal Dockyards. In the autumn of 1784 Howe made a surprise visit to Portsmouth Dockyard looking for faults[21] and then at the end of the year the Admiralty, in the name of saving money, decreed that all the extra clerks working in the dockyards be dismissed.[22] Howe also blocked Middleton's suggestion that John Marquand, who had constructed the marine barracks at Chatham, be appointed a general contractor for all dockyard buildings as well as his proposal to roof over all ships in stocks to protect them from the weather while building. In fact this idea could have had a profound effect on the Royal Navy by lengthening the useful life of warships.[23] All of this was futile and did not alter the fact that Pitt was bypassing Howe on many of the great issues concerning the Royal Navy by dealing directly with Middleton.[24]

During his time as First Lord of the Admiralty Howe became very unpopular among many members of the officer corps of the Royal Navy as well as with the friends and relations of officers in the House of Commons. Part of this discontent arose because of the technical innovations in the construction of warships and the building programme pushed by Middleton and Pitt.[25] However, by far the greater source of discontent with Howe among the officers of the Royal Navy was the great number of officers and the few available opportunities for promotion and assignments to ships at sea. There were no naval wars and few naval crises during the 1780s and while great sums of money were spent on the Royal Navy to repair and build ships, there were very few opportunities for employment of officers at sea. The number of seamen and marines borne on the naval establishment between 1783 and 1785 decreased from a wartime strength of 110,000 to 18,000 seamen and marines[26] with a corresponding decrease in the number of commissioned officers required for active service. The result was that during the time when Howe was First Lord of the Admiralty, there were scores of navy officers ashore, unemployed and on half pay. It was a situation very similar to that which confronted Sandwich in the 1770s. In 1786 the House of Commons attempted to deal with the discontent among unemployed navy officers when it petitioned the king requesting that superannuated captains, who had been passed over for promotion to rear admiral, receive a pension equal 'to their half pay as Senior Captains'.[27] The king approved this measure and granted the petition.[28] Nevertheless, the complaints continued about Howe's failure to grant employment and promotion to officers of the Royal Navy.[29]

On 24 September 1787 Middleton, while still controller of the navy, was promoted from post captain to the rank of rear admiral of the white.[30] Howe

Baltimore at Dublin River Jan:
12º 1745 - 6

Sir

Please to acquaint their Lordships
that this Morning I got Down to pool beg at the mouth
of this River & having Been Detain'd since y 5th of this
Ins.t for want of a fair wind, My Stay here will be
only till the weather Permits for my water & Beer
to be Brought Down to me the River being so Shoal
I was Oblig'd to leave them out, Some of the Bread
& having Been wet During the time the Sloop was
on Shore in the Bay, I laid a Survey on the Same
& found Three Thousand three Hundred & Sixty
Pounds wet & Damnefied & not fit for men to Eat,
as also some Beer which was taken on Board at
Kinsale the 1.st of last Dec.r Two Hundred & Eighty
Gallons of which was Sower & Spoild, Inclos'd with
this my weekly acct. which please to transmit to
their Lordships

I am
Sir
your most Humble Serv.t
Rich Howe

To
The Hon:ble Thom.s Corbett Esq.

1. A letter by Captain Richard Howe to the secretary of the Admiralty.
© **The National Archive.** ADM 1/1886.

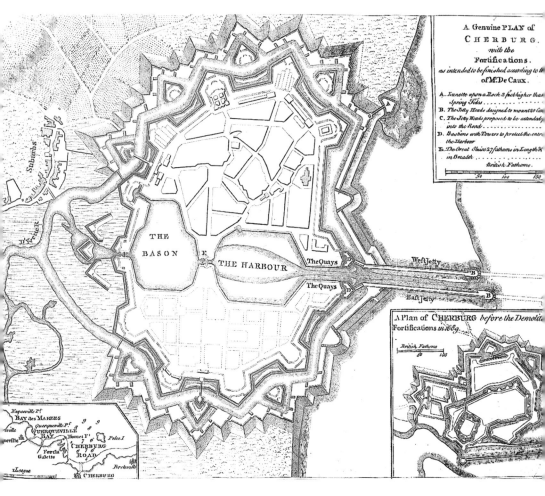

2. 'A Genuine Plan of Cherburg [sic] with the Fortifications as intended to be finished according to the Design of M. De Caux'. *Gentleman's Magazine*, 1758.

3. *Opposite:* 'The Coast of Britany between St Malo's and Cancale Bay where the English Army landed, June 1758'. *Gentleman's Magazine* 1758.

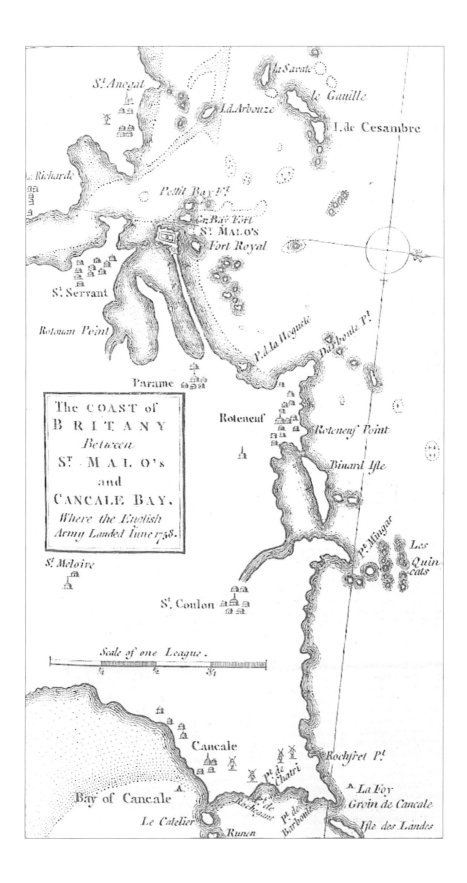

St. Anogat

la Savate

I.d.Arbouze

le Gauille

I. de Cesambre

la Richarde

Petit Bay F.t

Gr. Bay Fort
St. MALO'S
Fort Royal

St. Servant

Rotouan Point

P. d. la Hoguette

Darbouty P.t

Parame

The COAST of
B R I T A N Y
Between
St. M A L O's
and
CANCALE BAY.
Where the English
Army Landed June 1758.

Roteneuf

Roteneuf Point

Binard Isle

St. Meloire

St. Coulon

P.t Mingar

Les
Quin
cats

Scale of one League.

¼   ½   ¾

Cancale

Rochfret P.t

Pt. de
Chatri

La Foy

Bay of Cancale

Groin de Cancale

Le Catelier

Runen

Pt. de
Rochquant

Pt. de
Barboult

Isle des Landes

4. The Battle of Quiberon Bay, 20 November 1759 by Nicolas Pocock.
   © **National Maritime Museum, Greenwich, London.** BHC 0399.

5. *Above left:* Admiral Edward Hawke, the commander of the British squadron at
   the Battle of Quiberon Bay by John Charnock, *Biographia Navalis*, London
   1796, vol IV. © **The National Archive.** 359/331092

6. *Above right:* Benjamin Franklin, 1783. Artist unknown. © **National Portrait
   Gallery, London.** 327.

7. *Above left:* William Pitt, 1789 by James Gillray. © **National Portrait Gallery, London.** 135a.

8. *Above right:* Richard Howe, 1st Earl Howe by John Singleton Coply. © **National Maritime Museum, London.** BHC 2790.

9. *Above left:* Richard Howe, 1st Earl Howe. John Campbell, *Lives of British Admirals*, London 1817, vol VII. © **The National Archive.** 359/092.

10. *Above right:* Richard Howe, 1st Earl Howe. Artist unknown, 1798. © **National Portrait Gallery, London.** 3313.

11. *Left:* Richard Howe, 1st Earl Howe by Henry Singleton, 1799. © **National Portrait Gallery, London.** 75.

12. *Below:* The Battle of the First of June, 1794 by Philippe-Jacques de Loutherbourg. © **National Maritime Museum, Greenwich, London.** BHC 0470.

13. The Glorious First of June, 1794: Earl Howe on the deck of the *Queen Charlotte* by Mather Brown. © **National Maritime Museum, Greenwich, London.** BHC 2740.

14. The Battle of the First of June, 1794 by Philippe-Jacques de Loutherbourg. © **National Maritime Museum, Greenwich, London.** BHC 0469.

15. George III presenting a sword to Earl Howe, on board HMS *Queen Charlotte,*
26 June 1794. © **National Maritime Museum, Greenwich, London.** BHC 0476.

16. Relief of Gibraltar by Admiral Lord Howe, 11 October 1782 by George Paton.
© **National Maritime Museum, Greenwich, London.** BHC 0453.

used the opportunity of the controller's promotion to flag rank to attempt to rid himself of the troublesome Middleton. Learning of the impending promotion of Middleton, Howe in series of letters to Pitt, argued that if Middleton was promoted to flag rank then he must resign from the office of controller of the navy. Howe's argument was that the office of controller had always been held by a post captain and that when previous occupants of that office had achieved flag rank they had resigned from the position. Howe cited two examples to support his case. The first was Captain Savage Mostyn who had resigned from the controllership on 28 February 1755 when promoted to flag rank and then went to sea on active service as Boscawen's second in command. Howe's other example was Sir Hugh Palliser. Palliser, like Middleton, was awarded a baronetcy for his services as controller and then after becoming a Lord of the Admiralty had been promoted to the rank of rear admiral.[31] However, Pitt paid no attention to Howe's arguments and Middleton, while still controller, was promoted to flag rank.

Howe was hurt by the promotion of Middleton and by the failure of Pitt to see the validity of his arguments or the removal of that officer from the office of controller of the navy. According to the king, Howe believed 'himself lowered in the eyes of his Profession by the transaction concerning the Comptroller of the Navy' and believed that he had lost the confidence and support of Pitt. George III assured Howe that this was not the case.[32] Nevertheless, by the summer of 1788 Howe had decided to leave the Admiralty and on 16 July 1788 he resigned from the office of First Lord of the Admiralty.[33] The king, to show that Howe had resigned at his 'own request not occasioned by any disapprobation of his conduct created him Earl Howe and Baron Howe of Langar with revision in this honour in default of male issue to the female line'.[34] On Howe's death his oldest daughter Sophia would succeed to the baronetcy. This was a unique honour and within days of it becoming public, others requested that they be granted similar peerages.[35]

Howe, even though an aristocrat and an earl, was first and foremost a professional navy officer who made the proper functioning of the ships, squadrons and fleets under his command the centre of his professional life.[36] From almost the beginning of his career as a navy officer Howe introduced reforms designed to regularise and rationalise the methods of governance on board warships and the systems employed to command and control squadrons and fleets of warships at sea. In British warships before the Seven Years War there was no standardised system for organising a ship's company. It was for the most part left to each captain to organise, as he saw fit, the men on board his ship. This could, especially as ships increased in size and crews grew larger, result in disorganisation. In many instances the officers did not know the seamen they commanded. The problem was aggravated in wartime by the inclusion of many foreigners and landsmen in the crews of British warships. At the beginning of the War of Austrian Succession a 70-gun ship had a crew of 480 men. By the time of the Seven Years War a 74-gun ship, such as

HMS *Magnanime* which Howe commanded for much of that conflict, had a complement of 700 men. An answer to this problem was to organise the crew of a warship into divisions. This method was apparently first adopted by Rear Admiral Thomas Smith, commander of the Downs Squadron, in 1755. The crew of a warship was divided into several divisions each of which was placed under the command of a lieutenant. Each division was then divided into subdivisions under the command of a midshipman. The lieutenant in command of a division was responsible for the efficiency, discipline and welfare of the men of his division. The advantage of the divisional system was that it provided for the first time the means not only to exercise effective command of a warship's crew, but also an efficient way to oversee the welfare of the seamen.[37]

When in command of HMS *Magnanime*, in 1759, Howe had issued an order book which was the first step in cementing the divisional system in place by setting forth the duties of the crew of a warship. For instance, midshipmen in command of a subsection of a division were directed

> to keep an account of the clothing (linen particularly) belonging to each man, which they are to muster every Saturday or weekly; to see that the men continue provided with the means of keeping themselves clean and healthy, and have not disposed of or lost any of the clothing supplied or charged to them on the slop book; and to make report thereof to the officers of their different divisions accordingly.

This set of orders, while in some respects incomplete, is important for it is one of the first, and the earliest known to historians, concerning the governance of a warship's crew.[38]

In 1776 Howe, when in command of the squadron in America, had issued a second set of regulations for the governance of a warship's crew. These new regulations, which were issued to every ship under Howe's command in America, were fuller and went into more detail than those issued by Howe in 1759 when captain of HMS *Magnanime* and they are obviously the product of several years' reflection upon the problems of shipboard governance. Every aspect of the regulation and governance of a warship is set forth. For instance, Article XI directs that

> the lieutenant of the watch is to see marked in the log book all signals; every change of sails, the proportion of leeway the ship shall in his judgement make; and all other observations and occurrences that may happen while he is in charge of the ship by day and night, and attest such entries with his initial letters of his name.

These regulations, entitled 'the General Government and Discipline of Ships of War' were issued to every ship under Howe's command because he believed that 'an uniformed system of discipline established in this squadron would be productive of many essential benefits.'[39] These regulations were important for not only did Howe issue them in 1776 to every ship of the squadron in America, but they were again issued in 1782 to every ship of the Channel Fleet. Howe's regulations for 'The General Government and Discipline of Ships of War' were reissued by Lord Keith in 1796 and for years afterwards Howe's regulations served as a model system for the governance of the crews of British warships.[40]

Howe's greatest intellectual contribution to the Royal Navy was to revolutionise the command and control of squadrons and fleets of warships by formulating and introducing to the service innovations in signalling. Communications by means of signals – flags, lights, gunfire, and other means – were vital for the proper command and control of groups of ships at sea, for it was the only means by which the commander of a fleet or a squadron in the Age of Fighting Sail could make known his commands and intentions to the captains of various ships under his command. Without the ability to transmit by signals commands and other information between various ships of a fleet, it would have been impossible for a commander to exercise command and control and the force would be nothing more than a disorganised collection of ships. Signalling in the Age of Fighting Sail was all but indispensable for the conduct of all naval operations involving more than one ship. From the time when he first commanded a small squadron off the coast of Normandy in 1756, Howe understood the importance of signalling to the conduct of naval operations.

The first signals known to have been promulgated by Howe were issued in June of 1756 off the French port of Granville on the west coast of Normandy. Consisting of thirty-two signals, Howe's 1756 signals merely reinforced and clarified existing Admiralty signals.[41] Two years later on 25 May 1758, when in command of a squadron conducting amphibious attacks on the French coast, Howe issued a second set of signals which were an enlargement and rearrangement of the signals issued in 1756.[42] Howe's 1756 and May 1758 signals are not particularly innovative and were issued to their users in manuscript. Then on 24 July 1758, after the landings at St Malo and Cherbourg and before the second attack on St Malo, Howe at Spithead issued *Additional Signals & Instructions to be Observed by Ships of War*. These signals were a major innovation for they were the first signals issued as a printed reference book. The format of Howe's printed signal book was tabular with three columns: one column for the type of flag, another column for the place on the ship where the flag would be displayed, and a third column showing 'signification' or the meaning of a particular signal.[43] Again in 1762, when in command of another detached squadron, this time in Basque Road, Howe issued to the ships under his command a printed signal book again in tabular format. This book was in many respects an expanded and enlarged version of the 1758 printed signals.[44] Howe in

1758 and 1762 by issuing signals in the form of printed books with tabular formats was attempting to rationalise the signals employed by the Royal Navy by making the whole system 'user friendly'.

In the period after the Seven Years War Howe endeavoured to devise a system of signals and fighting instructions which would permit the commander of a fleet to achieve tactical advantage by being able to control the movements of the ships of his force in battle. Because the vast majority of the guns of a ship of the line were mounted in broadsides along the sides of the vessel, most naval battles of the 18th century were fought by fleets of ships of the line sailing in line ahead formations. Manoeuvring for the most part was a process by which the two opposing fleets, steering parallel courses, would close with each other with the objective of placing each ship abeam of her opposite number in the enemy line. When the two lines of opposing ships had closed within range of each other's guns the battle would begin and then be decided by weight of fire power and boarding. The conduct of a British ship in a battle was governed by fighting instructions issued by the Admiralty.[45] From time to time various admirals would attempt to gain tactical flexibility by supplementing and modifying the general fighting instructions and by issuing to captains of vessels under their command additional signals and instructions. Nevertheless, a majority of captains believed that the ultimate tactical objective in a naval battle was to lay one's ship alongside the opposite number in the enemy's line of battle. That is, the captain of a British warship, if his station in the line of battle was third from the front of the British line, could do little wrong if he engaged the enemy ship which was third from the front of the enemy's line of battle. This type of tactical thinking led to stalemate and many indecisive naval battles, for a doctrine which called for battles to be fought by parallel lines of ships firing broadsides at each other did not permit a commander of a fleet to gain tactical advantage by amassing overpowering weight of fire power against a particular part or portion of an enemy formation. Like other European navies during the 18th century, the British navy was in a tactical strait-jacket because of the doctrine of fighting naval battles in two parallel lines. Howe would bring tactical flexibility to the British navy and make possible the great naval victories of the French Revolutionary and Napoleonic Wars by rationalising and reforming the Royal Navy's system of signalling.

At the beginning of the American War when Howe arrived at New York on 12 July, even though France was not a belligerent and the Americans did not have a navy, he immediately began to organise the ships of his command to fight a major naval war. The admiral issued to the commanders of every ship in his squadron a printed signal book entitled *Signal Book for Ships of War*. The signals contained in this book were only for the use of ships under Howe's immediate command, and unlike other private signal books, there were no cross-references to the Admiralty's fighting instructions, but rather references to Howe's printed book of instructions entitled *Instructions for the*

Conduct of Ships of War, Explanatory of, and Relative to the Signals Contained in the Signal-Book herewith Delivered. These two books – one of signals and the other of instructions – while containing nothing revolutionary or any new doctrines for the tactical command and control of a fleet, were nevertheless important because Howe, by issuing them, was establishing for the ships of his squadron a system of command and control, separate and particular to the squadron under his command in America.[46] This point was reinforced when Howe on 1 July 1777 issued 'Additional Instructions Respecting the Conduct of the Fleet Preparative to and in Action with the Enemy'. These additional instructions were accompanied by a note stating that

> all signals contained in the general printed Signal Book which are likely to be needful on the present occasion being provided for in this signal book, the signals in the general printed Signal Book will only be made in conformity to the practice of some senior officer.[47]

What is primary to Howe's thinking is the principle that the actions and movements of ships in battle should not be governed by the Admiralty's fighting instructions, but rather by signals made by the commander of the fleet.

Howe was not the only officer during the American War working to improve methods by which British naval force were commanded and controlled in battle. Rodney and Kempenfelt, for instance, were also endeavouring to improve signals and battle tactics. It is clear that Rodney was thinking along the same lines as Howe concerning the primacy of orders from an admiral commanding a fleet over the Admiralty's fighting instructions. Captain Robert Carkett, of HMS *Stirling Castle*, was reprimanded by Rodney for following the dictates of the Admiralty's fighting instructions rather than the admiral's signals during a battle with the French fleet in 1780.[48] Howe, when in command of the Channel Fleet in 1782, and using the same signalling systems and standing orders as he employed in America in 1776–8,[49] believed, nevertheless, that the signalling systems for command and control employed by the Royal Navy were still in need of improvement. In 1789 Howe wrote:

> The Looseness of our present System of Tactics in the Navy, if any system may be properly said to exist, is such that I cannot say I have quite made up my mind upon a Plan that I would recommend for publication, were I in Circumstances for being called upon to give an opinion on the matter.[50]

In the years after the American War, while serving as First Lord of the Admiralty, Howe gave the problems of signals and command and control of fleets in battle considerable thought and was awaiting the opportunity to institute further reforms and improvements in the signals used for command and control of British fleets.

Such an opportunity came to Howe in the summer of 1790 when the Channel Fleet was mobilised during the Nootka Sound Crisis. When Howe was offered the command of the Channel Fleet he almost did not accept the appointment because he feared that there was a possibility that 'The gout should disable him at the moment that required the most activity.' However, these doubts were pushed aside by the intervention of George III and Howe accepted the appointment as commander of the Channel Fleet.[51] In some respects Howe's appointment as commander in chief of the Channel Fleet in 1790 was unprecedented. It was most unusual for a former First Lord of the Admiralty to be appointed to a subordinate position as a serving officer in the Royal Navy. Howe's commission was dated 13 May 1790, but the admiral remained in London working on a new signal book and making other preparations.[52] It was not until 8 July that Howe proceeded to Portsmouth and on 11 July he officially assumed command of the Channel Fleet.[53]

A new era in the Royal Navy's system of command and control of fleets and squadrons began when Howe warned the flag officers under his command that they would receive 'attested copies of the signals and regulations I have thought fit to establish for the general government of the fleet'.[54] In the days following Howe's assumption of the command of the Channel Fleet, the admiral issued a series of directives not only 'for maintaining an uniform discipline in the ships'[55] but also for overhauling the entire system of signals by which an admiral exercised command and control of a fleet. The centrepiece of Howe's new system of command and control was a printed signal book entitled *Signal Book for Ships of War* which was the first truly numerical signal system introduced into the Royal Navy. In Howe's new system each signal flag or combination of flags represented a number which in turn indicated the intended message. The signal book itself was divided into five columns. In the first column was entered the number of the signal. The second and third columns gave the 'purport' and 'signification' of the signal and the fourth and fifth columns contained the page and article number in the instructions referred to by the signal. There were in Howe's book spaces for 160 different signals. The signal numbers and many of the meanings of various signals were entered in handwriting and could as circumstances demanded be altered. Howe's numerical system of signalling for the first time provided the Royal Navy with a workable and flexible system of signalling by which a commander of a fleet, within the limits of existing technology, could exercise effective command over the ships of his formation in battle.[56] Howe's system of numerical signals would become standard throughout the Royal Navy and continue to be reissued until 1799; thereafter the system was incorporated into the first official Admiralty signal book which in turn would remain in service until 1816.[57]

The Channel Fleet, consisting of thirty-five ships of the line, as ordered by the Admiralty[58] sailed on 18 August to cruise thirty leagues to the westward of Ushant. Remaining at sea until 12 September Howe employed the opportunity to drill the ships of his command in the use of the new signal book and tactical exercises.[59] The Channel Fleet would remain in port for the crisis with Spain over Nootka Sound was quickly resolved. On 8 November Howe was given permission by the Admiralty to come ashore.[60] He was not placed in command of the Russian Armament of 1791 when the Royal Navy was again mobilised for a diplomatic crisis. Probably Howe did not return to active service during this crisis because he was suffering from an acute attack of the gout.[61] In June of 1792, with the death of Lord Rodney, Howe was appointed to the position of Vice Admiral of England – a sinecure worth £430 per annum.[62] Howe would not be employed again until 1793 when Britain went to war with Revolutionary France.

Notes

1. J C Sainty, *Admiralty Officials, 1660–1870* (London, 1975), pp. 133, 135.

2. A Francis Steuart, ed., *The Last Journal of Horace Walpole during the Reign of George III from 1771–1783* (London, 1910), vol. II, p. 482.

3. NA, ADM 3/97, 4 Feb. 1783.

4. Sir John Fortescue, ed., *The Correspondence of George the Third from 1760 to December 1782* (London, 1927–8) nos. 4095, 4096.

5. NA, ADM 3/97, 10 Feb. 1783.

6. NA, ADM 3/97, 11, 12 Feb. 1783.

7. Fortescue, *Correspondence*, nos 4126, 4127.

8. NA, ADM 1/4150, ff. 18, 19.

9. NA, ADM 3/97, 10 March 1783.

10. Sainty, *Admiralty Officials*, p. 133.

11. NA, 30/8/103, f. 19.

12. John Ehrman, *The Younger Pitt: The Years of Acclaim* (New York, 1969), pp. 131–3, 183–6.

13. P C Webb, 'The Rebuilding and Repair of the Fleet, 1783–1793', *Bulletin of the Institute of Historical Research* (1977), vol. 50, pp. 194–209.

14. Charles Derrick, *Memoirs of the Rise and Progress of the Royal Navy* (London, 1806), pp. 178–83, 249, 298.

15. Ehrman, *The Younger Pitt*, pp. 313–17.

16. Sir Richard Vessey Hamilton, ed., *Letters and Papers of Admiral of the Fleet Sir Thos. Byam Martin* (London, 1898–1903), vol II, p. 381.

17. Cf. Roger Morriss, *The Royal Dockyards during the Revolutionary and Napoleonic Wars* (Leicester, 1983), pp. 186–7.

18. Sir John Knox Laughton, ed., *Letters and Papers of Charles, Lord Barham, Lord Admiral of the Red Squadron, 1758–1813* (London, 1907–11) vol. I, p. xxiii.

19. NA, ADM 3/100, 24 Nov., 4 Dec. 1784.

20. Laughton, ed., *Barham Papers*, vol. II, pp. 178–91.

21. NA, ADM 3/99, 13 Sept. 1784; ADM 3/100, 10 Oct. 1784.

22. NA, ADM 3/100, 7 Dec. 1784; 6 Jan. 1785.

23. John E Talbott, *Pen & Ink Sailor: Charles Middleton and the King's Navy 1778–1813* (London, 1998), pp. 127–8.

24. Cf. Rd, 30/8/111, ff. 137–72.

25. E.g., *An Address to the Right Honourable the First Lord Commissioner of the Admiralty upon the pernicious Mode of Coppering the Bottoms of the King's Ships in time of Peace* (London, 1786).

26. Derrick, *Memoirs of the Rise and Progress of the Royal Navy*, p. 297.

27. *Journals of the House of Commons from January the 24th, 1786 ... to December 1786* (London, 1803), vol. 41, p. 800.

28. NA, ADM 1/4152, f. 26.

29. E.g., NA, PRO, 30/8/178, ff. 51–2.

30. David Syrett and R L DiNardo, *The Commissioned Sea Officers of the Royal Navy, 1660–1815* (Aldershot, Hants., 1994), p. 20.

31. NA, PRO, 30/8/146, ff. 176, 178–9, 180–1.

32. A Aspinell, ed., *The Later Correspondence of George III* (London, 1962), vol. I, no. 420.

33. Sainty, *Admiralty Officials*, p. 133.

34. NA, PRO, 30/8/103, ff. 299–300.

35. NA, PRO, 30/8/108, f. 3.

36. Cf. Roger Knight, 'Richard, Earl Howe, 1726–1799', *Precursors of Nelson: British Admirals of the Eighteenth Century*, Peter LeFevre and Richard Harding, eds (London, 2000), pp. 287–91.

37. N A M Rodger, *The Wooden World: An Anatomy of the Georgian Navy* (Annapolis, Md., 1986), pp. 216–17.

38. Brian Lavery ed., *Shipboard Life and Organisation, 1731–1815* (Aldershot, Hants., 1998), pp. 71–2, 74–5, 82–7.

39. W G Perrin, ed., *The Keith Papers selected from the Letters and papers of Admiral Viscount Keith* (London, 1927–55) vol. I, pp. 29–42.

40. Lavery, ed., *Shipboard Life and Organisation*, p. 65.

41. Julian S Corbett, ed., *Signals and Instructions, 1776–1794* (London, 1908), pp. 347–9.

42. Massachusetts Historical Society, Archibald Kennedy Papers, Signals for knowing each other by Day, 25 May 1758.

43. Corbett, ed., *Signals and Instructions*, pp. 350–1.

44. D Bonner-Smith, ed., *The Barrington Papers, Selected from the Letters and Papers of Admiral the Hon. Samuel Barrington* (London, 1937–41), vol. I, pp. 327–55.

45. Cf. Julian S Corbett, ed., *Fighting Instructions, 1530–1816* (London, 1909).

46. Brian Tunstall, *Naval Warfare in the Age of Sail: Evolution of Fighting Tactics, 1650–1815*, Nicholas Tracy, ed. (London, 1990), pp. 128–9.

47. Corbett, ed., *Signals and Instructions*, pp. 83–4.

48. Cf. David Spinney, *Rodney*, (London, 1969), pp. 322–4, 330–2.

49. Tunstall, *Naval Warfare*, p. 153.

50. HL, Howe to Curtis, 14 Oct. 1789.

51. Aspinell, *Later Correspondence of George III*, vol. I, no. 591.

52. HL, Howe to Curtis, 27 May 1790.

53. NA, ADM 2/120, pp. 214–17, 527–8.

54. BL, Add. MSS 35194, f. 37.

55. E.g., BL, Add. MSS 35194, ff. 37–8, 47–8, 51–3.

56. Corbett, ed., *Fighting Instructions, 1530–1815*.

57. Tunstall, *Naval Warfare*, pp. 194–5.

58. NA, ADM 2/1343, 3 Aug. 1790.

59. Corbett, ed., *Signals and Instructions*, p. 64. The dispatches for Howe's period of command of the Channel Fleet during the Nootka Sound Crisis are missing from the NA.

60. NA, ADM 2/592, p. 69.

61. E.g., HL, Howe to Curtis, 18 June 1791.

62. Cf. W G Perrin, 'The Vice-Admiral and Rear-Admiral of the United Kingdom', *The Mariner's Mirror* (June, 1928), vol. 14, pp. 26–31.

CHAPTER VII

The Glorious First of June, 1794

On 1 February 1793 the French Republic declared war on Great Britain. This was followed by a declaration of war by Britain and the mobilisation of the Royal Navy. Between the declaration of war and 1797 the number of seamen and marines in the Royal Navy increased from 16,000 men to a strength of 120,000 seamen and marines.[1] And by December of 1795 the strength of the Royal Navy stood at 385 ships and vessels of all classes.[2] The rapidity and scope of the mobilisation of the Royal Navy was made possible by the peacetime shipbuilding and repair programmes of the 1780s and the Pitt government's policy of stockpiling huge quantities of naval stores and other materials required for the fitting out of ships. The mobilisation of the Royal Navy in 1793 was the beginning of the largest sustained build-up of naval strength in the Age of Sail.

At the beginning of the French Revolutionary War Howe was appointed to the command of the Channel Fleet. Even though 67 years of age and because of recurrent attacks of gout not in the best of health, Howe's appointment to the command of the Channel Fleet in the event of a French war was all but inevitable. Rodney and George Darby were dead, Richard Hughes would be dead within a year, and Samuel Hood was slated to become commander in chief in the Mediterranean. All the fighting admirals from the American War, with the exception of Howe, were either dead or otherwise not available. Holding the confidence of the officer corps of the Royal Navy, with unsurpassed experience, and standing at the head of his profession, Howe was in 1793 a natural choice for the appointment. Vice Admiral Thomas Graves, one of the losers at Yorktown, and Rear Admiral Sir Alexander Hood, a man of difficult temperament, were respectively appointed second and third in command to Howe. And Captain Sir Roger Curtis would be Howe's captain of the fleet. Curtis, a man without much imagination, was long associated with Howe and would faithfully serve the admiral as a *de facto* chief of staff.

In 1793 France was politically isolated and threatened with foreign invasion. The once mighty French navy was decidedly inferior to the Royal Navy. France had eighty-two ships of the line compared to 158 ships of the same class in the Royal Navy. Not only was the French navy inferior in numbers to the Royal Navy in 1793, but the force was in a state of total disarray. Considered by the French revolutionary authorities to be a hotbed of royalism, many navy officers had been purged from the service and seamen were in short supply. The French Mediterranean fleet at Toulon would surrender to the British in August and a month later the French Atlantic fleet would mutiny.[3] The French navy in 1793 posed little or no threat to the security of Britain. Because of the weakened state of the French navy the assembling of ships for the Channel Fleet in 1793 was a slow process with first priority given by the government to the fitting and dispatch of ships to the Mediterranean.[4]

Howe assumed command of the Channel Fleet in the last week of May. Remaining in London until he learned of the departure from England of the last of the reinforcements for the Mediterranean,[5] Howe arrived at Portsmouth on 26 May to officially take command of the Channel Fleet.[6] The next day the Admiralty issued orders placing under Howe's command thirteen ships of the line, including the 100-gun ship of the line HMS *Queen Charlotte* which would serve as the admiral's flagship.[7] As the ships of the Channel Fleet were being made ready to proceed to sea, Howe and the Admiralty were formulating the strategy which would govern the operations of the force.

Early in the war against Revolutionary France neither Howe nor the Admiralty envisioned a strategy calling for the close blockade of the French coast. In 1793 the Admiralty perceived the main threat not to be major operations by the French navy, but rather attacks by small squadrons or individual warships on British merchant shipping in the Western Approaches to the English Channel.[8] Upon taking command of the Channel Fleet in 1793 Howe had sought out pilots and others with a knowledge of the navigation of the French coast.[9] Nevertheless, he rejected a strategy of a close blockade of the French coast, even though during the Seven Years War he had spent most of that conflict conducting operations, including close blockades, inshore near the French coast. In the years after the Seven Years War, however, he had come to the conclusion that a strategy of close blockade was a course filled with danger. In 1789 Howe declared:

> Stationing a large fleet off the coast of France was a very improper and hazardous measure. The ships particularly the large ones, were liable to receive great damage, the crews get sickly ... he could affirm from his own knowledge that a station off Brest was a dangerous station, and should never be taken but upon great emergencies.[10]

Considering Howe's appreciation of the dangers to his ships from operations close to the French coast and the estimation by the Admiralty that the major threat posed by the French would be attacks on British trade, it is hardly surprising that at the beginning of the French Revolutionary War the main task of the Channel Fleet would be cruising in the Western Approaches of the English Channel to protect British trade.

On 3 July 1793 the Admiralty issued instructions to Howe for the conduct of operations by the Channel Fleet. Howe was to cruise in the Western Approaches with fifteen ships of the line[11]

Upon such stations as your Lordship shall judge most proper for protecting the trade of His Majesty's subjects coming into or going out of, the Channel and for taking or destroying the enemy's ships of war, privateers, or trade, going into or out of, the Bay of Biscay, or navigating to or from any of the ports of west France.[12]

In separate instructions Howe was directed to protect from attack the ships of Britain's allies.[13] And in a letter from Philip Stephens, the secretary of the Admiralty, Howe was informed that a British convoy from Jamaica was soon expected in the English Channel and that the Admiralty had intelligence that a French convoy was expected to depart from St Domingo for France.[14] Upon receipt of these instructions it was Howe's intention that the Channel Fleet, after sailing from Spithead, should take station to the westward of Ushant.[15]

On the evening of 14 July the Channel Fleet sailed from St Helens and proceeded westward down the English Channel. On the morning of 19 July HMS *Majestic* and HMS *Bellerophon*, owing to 'a sudden Change of wind', crashed into each other. The foremast, bow sprit and maintopmast of HMS *Bellerophon* were carried away forcing Howe to have HMS *Ramillies* tow her into Plymouth for repairs. Then on the morning of 22 July the weather turned bad 'with a windy and very foggy appearance', forcing Howe to anchor in Torbay until the weather 'resumes any suitable or settled aspects'.[16]

The Channel Fleet remained at Torbay for several days and again put to sea on 25 July. Off the Start during the evening of 25 July Howe received intelligence to the effect that there was a French squadron – seventeen ships of the line and three frigates – cruising in the Bay of Biscay 'for the protection of a convoy daily expected from the West Indies'. Several days later the master of an intercepted American merchant ship also reported encountering a French squadron in the Bay of Biscay.[17] Upon receipt of this information Howe and the Channel Fleet entered the Bay of Biscay in an attempt to intercept the French squadron. On the morning of 31 July Howe was in the Bay of Biscay, some eighteen leagues south-west of Belle Ile, 'The supposed Station of the Enemy Fleet'. However, the wind forced the British ships north-east towards Belle Ile and that evening the French fleet was sighted 'about six or seven leagues to windward'. Howe then attempted to bring the French to battle, but failed in this endeavour for 'the intention of the Enemy seemed invariably to keep the same distance and position'. The French fleet was last seen on the evening of 1 August standing towards the Ile de Groix. For the next several days Howe and the Channel fleet continued to cruise in the Bay of Biscay off the southern coast of Brittany, after which Howe decided to return to the anchorage at Torbay. The admiral had concluded that it would be impossible to bring the French to battle off the southern coast of Brittany and that the French fleet in the Bay of Biscay posed little danger to the British trade in the English Channel. At the same time Howe also realised that until he had more information about the activities of the French at Brest he could not weaken the Channel Fleet by sending warships to the southward farther into the Bay of Biscay to attack French shipping. Then, after receiving information that at least one, if not two, British convoys had just entered and then passed up the English Channel, Howe decided to sail for Torbay where the Channel Fleet anchored on 10 August.[18]

While at anchor in Torbay the Admiralty informed Howe that the expected convoy from Jamaica had not arrived in England because its departure from the West Indies was delayed until 24 June and as a result of this the merchant ships were still at sea.[19] Then on 20 August the Admiralty informed Howe that the convoy from the West Indies was expected to make a landfall at Cape Clear in Ireland and the admiral was directed to put to sea with the Channel Fleet to protect the merchant ships from the West Indies from enemy attack.[20] It was apparently Howe's intention to cruise 'from 8 to 20 Leagues West from Cape Clear'. However, because of a failure to quickly resupply the ships with beer, Howe did not sail from Torbay until 23 August. On the evening of 1 September some fifty merchant ships of the Jamaica convoy were intercepted some twenty-five to thirty leagues from the Isles of Scilly. Howe and the Channel Fleet remained at sea in order to protect the remainder of the West Indies convoy before returning to Torbay where he arrived on 4 September.[21]

On 11 September Howe at Torbay received information that a French fleet, consisting of thirty-two ships of the line and three frigates, had been sighted several days before off the Isles of Scilly. Upon receiving this intelligence Howe immediately sent HMS *Phaeton*, HMS *Venus* and HMS *Southampton*, under the command of Captain Sir Andrew Douglas, to intercept and bring into Torbay two convoys, one proceeding to the Mediterranean and the other to the West Indies, which were at the time proceeding westward down the Channel. At the same time orders were issued to those ships of the Channel Fleet, which were being reprovisioned and restored at Plymouth, to rejoin the Channel Fleet at Torbay for Howe intended to sail and to seek out the enemy.[22]

As the ships of the Channel Fleet assembled at Torbay and the two outward-bound convoys were intercepted and directed to English ports, the intelligence received by Howe concerning the French fleet was far from clear. On 16 September it was reported by an American merchant ship that she had spoken with a French lugger who said the French fleet was at sea. At this time Howe also received a report that a fleet 'supposed to be French' had been sighted from the Isles of Scilly. On the basis of this information Howe decided to detain the two outward-bound trade convoys in British ports until he received further information about the movements of the enemy.[23] The Admiralty apparently had more nerve than Howe for on 20 September, in the absence of additional reports of the French fleet being in the English Channel, it directed the admiral to permit the convoys outward-bound to the Mediterranean and West Indies to sail.[24] Several days later it was learned by the British that the French fleet was in Quiberon Bay.[25]

On 13 September, as the Channel Fleet was being made ready to go to sea, the Admiralty informed Howe that a convoy from the Leeward Islands was approaching the western end of the English Channel.[26] Several days later, on 25 September, Howe was ordered by the Admiralty to sail from Torbay with the Channel Fleet to give protection from enemy attack not only to the approaching Leeward Islands convoy, but also to another convoy expected from Jamaica.[27] Howe in compliance with this order sailed from Torbay on 28 September. Arriving off the Start on 29 September with the wind at 'westsouthwest with the appearance of thick weather' Howe decided to return to Torbay because 'the heavier Sailing Ships were likely to be separated'. The Channel Fleet on 30 September anchored in Torbay. Several days later, on 4 October, Howe requested that the Admiralty postpone the sailing of the Channel Fleet for he had received information that the convoys from the West Indies had either arrived in English ports or had passed to the eastward up the English Channel.[28]

The Admiralty on 12 October ordered Howe to sail with the Channel Fleet from Torbay. The purpose of this cruise would be for the Channel Fleet to cover the departure for the West Indies and Mediterranean of several troop convoys sailing from English and Irish ports as well as to prevent the French from sending reinforcements to the West Indies.[29] Further, a number of trade convoys were also proceeding to England and required the protection of the Channel Fleet as they entered the English Channel. Over the next several days, the Admiralty sent Howe specific information concerning the convoys expected to arrive in the English Channel.[30] Howe, on 14 October, informed the Admiralty that he would 'put to sea therewith in execution of these orders'. On 24 October the Channel Fleet sailed from Torbay. However, that same evening off the Start the fleet encountered winds from the south-west and fearing being forced to the eastwards up the English Channel, Howe returned that evening to the anchorage at Torbay.[31]

Autumn and winter weather, especially with an instrument as cumbersome as the Channel Fleet, always rendered the conduct of naval operations in the English Channel somewhat problematic. Calms and then 'thick tempestuous weather' prevented the Channel Fleet from sailing from Torbay until 28 October. Encountering winds from the north-west and west as well as 'a considerable degree of swell and Head Sea' the Channel Fleet slowly made its way down the Channel to the westward. Ships were damaged by the weather; HMS *Bellona*, HMS *Montagu* and HMS *Tremendous* temporarily parted company with the main body of the fleet; and it was not until 6 November that Howe was off Land's End. Bad weather then forced the Channel Fleet back to the eastward. On 13 November Howe and the Channel Fleet were off The Lizard and still attempting, against contrary winds, to proceed to the westward.[32] The next day Howe received several dispatches from the Admiralty informing him that a number of French merchant ships and a frigate were thought to be approaching Europe from North America.[33] This information was in marked contrast to the intelligence Howe had been receiving from American merchant ships who had informed the admiral that French ships in American ports had abandoned any attempts to return to Europe.[34] On 14 November the wind came around to the south and the Channel Fleet again proceeded to the westward.[35]

On 18 November to the west of the Isles of Scilly the Channel Fleet encountered a force of French ships consisting of six ships of the line, two frigates, a brig and a schooner. Upon sighting the enemy the Channel Fleet in 'a very Fresh Gale from the South and S By E' chased the French. However, only the frigate HMS *Latona* could close with the enemy before dark and the next morning the French ships were not in sight from Howe's flagship. Over the next several days there were fleeting contacts between the British and French ships. The last intelligence about the enemy ships was obtained on 22 November when the British captured a small Danish lugger, with a French prize crew on board, and learned that there were probably three French ships of the line somewhere to the westward of the Channel Fleet.[36]

The Channel Fleet for the next several days, encountering easterly winds, cruised to the westward of the Isles of Scilly unable 'to get within the appointed limits of the Station off of Ushant'. By 10 December the Channel Fleet had been forced to the eastward and was off The Lizard. The next day the wind turned south-easterly and then 'west by south blowing a gale'. On the evening of 11 December, to prevent the Channel Fleet from 'being forced above the Start', Howe put into Torbay where he intended to remain until he received further directions from the Admiralty.[37]

The season for cruises by the Channel Fleet was over. All the ships of Howe's command had been damaged by the elements and were in need of repairs.[38] On orders from the Admiralty Howe sent eleven ships[39] to

Plymouth to be repaired and with thirteen remaining ships[40] sailed to Spithead.[41] Then Howe, who had received permission from the Admiralty to come ashore,[42] left HMS *Queen Charlotte* and went to London. Winter cruising in the Western Approaches of the English Channel was for a young man. Howe when he came ashore in December of 1793 was sick with 'Symptoms [which] bear much appearance of gouty irritation'. Within days of arriving in London Howe set out for Bath to recover his health.[43]

During this period of recuperation a unique system in the history of the Georgian navy was instituted for the command of the Channel Fleet. First from Bath and then at his house on Grafton Street in London, during the first months of 1794, Howe continued to exercise command of the Channel Fleet. Whilst ashore, either at Bath or in London, Howe continued to issue orders to the ships and officers of the Channel Fleet.[44] The commanders of ships and divisions of the Channel Fleet reported to and corresponded with Howe.[45] The admiral then passed the information in these communications on to the Admiralty.[46] And the Admiralty kept Howe informed of decisions it made concerning the officers and ships of the Channel Fleet.[47] This system of command, and especially considering the limitations of 18th-century communications, was somewhat confusing and at best cumbersome. Nevertheless it would be employed whenever Howe was ashore, until his retirement from active service in April of 1797.[48]

Howe during the first months of 1794 when he was ashore, by means of written directives, reports and other correspondence, attended to the health, welfare and training of the seamen of the Channel Fleet. The captains and other officers of the ships of the Channel Fleet were encouraged by Howe to reside on board their respective ships so that they could supervise the training of their men. Howe thought that the seamen of the Channel Fleet required additional training and believed 'that the care of their men in the exercise at Guns and Nautic duties should be deemed indispensable'.[49] Not only did Howe insist that the captains of the ships under his command supervise the training of the crews of their vessels, but he also at this time instituted several measures to preserve the health of the seamen serving in the Channel Fleet. For instance, Howe appointed a physician of the fleet.[50] This office had first been instituted by Rodney in the West Indies during the American War when Dr Gilbert Blane was appointed physician to the squadron in the Leeward Islands. Howe in 1782, at the end of the American War, following the example of Rodney, had appointed Dr Cuthbert Challoner physician of the Channel Fleet.[51] And on 3 April 1794 Howe appointed Dr Thomas Trotter, the second physician at Haslar Hospital, to be physician of the Channel Fleet.[52] Trotter was one of the leaders in the campaign to conquer scurvy.[53] In March of 1794, when confronted with increasing rates of sickness among the seamen of the Channel Fleet, Howe concluded 'that it may have been caused in part by dampness of the men's hammocks after washing them, which for the benefit of cleanliness (one essential requisite to the preservation of Health at Sea) is frequently necessary'. Howe's solution to this problem was to convince the Admiralty of the necessity of issuing two hammocks to each of the seamen of his command.[54] Howe's attention to the health and welfare of the men under his command earned the admiral the reputation among the seamen as being 'the sailor's friend'.[55]

Whilst ashore during the first months of 1794 Howe prepared for the next campaign in the Western Approaches of the English Channel by formulating and then arranging for the printing of all the signal books, standing orders, and the like required for the command, government, and control of the Channel Fleet. Howe made arrangements with firms of printers in London for the printing of signal books, instructions, and 'sheets for weekly returns'. Then when these documents had been printed the admiral made arrangements for the transportation of them as well as blank log books, pencils, and other items of stationery to Portsmouth for distribution to the ships of the Channel Fleet.[56] At the same time as overseeing all these arrangements the admiral was also ensuring that the ships under his command were supplied by the Navy Board with all the necessary signal flags and distinguishing vanes.[57]

On 21 March Howe arrived at Portsmouth to superintend the fitting out of the ships of the Channel Fleet for active service. It was his intention to remain at Spithead until he had to return to London to receive orders and instructions from the Admiralty concerning the future operations of the Channel Fleet,[58] which he did on 2 April.[59] Whilst it is obvious that Howe when in London discussed strategy with the Admiralty, and perhaps even with government ministers, there is no record of these discussions. On 13 April Howe returned to Spithead.[60]

The strategic situation confronting Britain in the eastern Atlantic and the Western Approaches to the English Channel was greatly altered from that which existed the year before. In 1793 the French navy was in chaos and in no condition to confront the Royal Navy. Miraculously, out of the confusion of the French Revolution the navy of the French Republic by the spring of 1794 had managed to regenerate itself into a credible fighting force. On 2 April the British learned from debriefing the officers of an American merchant ship that the French navy had intercepted and captured twenty-four merchant ships from a British convoy proceeding to England from Oporto, and furthermore that the French had amassed a force of twenty-two ships of the line which 'are well manned and discipline pretty well established in the crews' at Brest.[61] From all the available intelligence sources it was clear that the French in April of 1794 posed a threat not only to British maritime trade in the Eastern Atlantic, but perhaps also to the security of the British Isles. The Admiralty, when formulating the instructions to Howe for the operations of the Channel

Fleet in 1794, had to take into consideration the fact that the French now had a considerable force of ships of the line based at Brest.

On 17 April 1794 the Admiralty issued orders for the conduct of future operations by the Channel Fleet.[62] Howe was, as soon as wind and weather would permit, to sail with the Channel Fleet and escort the outward-bound trade, including an East India convoy, down the English Channel and out into the Atlantic. Off Ushant Howe was to detach a small squadron to escort the East India convoy to the southward across the Bay of Biscay. The British, from diplomats in the United States, had received intelligence that a large convoy of French merchant ships, loaded with provisions and West India produce, escorted by several French warships, was expected soon to arrive on the west coast of France.[63] Howe was directed, after escorting the British trade safely out into the Atlantic, to intercept this French convoy and to either capture or destroy the French merchant ships. Specifically Howe was directed to give orders to the commander of the ships escorting the East India trade southward across the Bay of Biscay to cruise, after he had seen the East India ships in safety to the southward, 'from Cape Ortegal to the latitude of Belle Isle' for the purpose of intercepting the expected French convoy from America. If Howe did not believe that this measure would result in the capture or destruction of the French convoy then the admiral was authorised to 'make a detachment of any other part of the fleet under your command for the performance of this service, as to your Lordship may appear most advisable'. Howe was 'further instructed to make such a general disposition' of the remaining ships of the Channel Fleet as 'he shall judge most proper' for the protection of British trade in the Western Approaches of the English Channel and for the taking and destroying of French ships of war, merchant vessels, and privateers. The admiral was further enjoined to always consider that the security of 'the Kingdoms of Great Britain and Ireland must form one of the most essential and constant objects of your care and attention'. The record does not show the extent of Howe's influence on the formulation of British strategy in 1794. But these instructions gave Howe great latitude in the conduct of operations and did not call for a close blockade of the French coast similar to the one instituted by Hawke during the Seven Years War.

Upon receipt of the Admiralty's 'Secret Instructions for the Conduct of the Channel Fleet' Howe immediately began to make preparations for sailing from Spithead.[64] Probably at the instigation of Dr Thomas Trotter, arrangements were made to obtain for the use of the fleet a quantity of lemon juice discovered to be in store at Haslar Hospital.[65] Directives were issued for the order of sailing and governance not only of the ships of the Channel Fleet, but also for the convoys of merchant ships while on passage down the English Channel and out into the Atlantic. The ships of the Channel Fleet were to be formed into two columns accompanied by a small detached squadron of four ships of the line[66] while the trade convoys, led by the East India convoy, were to be grouped together, and escorted by the ships of the Channel Fleet.[67] At the same time rendezvous and signals to be used by the ships of Howe's command in case of separation were issued.[68] And on 22 April Howe issued orders for the ships of the Channel Fleet to move down to St Helens and to prepare to sail.[69]

On 2 May the Channel Fleet, escorting a mass of merchant shipping, sailed from St Helens. As the ships of Howe's command passed down the English Channel they were joined by additional outward-bound merchant ships from the Channel ports to the westward of Portsmouth and on 4 May the Channel Fleet was off The Lizard where the convoy bound for the East Indies and its escort were detached.[70] The merchant shipping proceeding to the East Indies was to be escorted southward across the Bay of Biscay by a small squadron from the Channel Fleet consisting of six ships of the line and four frigates[71] under the command of Rear Admiral George Montagu. Howe's orders to Montagu called for the rear admiral to escort the East India ships as far south as the latitude of Cape Finisterre and then Montagu was to cruise with his squadron between Cape Ortegal and the meridian of 8° W to intercept the French convoy expected from America in the Bay of Biscay. Montagu was to remain on this station until 20 May unless he either intercepted the French convoy or obtained 'credible advice' that the French ships had passed to the eastward.[72] All of this was highly problematic for the British did not know when the French convoy had sailed from America or the course the French would follow. Montagu's interception of the French convoy while cruising across the mouth of the Bay of Biscay along 8° W would depend greatly on luck.[73]

After detaching and sending on their separate ways the outward-bound trade convoys, Howe arrived with the Channel Fleet off Ushant on 5 May. Brest Harbour was reconnoitred by HMS *Latona*: from a position off Point St Mathieu the frigate's captain, Sir Edward Thornborough, counted in Brest Harbour twenty-two large French ships which he 'took for Line of Battle ships, and a vast number of smaller vessels'. On 6 May the wind changed to the north-west and for several days continued to blow from the west and north-west. The Channel Fleet, to gain sea room, tacked to the northward. It was Howe's intention to return southward with the Channel Fleet and to take station off Ushant as soon as the wind and weather would permit.[74] When the Channel Fleet was again off Ushant on 19 May the British discovered that the French fleet had sailed from Brest. That same evening Howe received a dispatch from Montagu stating that he had captured the 20-gun French warship *Maire Quitton* escorting two prizes to Brest. Interrogation of the prisoners had revealed that a French squadron of five ships of the line and two large frigates, under the command of Rear Admiral Joseph-Marie Nielly, had captured these ships from a British convoy proceeding to Newfoundland. It was further learned that Nielly's squadron was waiting between 45° N and 48° N and about two degrees east or west of 16° 40' W for the arrival of the French convoy expected from America to escort it into a French port. However, the French prisoners were 'very backward in communicating what force may attend the homeward-bound convoy from America'. Upon receipt of this information Howe, fearing that Montagu's small squadron would be overwhelmed by superior French forces, ordered the Channel Fleet to sail south-west into the approaches of the Bay of Biscay to attempt to join the rear admiral. Then on 21 May Howe learned from the prize crews of several merchant ships which had been captured by the French from a Dutch convoy, that the French fleet was 'but a few leagues further to the westward'. The course of the Channel Fleet was altered to the west and on the morning of 28 May 'the Enemy was discovered far to windward'.[75]

When the French ships were sighted by British frigates at 6:30am on 28 May the positions of the two fleets were approximately 47° 34' N, 13° 39' W or about 430 miles west of Ushant. The British and French fleets in terms of numbers of ships of the line were evenly matched for each force consisted of twenty-six ships of the line.[76] But the combat capability of a fleet depends upon more than just the number of its ships. Howe was a skilful commander of vast experience and among the officers of the Channel Fleet were not only men of considerable sea and combat experience, but also others, such as Captain Cuthbert Collingwood, who would later distinguish himself as a commander of a fleet. Further, the Channel Fleet in 1794, even though Howe complained of a lack of tactical skill and knowledge among its officers, was perhaps the best constituted fleet with which Britain had ever begun a war in the 18th century. The French fleet on the other hand was a different proposition. It had been resurrected out of the chaos of the French Revolution and was commanded by Rear Admiral Louis Thomas, Comte de Villaret-Joyeuse (also known as Villaret de Joyeuse). Though only a lieutenant in 1791 and one of the few members of the nobility who would serve in the armed forces of the French Republic, Villaret-Joyeuse was an officer of exceptional ability who had worked hard to give his fleet a degree of tactical efficiency. Though most of his captains were men without command experience they would nevertheless fight their ships with some skill and with great determination.[77]

The French fleet was to windward of the Channel Fleet and the wind was out of the south-south-east. At about 9:30am the French ships, at a distance of about ten miles from the British, formed a rough line ahead formation on the port tack. Howe at 10:30am ordered the Channel Fleet, which was deployed in two columns, with a small detached squadron under the command of Rear Admiral Thomas Pasley off the weather bow, to turn in succession on to the same tack as the French. At 1pm the French were seen by the British to be making sail and tacking to avoid an action. Howe ordered the ships of Pasley's detached squadron to harass and attack the rear of the French line. At 2:30pm Howe ordered a general chase. Pasley's detached squadron, supported by several other British 74-gun ships of the line, was by 6pm attacking the rear of the French line. The last ship of the French line, the 100-gun ship *Révolutionnaire* was soon surrounded by British ships HMS *Marlborough*, HMS *Russell*, HMS *Bellerophon*, HMS *Leviathan*, HMS *Thunderer* and HMS *Audacious* – which with gunfire quickly smashed the French ship's rigging and toppled her mizzen mast. As darkness fell the *Révolutionnaire*, surrounded by British ships and battered into a wreck, ceased firing and appeared to be on the verge of surrendering. Certainly Captain the Hon. George Cranfield Berkeley of HMS *Marlborough* believed that the French ship had been struck and was taken possession of by HMS *Audacious*. However, in the darkness and confusion of battle these assumptions were ill-founded, for the next morning the battered wreck of the *Révolutionnaire* was still in French hands and would be towed by frigates into Rochefort. The British 74-gun ship HMS *Audacious* had also been so heavily damaged in the fight with the *Révolutionnaire* that she was forced to return to Britain. Even though the main bodies of the French and British fleets had not been engaged, the fighting on 28 May had reduced the strength of both fleets by one ship of the line.

The British and French fleets during the night of 28 May sailed south-east by east on parallel courses about three miles apart. The wind was south-south-west and the French were to windward of the Channel Fleet. In order to attack the rear of the French line Howe at 6am on 29 May ordered the British ships to tack in succession. Recognising the British manoeuvre, Villaret-Joyeuse, to support the rear of the French line, ordered the French ships to wear in succession and to run down the lee side of the French line in the opposite direction. As the van of the British line passed the rear of the French line there was a distant exchange of gunfire. These two manoeuvres brought the French and British ships on to parallel courses heading in the same direction with the French still to windward, but now the two lines of ships were much closer to each other. As the two lines of ships came on to parallel tracks gunfire was exchanged with the French in which several ships were damaged. At 11:30am Howe wanting to gain the weather gauge made the signal to tack in succession. Then considering the manoeuvre premature, Howe rescinded this order. The signal to tack in succession was again made at 12:30 but was only partially followed by some British ships being obscured by smoke; it was again rescinded to be repeated at 1:15pm. It was apparently Howe's intention to break the French line. However, the lead British ships, instead of going through the French line, passed down the line on an opposite course, to the leeward of the French formation, engaging the French centre and van. Howe, seeing that his orders were not being followed, had HMS *Queen Charlotte* tack, followed by HMS *Bellerophon* and HMS *Leviathan* out of succession and not in her turn, breaking through the French line between the sixth and fifth ships from the enemy's rear. As the ships of the main body of each fleet passed each other in opposite directions fighting became general and a number of ships on both sides were damaged. Two French ships – the *Tyrannicide* and *Indomptable* – from the rear of the French line were seen by Villaret-Joyeuse to be damaged and drifting to leeward. To save these two ships Villaret-Joyeuse wore the French line so as to pass between the British and the *Tyrannicide* and *Indomptable*. One of the French ships of the line, the *Montagnard*, did not, owing to battle damage, make the turn and continued on the port tack passing completely out of the battle area. After saving the *Tyrannicide* and *Indomptable* from possible capture and at the same time surrendering the weather gauge, Villaret-Joyeuse again wore and stood away from the British on the port tack. As night was falling and having gained the weather gauge Howe re-formed his line, decided to wait until the next day to renew the battle, and resolved to keep contact with the French during the night. The fighting on 29 May went in favour of the British for Howe not only gained the weather gauge but he had also forced the French ships of the line, *Montagnard* and *Indomptable*, out of the battle. Further, the *Tyrannicide* was so much damaged that she had to be towed by frigates for the next two days and during the fighting on 1 June.

The two fleets remained within about ten miles of each other with the French to the north-west off the British bow. During the night of 29 May the weather turned foggy. The next morning, 30 May, the fog cleared briefly and the French fleet was still to the north of the Channel Fleet. Then another fog descended, so thick that the British could not maintain their formation. On the morning of 31 May in clearer weather the British, to their surprise, saw to the north twenty-six French ships of the line. Later it was learned that Rear Admiral Joseph-Marie Nielly with three ships of the line[78] had on 30 May joined the French fleet. About 2pm Howe began to manoeuvre to bring the French to battle and by 5pm the two fleets were about five miles apart. Howe made the signal for his ships to attack their opposite number in the French line. However, this attack was called off at 7pm probably because Howe feared the confusion which would result from a night action. To prevent the French from breaking contact or seizing the weather gauge Howe stationed frigates about a mile to the leeward of the British main body to watch the enemy. During the night of 31 May the two fleets, steering west, remained on parallel courses.

At daylight on 1 June, with the wind south by west and the sea calm, the French fleet was on the port tack in a line ahead formation about five miles north and to the leeward of the Channel Fleet. Howe, after four days of manoeuvring, was at last in a position to bring the French to battle. At 5am he ordered that the British ships steer to the north-west and at 6am signalled that the Channel Fleet should head north directly towards the French fleet. At 7:15am Howe signalled that he would attack the centre of the French line and ten minutes later directed that the British ships should break through the enemy line and engage the French ships from leeward. This signal was modified at 8:30am by a signal directing each British ship to steer independently for and engage her opposite number in the enemy line. This last signal apparently led to some confusion among the captains of the British ships as to whether or not they were required to pass through the French line and then engage the enemy ships from leeward. As a result of this misunderstanding only six British ships would break through the enemy line.

In line abreast formation the ships of the Channel Fleet approached, at a speed of less than five knots, the French line of battle. At about 9:30am the French opened fire as the British ships came into range. Very quickly the firing became general. The majority of the British ships, as they neared the French line, turned to port, parallel to the French line, and engaged the French ships from the windward side. HMS *Queen Charlotte* was one of the six British ships which broke through, but as she approached the French line, heading for the stern of Villaret-Joyeuse's flagship the *Montagne*, the British ship was fired on by the *Vengeur* and *Achille*. Howe disregarded the *Vengeur* and fired on the *Achille* with the guns mounted on the upper decks of HMS *Queen Charlotte*, saving the fire of the lower tiers of guns for the *Montagne*. As HMS *Queen Charlotte* passed close astern of the *Montagne*, the British ship fired a broadside into the stern of the French flagship. Turning to port to engage the *Montagne* from leeward the British discovered that the French ship of the line was to leeward of Villaret-Joyeuse's flagship. *Queen Charlotte* then moved in between the two French ships engaging the *Montagne* to port and the *Jacobin* to starboard. HMS *Queen Charlotte*'s fore topmast fell by the wayside and at 10:15am both the *Montagne* and the *Jacobin* made more sail and pulled away from Howe's flagship. HMS *Queen Charlotte* then worked her way forward to engage the *Juste*. Howe made the signal for a general chase after concluding from the movements of the French ships that the enemy might be attempting to break off the battle.

Within minutes of the two fleets gaining contact and opening fire on each other the battle area was obscured by dense smoke and the fighting broke down into a series of bloody engagements between individual British and French ships in which the outcomes would be decided by the skill and determination of the officers and men of each ship. By 1pm most of the gunfire had ceased and the British and the French were each left with about a dozen heavily-damaged and dismasted ships.

As the gunfire stopped Villaret-Joyeuse in the *Montagne*, who after being engaged by HMS *Queen Charlotte* had pulled out of the battle, began to form a line of battle to leeward consisting of eleven ships of the line. At the same time a number of damaged French ships of the line, some being towed by frigates, began working their way to leeward towards the safety of Villaret-Joyeuse's line of ships. Seven other damaged French ships of the line could not make their escape being surrounded by British ships. Six of these – *Sans Pareil, Juste, América, Impétueux, Northumberland* and *Achille*

– were boarded and captured by the British and the seventh, the *Vengeur*, sank before she could be captured.

The British probably could have captured additional French ships if Howe had ordered a pursuit. The admiral was considering this course but his flag captain, Sir Roger Curtis, advised against it fearing that Villaret-Joyeuse might employ his newly-formed line of battle to capture damaged British ships which were drifting to leeward. Howe agreed with Curtis, ordering the Channel Fleet to form a line of battle and recalling two British ships which were approaching several damaged French ships with the intention of boarding and capturing the enemy vessels. In fact the danger did not exist for Villaret-Joyeuse's actions were wholly defensive and after collecting several damaged ships, the French fleet withdrew to the northward. The failure to order a pursuit during the afternoon of 1 June was perhaps Howe's greatest mistake during the five days of fighting and maneouvring. The failure to pursue the French, as was the case with Rodney at the Battle of Saints, was probably due to sheer physical and mental exhaustion. Howe, 68 years old and not in the best of health, was on the point of collapse after five days and four nights of commanding and supervising the Channel Fleet whilst in almost continuous contact with the enemy.[79]

Unfortunately victory over the French fleet in battle did not prevent the French convoy from America arriving in France which was the strategic objective of the campaign. Nevertheless, Howe, by taking six French ships of the line and sinking another, had gained a great victory. This victory was mainly attributable to superior British training and gunnery. Only six British ships managed to break through the French line. Howe made no attempt to concentrate his force on a part of the French line, but rather by having each ship engage her opposite number in the French line produced, which was his objective, a melee in which the issue would be decided by superior British gunnery.

Notes

1. Charles Derrick, *Memoirs of the Rise and Progress of the Royal Navy* (London, 1806), p. 298.
2. Julian S Corbett, ed., *Private Papers of George, Second Earl Spencer, First Lord of the Admiralty* (London, 1913–24) vol. I, p. 19.
3. Cf. W S Cormack, *Revolution and Political Conflict in the French Navy, 1789–1794* (Cambridge, 1995), pp. 143–226.
4. HL, Howe to Curtis, 9, 18 April 1793.
5. HL, Howe to Curtis, 24 May 1793.
6. NA, ADM 1/99, f. 11.
7. NA, ADM 2/124, p. 162.
8. Cf. John B Hattendorf et al, eds, *British Naval Documents, 1204–1960* (Aldershot, Hants., 1993), pp. 338–41.
9. NA, ADM 1/99, f. 22.

10. Quoted in Richard Saxby, 'The Blockade of Brest in the French Revolutionary War', *Mariner's Mirror* (Feb., 1992), vol. 78, p. 26.

11. *Queen Charlotte, Royal George, Royal Sovereign, Cumberland, Ramillies, Edgar, Bellerophon, Brunswick, Audacious, Sceptre, Majestic, Veteran.*

12. Roger Morriss, ed., *The Channel Fleet and the Blockade of Brest, 1793–1801* (Aldershot, Hants., 2001), pp. 30–1.

13. NA, ADM 2/124, pp. 263–4.

14. NA, ADM 2/1346, 3 July 1793.

15. NA, ADM 1/99, f. 64.

16. NA, ADM 1/99, ff. 78–81.

17. NA, ADM 1/99, ff. 88, 90, 95.

18. NA, ADM 1/99, ff. 92–4, 100–1.

19. Morriss, ed., *The Channel Fleet and the Blockade of Brest, 1793–1801*, p. 32.

20. NA, ADM 1/1346, 20 Aug. 1793.

21. NA, ADM 1/99, ff. 106, 113–14, 116, 120, 123–4.

22. NA, ADM 1/99, ff. 130, 133, 135, 137.

23. NA, ADM 1/99, ff. 140–1, 144, 155–6.

24. NA, ADM 2/601, p. 447.

25. NA, ADM 1/99, f. 170.

26. NA, ADM 2/1346, 13 Sept. 1793.

27. NA, ADM 2/1346, 25 Sept. 1793.

28. NA, ADM 1/99, ff. 185, 186.

29. Morriss, ed., *The Channel Fleet and the Blockade of Brest, 1793–1801*, pp. 32–3.

30. NA, ADM 2/602, pp. 70–1; ADM 2/1346, 12, 15 Oct. 1793.

31. NA, ADM 1/99, ff. 193, 195.

32. NA, ADM 1/99, ff. 203–5, 209–14.

33. NA, ADM 1/99, f. 215; ADM 2/602, pp. 269–70, 305.

34. NA, ADM 1/99, f. 217.

35. NA, ADM 1/99, f. 219.

36. NA, ADM 1/99, ft. 219–20.

37. NA, ADM 1/99, ff. 221, 229.

38. NA, ADM 1/99, ff. 233–6.

39. *Cumberland, Ganges, Bellona, Majestic, Alfred, Audacious, Ramillies, Tremendous, Venus, Southampton, Pegasus.*

40. *Queen Charlotte, Royal Sovereign, Royal George, Prince, London, Marlborough, Invincible, Brunswick, Russell, Edgar, Hebe, Niger, Lapwing.*

41. NA, ADM 1/99, ff. 198, 237.

42. NA, ADM 2/602, p. 458.

43. HL, Howe to Curtis, 26, 27, 30 Dec. 1793.

44. E.g., BL, Add. MSS 35194, ff. 249–50.

45. E.g., NA, ADM 1/603, pp. 420–1.

46. E.g., NA, ADM 1/100, f. 110.

47. E.g., NA, ADM 2/603, p. 401.

48. Morriss, ed., *The Channel Fleet and the Blockade of Brest, 1793–1801*, p. 16.

49. HL, Howe to Curtis, 31 Jan., 3 Feb. 1794.

50. HL, Howe to Curtis, 4 Feb., 14 March 1794.

51. David Syrett, *The Royal Navy in European Waters during the American Revolutionary War* (Columbia, S.C., 1998), p. 156.

52. Christopher Lloyd, ed., *The Health of Seamen* (London, 1965), pp. 132, 214.

53. Cf. Christopher Lloyd and Jack L S Coulter, *Medicine and the Navy, 1200–1900* (London, 1961), vol. III, pp. 322–5.

54. HL, Howe to Curtis, 8 March 1794; ADM 2/604, pp. 162–3.

55. Lloyd and Coulter, *Medicine and the Navy*, vol. III, p. 161.

56. HL, Howe to Curtis, 30 Jan., 4, 10, 14, 20 Feb., 1, 6, 8 March 1794.

57. HL, Howe to Curtis, 25, 27 Feb., 1 March 1794.

58. NA, ADM 1/100, f. 184.

59. NA, ADM 1/100, ff. 207, 212.

60. NA, ADM 1/100, f 237.

61. NA, ADM 1/100, ff. 212, 214–15.

62. Morriss, ed., *The Channel Fleet and the Blockade of Brest, 1793–1801*, pp. 34–6.

63. Michael Duffy, 'The Man who Missed the Grain Convoy: Rear Admiral George Montagu and the Arrival of Vanstabel's Convoy from America in 1794', *The Glorious First of June, 1794: A Naval Battle and its Aftermath*, Michael Duffy and Roger Morriss, eds (Exeter, 2001), p. 102.

64. NA, ADM 1/100, f. 245.

65. NA, ADM 1/100, ff. 246, 268; ADM 2/604, pp. 460–1

66. *Bellerophon, Russell, Marlborough, Thunder*.

67. BL, Add. MSS 35194, ff. 297–9, 301, 303–4.

68. NA, ADM 1/100, ff. 260–1.

69. BL, Add. MSS 35194, f. 305.

70. NA, ADM 1/100, ff. 320–1.

71. Ships of the line: *Hector, Arrogant, Theseus, Ganges, Bellona, Alexander*; frigates: *Pallas, Hebe, Venus, Circé*.

72. NA, ADM 1/100, ff. 257–8, 320.

73. Duffy, 'The Man who missed the Grain Convoy', p. 105.

74. NA, ADM 1/100, ff. 320–2.

75. NA, ADM 1/100, ff. 329–32, 361.

76. British ships: *Caesar, Bellerophon, Russell, Leviathan, Marlborough, Royal Sovereign, Audacious, Defence, Impregnable, Tremendous, Culloden, Invincible, Barfleur, Gibraltar, Queen Charlotte, Brunswick, Valiant, Orion, Queen, Ramillies, Alfred, Royal George, Montagu, Majestic, Thunderer*. French ships: *Eole, América, Terrible, Impétueux, Mucius, Tourville, Gasparin, Centurion, Trente-et-un-Mai, Juste, Tyrannicide, Montagne, Jacobin, Achille, Vengeur-Du-Peuple, Patriote, Northumberland, Entreprenant, Jemmapes, Neptune, Pelletier, Républicain, Scipion, Révolutionnaire, Indomptable, Sans Pareil*.

77. Brian Tunstall, *Naval Warfare in the Age of Sail: The Evolution of Fighting Tactics, 1650–1815*, Nicholas Tracy, ed. (London, 1990), p. 205.

78. *Sans Pareil, Trajan, Téméraire*.

79. This account of the five days and four nights of maneouvring and fighting, which is known as the Glorious First of June, is based on BL, Add. MSS 23207, ff. 12–14, 17, 40–1, 44–52, 62–3, 67–70, 72–5, 79–80, 99–100, 122–3; NA, ADM 1/100, ff. 361–5, 367–8; A T Mahan, *The Influence of Sea Power upon the French Revolution and Empire, 1793–1812* (London, 1892), vol. I, pp. 122–61; Tunstall, *Naval Warfare in the Age of Sail*, pp. 204–10; Roger Morriss, 'The Glorious First of June: The British View of the Actions', *The Glorious First of June, 1794*, pp. 46–100.

CHAPTER VIII

Retirement

On 13 June 1794 Howe and the Channel Fleet, escorting six French ships of the line captured on the Glorious First of June, arrived at Spithead to be greeted by salutes from the artillery guarding the anchorage. When Howe went ashore at Portsmouth he discovered that he had become a hero and was welcomed by cheering crowds and the band of the Gloucestershire militia playing 'The Conquering [sic] Hero Comes'.[1] George III being informed of the victory immediately wrote to Lady Howe a note of congratulation and ordered the First Lord of the Admiralty not to permit Howe to leave Portsmouth in order that he could visit the admiral's flagships and present Howe with a sword in recognition of the victory over the French fleet. Both Houses of Parliament voted their thanks to Howe and to the officers and men of the Channel Fleet.[2] Howe with the victory of the Glorious First of June, after more than fifty years of service in the Royal Navy, was a national hero.

There was in the last decade of the 18th century no established system of honours and awards to recognise the services of officers of the army and Royal Navy; the hierarchy of decorations and medals which now exist was established only in the 19th century. The system, if it can be dignified with such a word, employed to recognise the services of officers of the Royal Navy at the Glorious First of June was by general agreement defective.

On 26 June George III arrived at Spithead from Windsor, accompanied by several members of the royal family, courtiers and government ministers. The next day the king and queen were conveyed to HMS *Queen Charlotte* in Howe's barge which was steered by Captain Sir Andrew Snape Douglas. The barge carrying the king and queen was accompanied by the Lords of the Admiralty in their barge as well as barges carrying all the admirals and captains of the Channel Fleet. As the royal barge passed each of the ships of the Channel Fleet the king was saluted and the crews cheered. The king was received on board *Queen Charlotte* by Captain Sir Roger Curtis. Howe was then presented by George III with a diamond-hilted sword valued at 3,000 guineas.[3]

At this point the system of honours and awards began to break down. It was in the late 18th century customary to raise victorious admirals to the peerage. For example, Rodney, the victor of the Battle of the Saints, was made a baron of the Kingdom of England and his second in command, Rear Admiral Sir Samuel Hood, was made a baron of the Kingdom of Ireland. But Howe was already an English earl. While on board HMS *Queen Charlotte* George III told Howe that he intended to confer on the admiral for the victory of the Glorious First of June the Order of the Garter. However, before this award could be made, William Pitt decided that the honour of the Garter should instead be granted to the Duke of Portland, who had just been appointed home secretary, and that Howe should instead be advanced in the peerage to marquess.[4] The king learning of this scheme wrote to Pitt saying it was 'impossible' to comply with the request unless Howe agreed because he had already told the admiral that he would be made a member of the Order of the Garter. Pitt being anxious for political reasons that Portland should be granted the garter wrote to Howe saying that it would be 'beneficial for His Majesty's Service' if Portland received the garter. Howe acquiesced and agreed to forgo the honour of the garter to assist the king's service and in an ice cold note to Pitt refused to become a marquess. Portland became a member of the Order of the Garter in 1794 and the king would later in 1797 at his own instigation confer the Garter on Howe. This mismanaged affair created ill feeling.

The confusion over granting the Garter to Howe was not the only problem which generated ill feelings over the granting of awards and honours for the Glorious First of June. Howe in his first dispatch to the Admiralty, dated 2 June, telling of the victory, which was carried to England by his first captain, Captain Sir Roger Curtis, praised and mentioned by name only Curtis and Howe's second captain, Captain Sir Andrew Snape Douglas.[5] On 3 June Howe issued a memorandum to the flag officers and captains of the Channel Fleet directing that they write reports 'of their proceedings and observations' during the battle in order that he would be able 'to transmit to the Board of Admiralty a just representation of their meritorious conduct on those occasions'. The reports from the flag officers were also to include accounts of 'the services rendered by the captains of their respective divisions'.[6] On the basis of the reports received from the flag officers and captains of the Channel Fleet Howe composed on 6 June a second dispatch which was sent to the Admiralty along with the reports concerning the battle which had been drawn up by the flag officers and captains of the Channel Fleet.[7] Howe's two dispatches, but not the reports by the flag officers and captains of the Channel Fleet, were then published in the *London Gazette*.

Howe in his dispatch, dated 6 June, specifically singled out and named 'Those Officers therefore, who have such particular claim to my attention'. The officers named in Howe's dispatch were Admirals Thomas Graves and Sir Alexander Hood, the second and third in command of the Channel Fleet. Three junior flag officers, Rear Admirals Sir George Bowyer, Alan Gardener and Sir Thomas Pasley, are also named in the dispatch as are thirteen captains and two lieutenants.[8] The paragraph in which these names are contained ends with the cautionary statement:

> These selections however, should not be construed to the disadvantage of other Commanders, who may have been equally deserving of the approbation of the Lords Commissioners of the Admiralty, although I am not enabled to make a particular statement of their merits.

Howe's list of meritorious officers omitted several names, most notably Rear Admiral Benjamin Caldwell, the commander of the second division of the van squadron, and Captain Cuthbert Collingwood of HMS *Barfleur*. Both the king and Henry Dundas the Secretary of State for War, wondered why Caldwell was omitted from Howe's list[9] and the rear admiral after the event attempted to correct the record.[10] Collingwood was enraged at being omitted from Howe's list and blamed the whole affair, which he considered to be 'a libel on the fleet', on Curtis whom he believed to have actually written Howe's dispatch.[11] Obviously the list of names in Howe's dispatch had been composed in haste and without much thought. Nevertheless, this list was not only gazetted, but also was the list which governed the honours and awards which George III bestowed upon the officers of the Channel Fleet for the Glorious First of June.

The awards and honours conferred by George III on the officers named in Howe's dispatch of 6 June were many. Admirals Graves and Hood were created barons of the Kingdom of Ireland. Rear Admirals Sir George Bowyer, Alan Gardner, Sir Thomas Pasley and Howe's flag captain, Sir Roger Curtis, were made baronets. And because of their wounds Graves, Bowyer and Pasley were granted pensions of £1,000 per year. Captains Thomas Pringle, William Parker, Sir Roger Curtis, James Piggot and Thomas Mackenzie were promoted to rear admiral with seniority dated from 3 July. Captains James Gambier and Lord Hugh Seymour were appointed colonels of the marines.[12] And the four senior lieutenants of HMS *Queen Charlotte*, the two senior lieutenants of Graves's and Hood's flagships, as well as the senior lieutenant of every other ship of the line present at the Glorious First of June, were promoted to the rank of commander.[13] When George III visited HMS *Queen Charlotte* to present Howe with the sword, the flag officers and captains on Howe's list were told by the king that they would be presented with gold chains and gold medals to celebrate the Glorious First of June. These medals were designed by Thomas and Lewis Pingo and were struck at the mint. The inscription on Howe's medal read:

RICHARD EARL HOWE, ADMIRAL AND COMMANDER-IN-CHIEF ON THE 1 JUNE MDCCXCIV. THE FRENCH FLEET DEFEATED[14]

The recipients of these medals owing to delays in their manufacture did not receive them until 1797.[15] Because a number of officers, such as Collingwood, were not included in Howe's list of 6 June the whole process of awards and honours for the Glorious First of June led to bitterness among the officers of the Channel Fleet and the belief that Howe had caused, or had at least not prevented, a slur being placed on the reputations of some of the officers under his command.

On 3 August, after an absence in London and the country of several weeks, Howe returned to Spithead to prepare the Channel Fleet for the next cruise.[16] A major problem confronting Howe was the incorporation of a squadron of Portuguese ships into the Channel Fleet. On 5 August the Admiralty informed Howe that a Portuguese squadron of warships had arrived in England and that they were being placed under his command to be employed as the admiral 'shall judge best for HM Service'.[17] At the request of Howe, Commander Henry Raper, because of his knowledge of French and signalling, was assigned to assist the Portuguese admiral. Measures were also undertaken to assign British liaison officers and pilots to the Portuguese ships as well as to provide the Portuguese with all the necessary signal books, signal flags and provisions.[18] It was Howe's intention to employ the Portuguese ships as a detached squadron to act in the event of a general engagement 'against the unoccupied ships of the enemy's rear or to attack any of their separated ships as circumstances render advisable'.[19] From these tactical arrangements it is clear that Howe did not rate very highly the Portuguese combat effectiveness. Vice Admiral Sir Charles Middleton, who was a lord of the admiralty, wanted to employ the Channel Fleet to blockade the French fleet in Brest. Middleton's plan called for twenty-four British ships of the line and eight frigates to cruise 'as constantly as possible off Brest'.[20] Howe's instructions called for him to proceed with the Channel Fleet off Ushant and then to 'make such distribution of the force under your command as you shall judge most proper for the purpose of affording protection to the trade of His Majesty's Subjects and his Allies'. Specifically the Channel Fleet was to protect from attack the trade convoys from the East and West Indies and the Mediterranean expected to arrive in the Western Approaches of the English Channel.[21] There was also intelligence that a French convoy had sailed from America bound for the west coast of France.[22] The influence of Howe can be seen in these instructions for the admiral believed that a strategy of close blockade was not practicable and that a proper station for the Channel Fleet was offshore to the westward of Ushant.

The ships of the Channel Fleet by 23 August were at St Helens awaiting a fair wind to proceed down the English Channel.[23] However, it was not until 3 September that the Channel Fleet sailed from St Helens arriving off the Start on the evening of 4 September. That night the wind changed to the south-west and south with fog and rain. At 4am on 5 September, with visibility almost nil, while standing to the westward, the Channel Fleet encountered a convoy from the East Indies proceeding east up the English Channel. As the East India convoy was passing through the Channel Fleet the East Indiaman *Royal Charlotte* smashed into HMS *Queen* and the East Indiaman *Triton* carried away her masts when she ran into HMS *Latona*. Several other Indiamen and ships of the Channel Fleet were also damaged. Howe, because of the damage sustained by both the ships of the Channel Fleet and the East Indiamen from collisions as well as the 'Appearance of tempestuous weather', bore up and anchored in Torbay on the morning of 5 September.[24]

The damage to the ships was soon repaired and the Channel Fleet sailed from Torbay on 7 September. Arriving off Ushant the next day Howe soon learned that the French fleet was in Brest harbour. On 9 September the wind turned to the east and the Channel Fleet stood off Ushant. Over the next few days Howe received intelligence that convoys from the Leeward Islands and Jamaica had arrived in the Western Approaches – and concluded from this information that the two convoys had passed up the Channel. With the wind out of the west and in 'tempestuous' weather, Howe could not proceed farther to the westward 'where the Enemy, if they had any force detached from Brest to intercept the homeward bound convoys, would probably take their station'. The Channel Fleet bore up and on 20 September put into Torbay. Two of the Portuguese ships and four British ships of the line were damaged by the elements during this cruise and were in need of repairs.[25]

When the Channel Fleet returned to Torbay Howe concluded that the men and ships of the Portuguese squadron were not suitable for autumn cruises in the Western Approaches of the English Channel. After discovering that the Portuguese 'suffered so much by fatigue and sickness since the[y] last put to sea', Howe recommended to the Portuguese commander that his squadron should repair to Plymouth Sound and wait there until receipt of orders from the Portuguese government for the future employment of the Portuguese ships.[26] The Portuguese squadron did not operate again in conjunction with the Channel Fleet.

On 26 September the Admiralty issued additional orders to Howe. Because two more convoys were expected, one from the Mediterranean and the other from Jamaica, to arrive in the English Channel and the French with ships based at Brest might attempt to intercept the British merchant ships, Howe was directed to protect these convoys with either a detachment from his force or with the entire Channel Fleet.[27] Because of adverse winds the Channel Fleet could not sail from Torbay until 12 October. However, before the ships of the Channel Fleet could proceed to the westward of the Start, Howe received orders from the Admiralty calling for him to complete the stores and provisions of seven ships of the line to enable these vessels 'to sail at the shortest notice' for the Leeward Islands. Howe upon receipt of these orders concluded that the provisioning and storing of the ships to be detached to the Leeward Islands had priority over other missions and returned to Torbay with the Channel Fleet.[28]

Howe, after storing and provisioning the seven ships to be sent to the Leeward Islands, intended immediately to put to sea with the Channel Fleet. However, on the night of 13 October a 'hard easterly wind, which lasted for a whole day', came up damaging a number of ships. It was not until 21 October that the Channel Fleet sailed from Torbay. Once out of the anchorage Howe stood southward across the English Channel towards Ushant. On 22 October, with the wind blowing from the south and west, the Channel Fleet was forced away from the French coast to the northward. However, that evening the wind changed to the north-west and Howe 'deemed it requisite to steer immediately for gaining a position, on the possible track of any ships, which might have sailed from Brest on a southern course'. For the next several days the Channel Fleet cruised in 'tempestuous weather' sixty to eighty leagues south-west of Ushant until the weather forced the British ships into the English Channel. On 31 October the ships of the Channel Fleet anchored in Torbay.[29]

On 8 November Howe and the Channel Fleet again sailed from Torbay to protect from attack, by a French squadron thought to be at sea, several trade convoys which were expected to arrive in the English Channel. The Channel Fleet stood to the southward across the English Channel. However, the British ships because of adverse weather could not approach nearer to the French coast than ten leagues. One of the British trade convoys, from the Mediterranean, passed the Channel Fleet proceeding up the Channel. Howe in order to protect the other convoy, also expecting to enter the English Channel, proceeded with the Channel Fleet to the westward heading for the region where intelligence indicated that a French squadron might be cruising. For the next several days the Channel Fleet, with a 'SW wind in this tempestuous season of the year' criss-crossed, to the westward of the Isles of Scilly, the Western Approaches of the English Channel. On 26 November Howe stood to the east in order to pick up intelligence, as well as any dispatches from the Admiralty, which might be 'lodged' at Falmouth. However, the wind came around to the south-east and the Channel Fleet was forced eastward up the English Channel. On 29 November the ships of the Channel Fleet anchored at St Helens.[30]

The autumn cruises of the Channel Fleet while without tangible strategic results did place a great strain on both the ships and the men of the Channel Fleet. Many of the ships were damaged by the elements and Howe, a man of 68 years of age and suffering from gout, was probably driven to near collapse by the physical and mental demands placed on him during the 1794 autumn cruises of the Channel Fleet. On 1 November, from Torbay, Howe requested that he 'be relieved in command of the fleet, the important duties of which my infirmities render me unable to discharge'. Howe wished to go to Bath to regain his health. Several days later the Admiralty, on 3 November, promised Howe 'that leave will be given for Your Lordship to go to Bath for the recovery of it, when you return from the present intended service'.[31] And on 2 December with the end of active operations Howe turned over command of the Channel Fleet to his second in command, Lord Bridport, came ashore, and went to Bath to regain his health.[32] While at Bath Howe concluded that because of his age and ill health remaining in command of the Channel would be of 'prejudice to His Majesty's Service'. On 29 December the admiral wrote to the Admiralty requesting that he be relieved of command for reasons of health.[33]

Howe returned to London on the first day of 1795 believing that his resignation of the command of the Channel Fleet would be accepted by the Admiralty.[34] However, this would not come to pass for George III and Lord Spencer, who had replaced Chatham as First Lord of the Admiralty, would not permit Howe to retire from the command of the Channel Fleet. Spencer believed, and the king agreed with him, that Howe leaving the command of the Channel Fleet would 'be attended with consequences so highly prejudicial to your Majesty's interest and the welfare of the country that no probable means ought to be left untried to prevent his coming to such a determination'.[35] After consulting with Spencer as to the best manner to proceed, George III, on 7 January, wrote to Howe:

> I know Earl Howe's attachment to my person as well as to the service, and therefore point out to him that his forming any idea of retreat at the present would be highly detrimental to me, at an hour when some shew a timidity very fatal to the great cause in which I am engaged, any failure from him who I think a sheet anchor would be the cause of much evil than I cause to express

That same day Howe wrote to the king assuring him that he would not retire from the Command of the Channel Fleet.[36] Howe just could not refuse such a request from George III.

After agreeing to remain in command of the Channel Fleet Howe began to make the necessary preparations for the next series of operations in the English Channel by drawing up all the necessary directives and placing orders for the printing of signal books.[37] On 12 January the Admiralty issued directives placing some forty warships at Portsmouth and Plymouth under the command of Howe.[38] On 15 January Howe returned to Portsmouth to resume command of the Channel Fleet.[39] And on 20 January the Admiralty issued orders to Howe for the conduct of the next operation to be undertaken by the Channel Fleet. Howe was informed by the Admiralty that intelligence had been received that a French fleet, consisting of between thirty-one and thirty-four ships of the line, ten frigates, and a number of smaller vessels had sailed from Brest to cruise to the westward of the Isles of Scilly with the objective of intercepting a number of convoys of merchant ships which were about to sail from the British ports. Howe in the light of this information was to sail with thirty-one ships of the line and escort the trade convoys assembled at Plymouth out into the Atlantic. After safely escorting the trade convoys offshore Howe, if he had intelligence telling of the location of the French fleet, was to seek out the enemy and bring them to battle. If Howe did not know the location of the French fleet, the Channel Fleet was to take station, after detaching the trade convoys, off Ushant. Upon arrival off Ushant, if the French fleet was in Brest, the Channel Fleet was to return to England. On the other hand if Howe, upon arrival off Ushant, discovered that the French fleet was not in Brest then the Channel Fleet was to cruise to the westward of Ushant until further orders.[40]

Because a number of the ships of the Channel Fleet were based at Plymouth and the merchant ships of outward-bound trade convoys had also assembled at that port the plan called for Howe to sail with the bulk of the Channel Fleet from Spithead, proceed down the Channel, and then off Plymouth to be joined by the ships from that port. The weakness of this scheme was that Howe and the Channel Fleet would have to remain off Plymouth for at least two days to be joined by the shipping from that port, for it was estimated that at least forty-eight hours, with a fair wind, would be required to move all the merchant shipping out of the Homoze. Further, if the wind was blowing out of the south, it would be impossible for the ships to depart from Plymouth.[41]

On 29 January Howe and the Channel Fleet sailed from Spithead. The next day the fleet was off the Start, but the wind shifted to the southward preventing the ships in Plymouth from joining Howe. For two days the Channel Fleet, with southerly winds, remained off the Start, and then the force put into Torbay. Howe informed the Admiralty of the situation and pointed out that it was dangerous for the Channel Fleet to remain off Plymouth in the winter and recommended that in future all convoys, along with their escorts, should be assembled in the anchorage at Spithead. This would permit the whole force, warships and merchant ships, to sail together down the English Channel and out into the Atlantic with an easterly wind.[42]

On 4 February the Admiralty ordered Howe, and all the shipping at Plymouth, if the wind continued to the west, to proceed to Spithead where the outward-bound convoys would be reassembled and then sail down the English Channel under escort of the Channel Fleet.[43] However, for the next several days, adverse weather prevented the ships of the Channel Fleet at Torbay and the shipping at Plymouth from proceeding up the Channel to Spithead.[44] It was not until 14 February that Howe and the ships of the Channel Fleet were able to sail from Torbay. The wind was out of the north-west which also enabled the merchant shipping to depart from Plymouth. Proceeding westward, and not as ordered to Spithead, out into the Atlantic Howe detached the convoys sailing to the West Indies and then several days later off Finisterre the merchant ships bound to Iberian ports and the Mediterranean were sent on their way. The only enemy ship encountered was a 16-gun French brig bound for Brest from Norway. Not gaining any intelligence from this ship of the movements of the French fleet, Howe returned to England and the Channel Fleet anchored at Spithead on 25 February.[45]

The February voyage, escorting the trade across the Bay of Biscay to Cape Finisterre, was Howe's last active command at sea. During the last days of the voyage Howe was confined to bed 'by a severe fit of gout' and on arrival at Spithead requested to be relieved of command. On 28 February Howe turned command of the Channel Fleet over to his second in command, Admiral Lord Bridport.[46] After lingering at Portsmouth for over a month in hopes of recovering his health, Howe went to Bath at the beginning of April. It was the admiral's intention to remain at Bath for only two weeks to recover his health and then return to Portsmouth to attend a court-martial.[47] However, Howe's health only slowly improved and for most of his stay at Bath the admiral was 'too infirm to stand any time without support of my Crutches' and had to be carried each day to the waters in a sedan chair.[48] By 15 May Howe's health was such that he could return to Portsmouth and resume command of the Channel Fleet.[49]

Howe, still suffering from the gout, did not remain long at Portsmouth. On 20 May the admiral received permission from the Admiralty for a leave of absence 'to avail yourself of the Change of Air & Exercise to remove the effects of your late Complaint'.[50] And at the end of May Howe left Portsmouth and went to his country residence outside London at Porters Lodge in Barnet in Hertfordshire. While Howe was in Hertfordshire, on 6 June the Admiralty issued orders to the admiral to proceed to sea with the Channel Fleet to protect troop convoys and other forces to be employed landing French loyalist forces on the coast of France in the Bay of Biscay.[51] These orders were accompanied by a letter from Evan Nepean, secretary to the Lords of the Admiralty, informing Howe that:

If however, your Lordship should not feel your health sufficiently re-established to undertake service of that nature in the present moment, I have it in command from their Lordships to signify their direction to you, to order the officer next in seniority to you, to carry into execution the orders and instructions therein contained.[52]

Upon receipt of these orders Howe, whose health had not and would not improve, sent the Admiralty's orders and instructions on to his second in command, Admiral Lord Bridport, with a directive ordering Bridport to put to sea and execute the Admiralty's orders.[53] Howe for the next eighteen months, remaining ashore in London, Hertfordshire, or at Bath, while still legally the commander in chief of the Channel Fleet, became in effect a conduit through which the Admiralty passed orders to Bridport who was in all but name the commander in chief of the Channel Fleet. This unusual command arrangement gave rise to a number of misunderstandings and disagreements.

Admiral Lord Bridport, who at the best of times did not have an easygoing personality, chafed in a situation where he had all the responsibilities of the commander in chief of the Channel Fleet, but not the actual title nor the prestige of the position. Bridport showed his annoyance by not recognising Howe as his superior officer and commander in chief of the Channel Fleet. Bridport simply did not acknowledge the receipt of orders from Howe nor did he send Howe any reports or returns.[54] Bridport's conduct at first mystified and then soon enraged Howe. On 6 July 1795 Howe noted:

I have not received a Line from the Admiral [Bridport] since he went from Spithead, but have never been informed by himself that he received his Sailing Orders. Whether this omission proceeds from interesting occurrences engaging the attention, or inadvertency, I cannot judge. But suppose he could not be apprised that a Report of his proceeding should be made to the authority from which his Line of conduct was marked out for him, as well with the Admiralty.[55]

Bridport did not write to Howe until 15 September when he claimed that under the terms of his orders from the admiral it was his 'weak understanding, that your Lordship did not expect to be troubled with business in your retirement at Porters Lodge' and that all reports, returns and the like should be directed to Nepean for the information of the Lords Commissioners of the Admiralty.[56] Howe thought this letter insulting and vowed never again to serve with Bridport.[57] Relations between Howe and Bridport were exacerbated, when Howe not only successfully claimed a commander in chief's share of all prize money earned by the Channel Fleet during 1795, but also insisted that his first captain, Sir Roger Curtis, receive a flag officer's share of the prize money.[58] The breakdown of relations between Howe and Bridport in 1795, in the absence of goodwill on all sides, showed the limitations of attempting before the age of electronic communications to command the Channel Fleet from ashore. Nevertheless, Howe, owing mainly to the government's inability to find a suitable replacement, would remain nominally as commander in chief of the Channel Fleet until 10 April 1797.[59]

On 12 March 1796, upon the death of Admiral of the Fleet John Forbes, Howe was promoted to the rank of admiral of the fleet and assumed the sinecure of general of the marines.[60] Howe was not overjoyed with this promotion and said that he had 'gained it however, by the least eligible of all titles – that of Age, almost universally, and survivorship'. Howe had held the brevet rank of admiral of the fleet since 1790, and when he assumed the actual rank of admiral of the fleet, he had to give up the position of vice admiral of England. From Howe's viewpoint the bitterest part of this transaction was the fact that upon his promotion to admiral of the fleet the position of vice admiral of England passed to Bridport.[61]

In April 1796 Howe was ordered to Portsmouth to take part in the court-martial of Vice Admiral Sir William Cornwallis.[62] The Cornwallis court-martial was nearly Howe's last official act as commander in chief of the Channel Fleet for gout had reduced the admiral to the condition of almost an invalid. For instance, at the beginning of 1797 Howe could only 'walk across the room three or four times on my Crutches at Intervals'.[63] Though he was crippled with gout, Howe's mind was clear and the admiral continued to take an active interest in naval affairs. In February 1797 Howe sent to Portsmouth from Bath a number of 'Signals and Instruction Books' containing corrections and alterations for the use of the Channel Fleet.[64]

At the end of February 1797, while at Bath, Howe received four anonymous petitions,[65] supposedly written by the seamen of four ships[66] belonging to the Channel Fleet, asking that the admiral, as commander, request that the Lords of the Admiralty increase the pay of seamen. These four petitions only requested an increase in seamen's pay and in no way threatened mutiny or any refusal of duty. An increase in seamen's pay was not an illogical request for the 1790s was a period of inflation, the pay of soldiers had been increased several years before, and that of seamen had remained the same since 1652. Howe upon reading these petitions was at first suspicious suspecting them 'to be the fabrications of some person'. Nevertheless, Howe decided to bring the seamen's petitions to London and submit them to the First Lord of the Admiralty.[67] Before departing from Bath for London he wrote 'to the officer at Portsmouth', probably not his first captain, Rear Admiral Sir Roger Curtis,[68] to enquire if there was 'any such dissatisfaction in the fleet' as mentioned in the petitions and received in return assurances that none existed. And upon his arrival in London on 22 March Howe turned over the seamen's petitions to the Admiralty.[69] At the time Howe probably thought this must be the end of the matter, as far as he was concerned, for such complaints about seamen's pay were not so unusual and he was at the end of his active service in the Royal Navy.

On 10 April 1797 the Admiralty at last accepted Howe's resignation as commander in chief of the Channel Fleet.[70] On every other occasion since coming ashore in 1794, when Howe had requested permission to resign from the command of the Channel Fleet, the Admiralty had only granted him a leave of absence. Now at last it seemed that he could retire completely from active service. However, the acceptance of Howe's resignation by the Admiralty was not the end of the admiral's connection with the Royal Navy; for in the middle of April 1797 the seamen of the ships of the Channel Fleet stationed at Spithead mutinied.

The causes of the great mutiny at Spithead in 1797 by the seamen of the Channel Fleet were many.[71] Pay, working conditions, and the ideological influences of the time were of first importance, but the command arrangements of the Channel Fleet wherein since the end of 1794 authority and responsibility were divided between Bridport on board his flag ship HMS *Prince George*, Howe ashore in Bath, London or Hertfordshire, and the Admiralty in London must have facilitated the growth of dissatisfaction among the seamen of the fleet. For instance, Bridport did not learn of the petitions sent to Howe until 12 April. Dual command and divided responsibilities slowed the reaction of the authorities both at Spithead and London to the increasing discontent of the seamen. Nevertheless, the government and the command structure of the Royal Navy, once the nature of the mutiny was understood, quickly realised that measures must be undertaken to meet the demands of the seamen. Efforts were made to improve rations, legislation was passed by Parliament to increase the pay of the seamen, a blanket royal pardon was issued, and serious negotiations entered into with their representatives. These measures by the middle of May seemed to be successful for the seamen appeared to be on the verge of returning to their duty. The government, to ensure that there was not further misunderstanding of its intentions and recognising the difficulties of winning back the allegiance of the seamen decided to bring Howe out of retirement and to send him to Spithead to explain to the seamen of the Channel Fleet the government's measures for conciliation in order to bring the mutiny to an end.[72]

The dispatch of Howe by the government to Spithead to convince the mutinous seamen to return to duty was an astute move. Howe, because of his long service, and being the victor of the Glorious First of June, had vast prestige. He had carried out a similar mission when First Lord of the Admiralty at the end of the American War. And the admiral was popular among the seamen of the Channel Fleet. Considered by many to be an even-handed disciplinarian who had always sought to promote the welfare of his men, Howe was allegedly nicknamed by the seamen 'Black Dick, the sailor's friend'. Perhaps most important of all was the fact that Howe understood the need for conciliation if the mutiny was to be ended. Even Bridport saw the wisdom of Howe's mission to allay the fears of the mutineers, and he briefly put aside his personal animosities towards his former commander.[73]

On 10 May Howe, accompanied by Lady Howe, set out from London for Portsmouth. Arriving before noon on 11 May, and in spite of his age and suffering from gout, Howe immediately went on board Bridport's flagship HMS *Royal George* at St Helens and that same afternoon visited his old flagship HMS *Queen Charlotte* as well as HMS *Duke*. Howe, unlike the Admiralty, recognised the authority of the delegates appointed by the mutinous seamen and spoke at length to groups of seamen in a conciliatory manner telling them that the government would grant everything that they demanded and that, as they knew, legislation for increasing their wages had already been enacted by Parliament. Also Howe read to them the proclamation of royal pardon for their past mutinous actions. Over and over again Howe told the seamen that the government intended to grant them everything it had promised.[74] It quickly became apparent to Howe that the seamen were deeply suspicious of the government believing that it intended to deceive them. Further, the only way to end the mutiny would be for a number of those officers who had been forced to leave their ships by the mutinous seamen not to be permitted to return. To allay fears of government deceit and of reprisals Howe requested from the Admiralty printed copies of the royal pardon and the authority not to permit certain officers to return to their ships.[75] The Admiralty at first did not want to concede the point that some officers should not be permitted to return to their ships because it would be an admission that the Articles of War had been too harshly applied and it would also set the precedent of appearing to give common seamen a veto over the appointment of officers. However, in the end the Admiralty was forced to concede this point and about half of the officers – 114 in all – who were sent ashore by the mutinous seamen never returned to their ships. Over the next several days Howe went from ship to ship at Spithead and St Helens addressing groups and negotiating with their delegates. The seamen were always suspicious of the motives of the Admiralty and government, but unlike with the rebellious Americans twenty-one years before, Howe understood the seamen and he was trusted by them. Ever so slowly, by force of personality, Howe's assurances that the government was really addressing their grievances was accepted. By the evening of 14 May the mutiny at Spithead appeared to be over. This was Howe's last service to the Royal Navy and it ended on 15 May on a note of triumph with feasting and processions as Howe made a grand tour of the fleet.[76]

Howe during the last two years of his life passed his time mainly at his residence at Grafton Street in London or at his country house at Barnet in Hertfordshire. During his retirement Howe maintained an interest in current events and naval affairs. For instance in May of 1799 he had the Admiralty send him 'a copy of the "amended" Signal Book and Instruction' and upon inspecting these documents concluded 'that the Author (not unindustrious) has different concept of Naval Tactics, in the practice as well as Theory, from those occurring to me'.[77] However, for long periods Howe was in pain and crippled with gout which made all movement very difficult. In 1798 the admiral would write:

> My most spirited Efforts don't yet exceed a movement farther than from one Room to the other, without crutches. But tho' I have been for many Weeks but stationary in my progress to amendment, I think within the last 8 or 10 days I am getting forward again.[78]

During the summer of 1799 in an effort to obtain relief from the gout Howe undertook a series of treatments consisting of electric shocks.[79] According to one account the electricity, on 5 August 1799, drove the gout into Howe's head killing the admiral.[80] Howe's obituary in *The Times* said that the admiral 'had been for many years affected with the gout, which had much impaired his health. At last it attacked him in the stomach, which terminated in his death'.[81] On 18 August Howe's remains were placed in the family vault at Langer in Nottinghamshire with the following inscription on the coffin:

> Richard Howe
> Earl and Viscount Howe
> Viscount Howe and Baron Clenawley, in Ireland
> Admiral of the Fleet
> General of His Majesty's Marine Force, and Knight of
> the most noble Order of the Garter
> Died 5th August 1799,
> Age 73 years[82]

Notes

1. Roger Morriss, ed., *The Channel Fleet and the Blockade of Brest, 1793–1801* (Aldershot, Hants., 2001), p. 43.
2. Aspinell, ed., *The Later Correspondence of George III* (Cambridge 1962–70) vol. II, nos 1081, 1082, 1085, 1086, 1090.
3. Oliver Warner, *The Glorious First of June* (New York, 1969), pp. 89, 144.
4. NA, 30/8/146, ff. 221, 228; HL, Howe to Curtis, 18 July 1794; Aspinell, *Later Correspondence of George III*, vol. II, nos 1093, 1095, and p. 224n.
5. BL, Add. MSS 23207, ff. 12–14.

6. BL, Add. MSS 35194, f. 324.

7. NA, ADM 1/100, ff. 367–9.

8. Captains: Lord Hugh Seymour, Hon. Thomas Pakenham, Hon. George Cranfield Berkeley, James Gambier, John Hervey, John Willett Payne, William Parker, Henry Hervey, Thomas Pringle, John Thomas Duckworth, John Elphinston, Henry Nicholls, William Johnstone Hope; Lieutenants: John Monkton and Ross Donnally.

9. Aspinell, *The Later Correspondence of George III*, vol. II, no. 1090.

10. NA, ADM 1/101, f. 16.

11. Edward Hughes, ed., *The Private Correspondence of Admiral Lord Collingwood* (London, 1957), pp. 48–50.

12. Warner, *The Glorious First of June*, pp. 157n, 162.

13. NA, ADM 2/606, pp. 60–1.

14. Warner, *The Glorious First of June*, pp. 157–8.

15. Aspinell, *The Later Correspondence of George III*, vol. II, nos 1472, 1476.

16. NA, ADM 1/101, f. 28.

17. NA, ADM 2/126, pp. 318–19.

18. NA, ADM 1/101, ff. 35–6; ADM 2/606, pp. 350–2.

19. BL, Add MSS 35195, f. 30.

20. Morriss, ed., *The Channel Fleet and the Blockade of Brest, 1793–1801*, p. 47.

21. NA, ADM 2/1348, 16, 17 Aug. 1794.

22. NA, ADM 2/606, pp. 438, 458.

23. NA, ADM 1/101, f. 63.

24. NA, ADM 1/101, ff. 68–9.

25. NA, ADM 1/101, ff. 72–3.

26. NA, ADM 1/101, ff. 76–7, 82–106.

27. NA, ADM 2/1348, 26 Sept. 1794.

28. NA, ADM 1/101, ff. 115, 118, 121; ADM 2/1348, 10 Oct. 1794.

29. NA, ADM 1/101, ff. 120, 123, 134, 135.

30. NA, ADM 1/101, ff. 151–2, 153.

31. NA, ADM 1/101, f. 135; ADM 2/606, p. 481.

32. NA, ADM 1/101, f. 154.

33. NA, ADM 1/101, f. 159.

34. HL, Howe to Curtis, 2 Jan. 1795.

35. Julian S Corbett, ed., *Private Papers of George, Second Earl Spencer, First Lord of the Admiralty, 1794–1801* (London, 1913–24), vol. I, pp. 26–7.

36. Aspinell, *The Later Correspondence of George III*, vol. II, nos 1186, 1187.

37. HL, Howe to Curtis, 8, 12 Jan. 1795.

38. NA, ADM 2/127, pp. 270–1.

39. NA, ADM 1/ 102, f. 7.

40. NA, ADM 2/1349, pp. 5–8.

41. NA, ADM 1/102, ff. 11, 13.

42. NA, ADM 1/102, f. 24.

43. NA, ADM 2/1349, pp. 16–17.

44. NA, ADM 1/102, ff. 28, 29.

45. NA, ADM 1/102, ff. 32, 34–5.

46. NA, ADM 1/102, ff. 33, 39.

47. NA, ADM 1/102, f. 44.

48. HL, Howe to Curtis, 13, 17 April 1795.

49. NA, ADM 1/102, f. 49; ADM 2/1336, Nepean to Howe, 15 May 1795.

50. NA, ADM 2/1326, Nepean to Howe, 20 May 1795.

51. NA, ADM 2/1349, pp. 111–13.

52. NA, ADM 2/1349, p. 97.

53. BL, Add. MSS 35195, ff. l75–6; NA, ADM 1/102, f. 69; Morriss, ed., *The Channel Fleet and the Blockade of Brest, 1793–1801*, pp. 78–9.

54. Morriss, ed., *The Channel Fleet and the Blockade of Brest, 1793–1801*, p. 89.

55. HL, Howe to Curtis, 6 July 1795.

56. BL, Add. MSS 35916, ff. 234–5.

57. HL, Howe to Curtis, 24 Sept. 1795.

58. HL, Howe to Curtis, 29, 30 Sept., 9 Oct. 1795.

59. NA, ADM 2/133, p. 152.

60. David Syrett and R L DiNardo, *Commissioned Sea Officers of the Royal Navy, 1660–1815* (Aldershot, Hants., 1994), p. 231.

61. HL, Howe to Curtis, 14 March 1796.

62. HL, Howe to Curtis, 31 March 1796; NA, ADM 2/130, p. 295.

63. HL, Howe to Curtis, 28 Jan. 1797.

64. HL, Howe to Curtis, 24, 27 Feb. 1797.

65. BL, Add. MSS 35197, ff. 81–2.

66. *Royal George, Formidable, Ramillies, Queen Charlotte.*

67. HL, Howe to Curtis, 4 March 1797.

68. Cf. Harding Craig, 'Black Dick Howe, The Sailor's Friend', *The Mariner's Mirror* (Jan., 1949), vol. 35, p. 21.

69. *The Parliamentary History of England from the earliest period to the year 1803* (London, 1818), vol. XXXIII, col. 476.

70. NA, ADM 2/133, p. 152.

71. Cf. Conrad Gill, *The Naval Mutinies of 1797* (Manchester, 1913); G E Manwaring and Bonamy Dobree, *The Floating Republic. An Account of the Mutinies at Spithead and the Nore in 1797* (London, 1935); James Dugan, *The Great Mutiny* (New York, 1965).

72. Morriss, ed., *The Channel Fleet and the Blockade of Brest, 1793–1801*, pp. 191–6.

73. Morriss, ed., *The Channel Fleet and the Blockade of Brest, 1793–1801*, p. 229.

74. Gill, *The Naval Mutinies of 1797*, pp. 74–5.

75. Morriss, ed., *The Channel Fleet and the Blockade of Brest, 1793–1801*, pp. 230–l.

76. Gill, *The Naval Mutinies of 1797*, pp. 76–83; Manwaring and Dobree, *The Floating Republic*, pp. 106–16.

77. HL, Howe to Curtis, 28 May 1799.

78. HL, Howe to Curtis, 16 May 1798.

79. HL, Howe to Curtis, 3, 18 June, 6 July 1799.

80. *The Dictionary of National Biography* (London, 1921–22 reprint), vol X, p. 100.

81. *The Times*, 6 Aug. 1799.

82. *Gentleman's Magazine*, vol. LXIX, pp. 807–8.

CHAPTER IX

Conclusion

Admiral Lord Howe was one of the great figures in the history of the Hanoverian Royal Navy. Howe, who fought in four wars – Austrian Succession, Seven Years, American, and French Revolutionary Wars – and whose career spanned the Age of Fighting Sail, from Anson's voyage around the world to the Glorious First of June, took part in many of the great naval events of the last half of the 18th century.

Howe entered the Royal Navy in 1739 at the age of 13 and rose quickly through the ranks of commissioned officers to become a post captain at 20 years of age. Then as a captain and later as a commodore during the Seven Years War, Howe compiled a distinguished record as a combat commander. He fired the first shot at sea of the Seven Years War and his ship led the British attack at Quiberon Bay. But more importantly, as a commodore Howe commanded a squadron conducting amphibious operations on the coasts of Normandy and Brittany. It was during the Seven Years War that Howe first showed his skill as an organiser and staff officer, by not only drawing up and issuing the orders and directions required to organise a ship's crew by divisions, but also by formulating and codifying British doctrine for the conduct of amphibious operations.

In the years of peace after the Seven Years War, Howe as a Member of Parliament representing Dartmouth in the House of Commons, became a political figure who for the most part appears only to have dabbled in politics. Even though Howe in the 1760s held several minor offices, such as the treasurership of the navy, he was a political independent. To Howe politics were to a large extent personal and non-ideological and non-partisan. In fact it is virtually impossible for the historian at this late date to discover just what political positions, if any, Howe, had on the great issues of the time. Perhaps Howe's greatest achievement in Parliament in the years before the American War was to lead a non-partisan movement in the House of Commons to obtain an increase of half pay for junior captains in the Royal Navy. In 1770, during the Falkland Islands crisis, Howe was promoted to flag rank and would have commanded the squadron in the Mediterranean in the event of war with Spain.

155

Howe's attempt to settle the Anglo–American constitutional crisis by negotiations with Benjamin Franklin is one of the most mysterious episodes in the life of the admiral. Before the end of 1774 there is no record of Howe showing any interest in American affairs. Nevertheless, at the end of 1774 Howe approached Benjamin Franklin and attempted to open negotiations with a view to bringing an end to a constitutional crisis between America and Great Britain. Franklin characterised the resulting talks as 'spitting in the soup', for they led nowhere beyond the Pennsylvanian restating the American position and the admiral floating the idea of sending a commissioner to America to undertake peace negotiations. The whole affair is an enigma for no one knows what motivated Howe to approach Franklin. There are other questions arising from this episode as well. For instance, was the admiral seeking personal glory and acting on his own instigation or was he acting as an intermediary for the government? Further, the existing record, which is admittedly incomplete, does not indicate what Howe envisioned as a suitable solution to the crisis in Anglo–American relations.

In a swirl of politics, both personal and public, Howe was appointed a commissioner for restoring peace in America and commander in chief of the Royal Navy's squadron in America. In this latter capacity Howe was ordered, in conjunction with the British army, to suppress by force of arms the rebellion in America. At the same time as a commissioner for restoring peace to America, Howe, along with his brother General the Hon. William Howe, commander in chief of the British army in America, was authorised to grant pardons to those Americans 'who shall return to their allegiance' and to declare any colony, which recognised the authority of Parliament and had abandoned the rebellion, to be returned to a state of peace. Armed with these powers Howe on 11 May 1776 sailed for America to re-establish royal authority in that land.

When Howe arrived at New York in July of 1776 he was confronted with a military and political situation without precedent. America was a continent swept by an ideologically motivated armed rebellion. At first Howe attempted to end the rebellion in America by negotiations, but the effort was soon abandoned as futile. When Howe, at Staten Island on 11 September 1776, met with three leaders of the American revolutionary movement – John Adams, John Rutledge and Benjamin Franklin – the three Americans made it absolutely clear to the admiral that America would not under any circumstances end the rebellion and submit to royal authority. As a result any hopes that Howe might have entertained of bringing the rebellion in America to an end by means of negotiations vanished. Howe, from the beginning of the talks with Franklin in London at the end of 1774 to the collapse of negotiations with the Americans at Staten Island in September of 1776, had totally misread American politics. Equally surprising as Howe's complete and total misunderstanding of the politics of the American Revolution is the fact that at no point during the discussions with the Americans or with the North government over the terms of the peace commission is there on the record a statement of just what the admiral himself believed to be the terms of a proper and just settlement of the American problem. After the abortive meeting with the Americans on Staten Island there was open to Howe no other alternative but to employ the Royal Navy's squadron in America to crush the rebellion by force of arms.

Lord Howe played a secondary role, compared to that of his brother General Howe, in the British attempt to suppress the rebellion in America by force of arms during the years 1776–7, for the ships of the Royal Navy were for the most part employed to support the British army and to blockade the coast of America. Scores of warships of Howe's squadron were deployed supporting amphibious operations, escorting military supply ships, and guarding British bases and enclaves in America while other British warships were stationed along the American coast on blockade duty. Perhaps the American rebellion could have been crushed by force of arms if the British had destroyed Washington's army and effectively blockaded the American coast. However, the British could not destroy Washington's army and from the beginning the blockade was a failure for it never prevented American cruisers from putting to sea nor the Americans from importing the munitions and military stores required to carry on the war. The American coastline was too long to be blockaded by the number of ships available to Howe and Washington's army proved to be too elusive an enemy to be trapped and destroyed by the British army.

At the end of 1777 the campaign in America, with the surrender of Burgoyne's army at Saratoga, the British attempt to subdue the rebellion in America was at a dead end. Howe wished to be relieved of his command and return to England to defend his conduct in America. The admiral knew that he and his brother would be blamed for the failure of British arms in America and wished to defend his reputation in the House of Commons. However, the impending French entry into the war and the possible arrival of a French fleet in American waters prevented the immediate departure of Howe for England.

In July of 1778, just after the British evacuation of Philadelphia, a powerful French squadron under the command of Comte d'Estaing arrived on the coast of America. The British position in America was now faced with the possibility of a combined Franco–American attack. However, in a series of skilfully conducted manoeuvres and actions off New York and Rhode Island Howe, though out-numbered by the enemy, defeated all attempts to overcome the British forces. Howe's skilful and successful actions in 1778 salvaged from the debacle of the British defeat in America his reputation as an admiral.

Returning to England at the end of 1778 Howe, in conjunction with his brother, attempted in the House of Commons, by means of the enquiry into the conduct of the war in America, to force the North government to accept responsibility for the failure of the British effort. Howe emerged from the political maelstrom – the Keppel–Palliser affair and the inquiry into the conduct of the war in America – as one of the major naval personages within the ranks of the opposition. When the North government fell from power at the end of 1781 Howe was created an English viscount and placed in command of the Channel Fleet by the Rockingham–Shelburne government. As commander of the Channel Fleet in 1782 Howe concluded the American war on a note of triumph by successfully undertaking the third relief of Gibraltar. At the end of the American War Howe was one of the best known and most successful admirals to emerge from that conflict.

At the beginning of 1783 Howe briefly served in the Shelburne government as First Lord of the Admiralty. Then on the last day of 1783 he was again appointed First Lord of the Admiralty in the government of William Pitt and would serve in that post for more than four years; however, it was a frustrating experience for him as he was largely ignored by Pitt in his effort to strengthen the Royal Navy. In July of 1788 Howe resigned from the Admiralty after a dispute with Pitt over the promotion of Sir Charles Middleton to flag rank. Howe had not been a dynamic First Lord of the Admiralty, but as a mark of royal favour when he left office he was made an earl by George III. Moreover, in 1790 during the naval mobilisation for the Nootka Sound Crisis, Howe was placed in command of the Channel Fleet.

When in command of the Channel Fleet in 1790 Howe introduced into use by the Royal Navy a numerical system of signals. Howe was one of the leaders in the movement to reform and rationalise not only the signals employed by the king's ships, but also other aspects of the Royal Navy. Howe was not only one of the prime movers in the effort to reform signalling within the navy, but also one of the first officers to employ the divisional system for the governance of a ship's crew, the driving force behind the formulation of a doctrine of amphibious warfare, as well as an early advocate for improving gunnery by the introduction of locks to fire ship's guns. The introduction of a numerical system of signalling by Howe in 1790 was the culmination of an intellectual effort that had begun as early as the Seven Years War.

At the beginning of the French Revolutionary War in 1793, Howe was placed in command of the Channel Fleet. The first operations of the Channel Fleet during this war consisted for the most part of escorting British convoys in and out of the English Channel and cruising for the protection of British trade. The main naval threat in 1793 was perceived as coming from single enemy warships or small squadrons of French ships attacking British merchant shipping and not from the operations of large squadrons of the French navy. Neither Howe, nor the Admiralty, at the beginning of the French Revolutionary War considered a strategy of close blockade of the French coast to be either practical or expedient.

In the spring of 1794, at a battle known to history as the Glorious First of June, the Channel Fleet under the command of Howe fought and defeated the French fleet. The Glorious First of June was the culmination of a series of naval movements designed by the French to protect, and intended by the British to intercept and destroy, a large French convoy expected to arrive in Europe from America. Howe and the Channel Fleet never did intercept the French convoy, but on 28 May, some 430 miles west of Ushant, the Channel Fleet, consisting of some thirty-six ships of the line, intercepted a French fleet of equal strength. For the next four days the British and French ships manoeuvred, and at times exchanged gunfire, with Howe seeking the weather gauge so as to be able to advantageously engage the French. On the morning of 1 June Howe and the ships of the Channel Fleet, from a windward position, bore down and engaged the French. Only six British ships of the line broke through the French line and most of the British ships engaged the windward side of the French ships. British gunners however, decided the issue and when the firing ceased in the early afternoon, the British had sunk one French ship and captured six others. The Glorious First of June was the first great British naval victory of the French Revolutionary and Napoleonic Wars.

Howe, after the Glorious First of June, would continue to command the Channel Fleet. However, old age and increasingly severe attacks of gout would force his retirement from active service. In February of 1795 after a voyage, in command of the Channel Fleet, across the Bay of Biscay to Cape Finisterre, during the course of which Howe suffered greatly from the gout, the admiral requested that he be permitted to come ashore and retire from active service. However, the king and the First Lord of the Admiralty, Lord Spencer, were reluctant to permit Howe to retire even though the admiral was obviously physically incapable of going to sea. While ashore a semi-invalid Howe would remain nominally in command of the Channel Fleet until 10 April 1797 when finally he was permitted to officially retire from active service.

The great mutiny of 1797 at Spithead was the occasion of Howe's last service to the Royal Navy. Called out of retirement Howe went to Spithead to supervise the ending of the mutiny among the seamen of the Channel Fleet. Howe convinced the government to reassign a number of officers objected to by the mutinous seamen and through force of personality convinced the seamen to return to their duty.

Howe, when he died on 5 August 1799, was the most famous admiral in Great Britain. The victory of the Glorious First of June, capping off a long and distinguished career in the Royal Navy propelled Howe into the ranks of late Georgian celebrities. In the wake of the Glorious First of June, to celebrate the victory and Howe's new-found status as a celebrity, there appeared several curiosities such as mugs adorned with his image and ceramic figures of the admiral.[1] In 1803 the government commissioned the sculptor John Flaxman, at the cost of 6,000 guineas, to produce a monument to Howe which was placed in St Paul's.[2] Howe was the first person to enter the pantheon of naval heroes of the French Revolutionary and Napoleonic Wars.

Though several of the Royal Navy's capital ships would be named after the admiral, Howe would soon be eclipsed in the public consciousness by Nelson. Today, more than two hundred years after the victory of the Glorious First of June and the death of the admiral, Howe is little known except to naval historians and students of the American Revolution.

Notes

1. Barbara Tomlinson, 'The Battle Sanctified: Some Memorials and Relics', *The Glorious First of June, 1794: A Naval Battle and Its Aftermath*, Michael Duffy and Roger Morriss, eds, (Exeter, 2001) , pp. 166–7.
2. David Irwin, *John Flaxman, 1755–1826: Sculptor, Illustrator, Designer* (New York, 1979), pp. 155–6.

Bibliography

Manuscripts
American Philosophical Society:
The Sol Feinstone Collection of the American Revolution.

British Library (BL):
Naval Papers, Add. MSS 23207.
Newcastle Papers, Add. MSS 32880, 32881, 32883, 32056.
Auckland Papers, Add. MSS 34412.
Nelson Papers, Add. MSS 43903.
Bridport Papers, Add. MSS 35194, 35195, 35197.
Hardwicke Papers, Add. MSS 35595.

Huntington Library (HL):
Howe-Curtis correspondence. Transcripts made by the late Dr. Richard Boulind.
Ipswich and East Suffolk Record Office:
Keppel Papers.

Massachusetts Historical Society:
Archibald Kennedy Papers.

The National Archive:
ADM 1/89, 91, 97, 99, 100, 101, 102, Admiral's dispatches, Channel.
ADM 1/368, Admiral's dispatches, Mediterranean.
ADM 1/487, 488, 489, Admiral's dispatches, North America.
ADM 1/1886, 1888, 1889, 1890, 1891, 1892, 1893, 1895, 1896, 1898, 2217, Captain's letters.
ADM 1/4122, 4128, 4147, 4150, 4152, Letters from Secretary of State.
ADM 2/65, 69, 74, 75, 76, 78, 79, 80, 81, 82, 87, 88, 89, 100, 103, 120, 124, 126, 127, 130, 133, Orders and instructions.
ADM 2/511, 557, 592, 601, 602, 603, 604, 606, Secretaries letters.
ADM 2/1326, 1331, 1332, 1341, 1343, 1346, 1348, 1349, Secret orders.
ADM 3/27, 71, 72, 73, 95, 96, 99, 100, Admiralty minutes.
ADM 6/16, 17, 18, Commission and warrant books.
ADM 6/86, Lieutenant's passing certificates.
ADM 36/435, 2403, 4013, 4042, 4086, Ship's muster books.

ADM 51/80, 258, 270, 320, 389, 412, 786, 888, 1005, 4133, Captain's logs.
ADM 107/6, Lieutenant's passing certificates.
ADM 118/26, Commissioned sea officers.
CO 5/92, 94, 96, 236, 487, Military dispatches, America.
CO 5/177, Peace commission reports.
PC 2/111, Privy council registers.
NA 30/8/45, 68, 103, 108, 111, 146, 178, Chatham papers.
SP 42/37, State papers, naval.

University of Virginia:
Hamond Papers.
William L. Clement's Library, University of Michigan:
Clinton Papers.
Sackville-Germain Papers.
Sackville-Germain Papers, military dispatches, 1775–1782.

Printed Documents
Abbot, W W et al (eds), *The Papers of George Washington: Revolutionary War Series*, Charlottesville, Va: University of Virginia Press, 1985–.
Anson, William (ed.), *Autobiography and Political Correspondence of Augustus Henry, Third Duke of Grafton*, London: John Murray, 1989.
Aspinell, A (ed.), *The Later Correspondence of George III*, Cambridge: CUP, 1962–70.
Barnes, G R, and Owen, J H (eds), *The Private Papers of John, Earl of Sandwich First Lord of the Admiralty, 1772–1782*, London: Navy Records Society, 1932–8.
Bonner-Smith, D (ed.), *The Barrington Papers. Selected from the Letters and Papers of Admiral the Hon. Samuel Barrington*, London: Navy Records Society, 1937–41.
Brown, Gerald Saxon (ed.), *Reflections on a Pamphlet Intitled 'A Letter to the Right Hon. Lord Vist. H—e'*, Ann Arbor, Mich: University of Michigan Press, 1959.
Carswell, John and Dralle, Lewis Arnold (eds), *The Political Journal of George Bubb Dodington*, Oxford: Clarendon Press, 1965.
Clark, William Bell at al, *Naval Documents of the American Revolution*, Washington DC: US Government Printing Office, 1964–.
Corbett, Julian S (ed.), *Signals and Instructions, 1776–1795*, London: Navy Records Society, 1908.
_____ *Fighting Instructions, 1530–1816*, London: Navy Records Society, 1909.
_____ *Private Papers of George, Second Earl Spencer, First Lord of the Admiralty*, London: Navy Records Society, 1913–24.
Davies, K G (ed.), *Documents of the American Revolution*, Dublin: Irish University Press, 1972–81.
Doniol, Henri (ed.), *Histoire de la participation de la France à l'établissement des Etats-Unis d'Amérique*, Paris: Imprimerie nationale, 1886–92.
Erskine, David (ed.), *Augustus Hervey's Journal*, London: William Kimber, 1953.
Ford, Worthington Chauncey et al (eds), *Journals of the Continental Congress 1774–1789*, Washington, DC: US Government Printing Office, 1904–37.
Fortescue, Sir John (ed.), *The Correspondence of George III from 1760 to December 1782*, London: Frank Cass, 1972 (reprint).
Hamilton, Sir Richard Vessey (ed.), *Letters and Papers of Admiral of the Fleet Sir Thos.*

Byam Martin, London: Navy Records Society, 1898–1903.

Hammond, Otis G (ed.), *Letters and Papers of Major-General John Sulliban, Continental Army*, Concord, NH: New Hampshire Historical Society, 1930–9.

Hattendorf, John B et al (eds), *British Naval Documents, 1204–1960*, Aldershot: Scolar Press for the Navy Records Society, 1993.

Historical Manuscripts Commission, *Report on the Manuscripts of Mrs Stopford-Sackville of Drayton House, Northamptonshire*, London and Hereford: printed for HMSO by Eyre & Spottiswoode, 1904–10.

_____ *Report on Manuscripts in Various Collections*, Dublin and Hereford: printed for HMSO by Mackie & Co., 1904–14.

_____ *Report on Manuscripts of the Late Reginald Hastings Esq. of Manor House, Ashby de la Zouche*, London: HMSO, 1928–47.

Hughes, Edward (ed.), *The Private Correspondence of Admiral Lord Collingwood*, London: Navy Records Society, 1957.

Hutchinson, Peter Orlando (ed.), *The Diary and Letters of His Excellency Thomas Hutchinson Esq.*, London: S Low, Marten Searle & Rivington, 1883–86.

Kielmansegge, Frederick (ed.), *Diary of a Journey to England in the Years 1761–1763* (trans. Countess Kielmansegge), London: Longman, 1902.

Labaree, Leonard W, et al (eds), *The Papers of Benjamin Franklin*, New Haven, Ct: Yale University Press, 1959–.

Laughton, Sir John Knox (ed.), *The Naval Miscellany*, London: Navy Records Society, 1901.

_____ *Letters and Papers of Charles, Lord Barham, Admiral of the Red Squadron, 1758–1813*, London: Navy Records Society, 1907–11.

Lavery, Brian (ed.), *Shipboard Life and Organisation, 1731–1815*, Aldershot: Ashgate for the Navy Records Society, 1998.

Lewis, W S et al (eds), *Horace Walpole's Correspondence with Sir Horace Nann*, London: Yale University Press, 1967

Lloyd, Christopher (ed.), *The Health of Seamen*, London: Navy Records Society, 1965.

Mackay, Ruddock (ed.), *The Hawke Papers*, Aldershot, Hants: Ashgate for the Navy Records Society, 1990.

Morriss, Roger (ed.), *The Channel Fleet and the Blockade of Brest 1793–1801*, Aldershot, Hants: Ashgate for the Navy Records Society, 2001.

New York Historical Society Collections, *The Montressor Journals*, New York, 1881.

_____ *Kimble Papers*, New York, 1884–5.

Partridge, Bellamy, *Sir Billy Howe* (New York, 1932)

Pearsall, A W H (ed.), 'The Naval Aspects of the Landings on the French Coast, 1758', *The Naval Miscellany* (N A M Rodger, ed.), London: George Allen & Unwin for the Navy Records Society, 1984.

Perrin, W G (ed.), *The Keith Papers selected from the Letters and Papers of Admiral Viscount Keith*, London: Navy Records Society, 1927–55.

Smith, Paul H (ed.), *Letters of the Delegates to Congress, 1774–1789*, Washington, DC: US Government Printing Office, 1979–.

Smith, William James (ed.), *The Grenville Papers: Being the Correspondence of Richard Greville Earl Temple, K. G., and the Right Hon. George Greville, Their Friends and Contemporaries …* , London: John Murray, 1852–3.

Steuart, A Francis (ed.), *The Last Journal of Horace Walpole during the Reign of George III from 1771 to 1783*, London: John Lane at the Bodley Head, 1910.

Tatum Jr, Edward H (ed.), *The American Journal of Ambrose Serle*, San Marino CA: Huntington Library Publications, 1940.

Thomas, P D G, 'Parliamentary Diaries of Nathaniel Ryder, 1764–7', *Camden Miscellany* (4th series), London: Royal Historical Society, 1969.

Walpole, Horace, *Memoirs of the Reign of George III* (Derek Jarret, ed.), New Haven Ct: Yale University Press, 2000.

_____ *Memoirs of the Reign of George III*, London: Lawebec & Bullen, 1894.

Wheatley, Henry B (ed.), *The Historical and Posthumous Memoirs of Sir Nathaniel William Wraxall, 1722–1784*, London: Bickers & Son, 1884.

Willcox, William B (ed.), *The American Rebellion: Sir Henry Clinton's Narrative … *, New Haven Ct: Yale University Press, 1954.

Williams, Glyndwer (ed.), *Documents relating to Anson's Voyage round the World, 1740–1744*, London: Navy Records Society, 1967.

Woods, John A (ed.), *The Correspondence of Edmund Burke*, Cambridge: CUP, 1958–78.

Wright, John (ed.), *Sir Henry Cavendish's Debates … *, London: Longman, 1841–3.

Contemporary Publications

A Letter to the Right Hon. Lord Howe on his Naval Conduct in the American War, London, 1779.

A List of the General Officers and Field Officers as they Rank in the Army, London, 1763.

A List of the General Officers and Field Officers as they Rank in the Army, London, 1771.

An Address to the Right Hon. the First Lord Commissioner of the Admiralty upon the pernicious Method of Coppering the Bottoms of the King's ships in time of peace, London, 1876.

An Address to the Right Hon. First Lord Commissioner of the Admiralty upon the Visible Decreasing Spirit, Splendour and Discipline of the Navy, London, 1787.

Commissioners of Inquiry into the Fees and Emoluments received in Public Offices: Fourth Report. Treasurer of the Navy, London, 1808.

[Galloway, Joseph], *A Letter to the Right Hon. Viscount H—E on his Naval Conduct in the American War*, London, 1779.

Gentleman's Magazine

Journals of the House of Commons from January the 24th, 1786 … to December 1786, London, 1803.

[O'Beirne, Thomas], *Candid and Impartial Narrative of the Transactions of the Fleet under the Command of Lord Howe*, 2nd edn, London, n.d.

Parliamentary Register; or History of the Proceedings and Debates of the House of Commons, London, 1779.

Regulations and Instructions relating to His Majesty's Service at Sea, London, 1745.

The Parliamentary History of England from the earliest Times to the Year 1803, London, 1813.

The Times

Whitehall Evening Post

Secondary Works

Allen, Garner W, *A Naval History of the American Revolution*, Williamstown, Mass.: Corner House Publishers, 1970 (reprint).

Anderson, Troyer Steele, *The Command of the Howe Brothers during the American Revolution*, New York: OUP, 1936.

Austen-Leigh, Richard Arthur, *The Eton College Register, 1698–1752,* Eton: Spottiswoode, Ballantyne & Co., 1927.

Baily, Thomas, *Annals of Nottinghamshire: Nottingham including the Borough,* London: Simpkin Marshall, 1853.

Barker, G F R and Steiving, Alan H, *The Records of Old Westminsters,* London: Chiswick Press, 1928.

Barrington, Shute, *The Political Life of William Wildman, Viscount Barrington,* London: W Bulmer, 1814.

Barrow, Sir John, *The Life of Richard Earl Howe KG, Admiral of the Fleet and General of the Marines,* London: John Murray, 1838.

Beatson, Robert, *Naval and Military Memoirs of Great Britain from 1727 to 1783,* London: Longman, 1804.

Brewer, John, *Party Ideology and Popular Politics at the Accession of George III,* Cambridge: CUP, 1976.

Buel, Richard, *In Irons: Britain's Naval Supremacy and the American Revolutionary Economy,* New Haven Ct: Yale University Press, 1998.

Charnock, John, *Biographia Navalis: or, Impartial Memoirs of the Lives and Characters of Officers of the Royal Navy of Great Britain,* London: R Faulder, 1793–8.

Christie, I R, *The End of North's Ministry, 1780–82,* London: Macmillan, 1958.

Corbett, Julian S, *England in the Seven Years War,* London: Greenhill, 1992.

Cormack, W S, *Revolution and Political Conflict in the French Navy, 1789–1794,* Cambridge: CUP, 1995.

Craig, Harding, 'Back Dick Howe, The Sailor's Friend', *The Mariner's Mirror,* vol. 35, (January 1949).

Derrick, Charles, *Memoirs of the Rise and Progress of the Royal Navy,* London: Blacks & Perry, 1806.

Dictionary of National Biography, London, 1921–2.

Donoughue, Bernard, *British Politics and the American Revolution: The Path to War 1773–75,* New York: St Martin's Press, 1964.

Duffy, Michael, 'The Man who Missed the Grain Convoy', *The Glorious First of June, 1794: A Naval Battle and its Aftermath,* (Duffy, Michael and Morriss, Roger, eds), Exeter: University of Exeter Press, 2001.

Dugan, James, *The Great Mutiny,* New York: G P Putnam's Sons, 1965.

Dull, Jonathan R, *The French Navy and American Independence: A Study in Arms and Diplomacy 1774–1787,* Princeton, NJ: Princeton University Press, 1975.

Ehrman, John, *The Younger Pitt: The Years of Acclaim,* New York: Dutton, 1969.

Ford, Worthington C, 'Parliament and the Howes', *Proceedings of the Massachusetts Historical Society* (1910), vol. 44.

Freeman, D S, *George Washington,* New York: Scribner, 1948–57.

Gipson, Lawrence Henry, *The British Empire before the American Revolution. The Great War for Empire,* New York: Alfred A Knopf, 1958–70.

Gill, Conrad, *The Naval Mutinies of 1797,* Manchester: Victoria University Historical Series, 1913.

Granier, Hubert, *Marins de France au Combat, 1715–1789,* Paris: Editions France-Empire, 1995.

———— *Histoire des marins français, 1789–1815,* Nantes: Marines édition, 1998.

Gruber, Ira D, *The Howe Brothers and the American Revolution,* New York: Atheneum, 1972.

Hackman, William Kent, *English Military Expeditions to the Coast of France 1757–1761*, unpublished PhD dissertation for University of Michigan, 1969.

Harding, Richard, *Amphibious Warfare in the Eighteenth Century: The British Expedition to the West Indies 1740–1742*, Woodbridge, Suffolk: Boydell Press for the Royal Historical Society, 1991.

Harte, C R, 'River Obstructions of the Revolutionary War', *Annual Report of the Connecticut Society for Civil Engineers*, vol. 62, 1946.

Higginbotham, Don, *The War of American Independence: Military Attitudes, Politics and Practices, 1763–1783*, New York: Macmillan, 1971.

Hoffman, Ross J F, *Marquis: A Study of Lord Rockingham*, New York: Fordham University Press, 1973.

Holdem, J A, 'Description of the Howe Monument, Westminster Abbey', *New York Historical Society Proceedings*, vol. X, 1911.

Irwin, David, *John Flaxman, Sculptor, Illustrator, Designer*, New York: Rizzoli International Publications Inc., 1974.

Jesse, J Heneage, *Memoirs of the Life and Reign of George the Third*, London: Tinsley Brothers, 1867.

Jones, Maldwyn A, 'Sir William Howe: Conventional Strategist', *George Washington's Opponents* (George Athen Billas, ed.), New York: Morrow, 1969.

Knight, Roger, 'Richard Howe, 1726–1799', *Precursors of Nelson: British Admirals of the Eighteenth Century* (Peter Le Fevre and Richard Harding, eds), London: Chatham Publishing, 2000.

Lewis, Michael, *A Social History of the Navy, 1793–1815*, London: George Allen & Unwin, 1960.

Lloyd, Christopher and Coulter, Jack L S, *Medicine and the Navy, 1200–1900*, London: Livingstone, 1961.

Lowell, Edward J L, *The Hessians and other German Auxiliaries of Great Britain in the Revolutionary War*, Williamstown, Mass: Corner House Publishing, 1970.

Mackesy, Piers, *The War for America, 1775–1783*, London: Longmans, Green, 1964.

Mahan, A T, *The Influence of Sea Power upon the French Revolution and Empire, 1793–1812*, London: Sampson Low, Morston & Co., 1892.

Manwaring, G E and Dobree, Bonamy, *The Floating Republic. An Account of the Mutinies at Spithead and the Nore in 1797*, London: Geoffrey Bles, 1935.

Middleton, Richard, *The Bells of Victory: The Pitt-Newcastle Ministry and the Conduct of the Seven Years War, 1757–1762*, Cambridge: CUP, 1985.

Moomaw, William Hugh, *The Naval Career of Captain Hammond, 1775 – 1779*,unpublished PhD dissertation for University of Virginia, 1955.

_____ 'The Denouement of General Howe's Campaign of 1777', *English Historical Review*, vol. 79, July 1964.

Morriss, Roger, *The Royal Dockyards during the Revolutionary and Napoleonic Wars*, Leicester: Leicester University Press, 1983.

_____ 'The Glorious First of June: The British View of the Actions of 28, 29 May & 1 June 1794', *The Glorious First of June, 1794: A Naval Battle and its Aftermath* (Michael Duffy and Roger Morris, eds), Exeter: University of Exeter Press, 2001.

Namier, Sir Lewis, *The Structure of Politics at the Accession of George III*, London: Macmillan, 1957.

Namier, Sir Lewis and Brooke, John, *The History of Parliament: The House of Commons, 1754–1790*, London: HMSO, 1964.

Perrin, W G, 'The Vice-Admiral and Rear-Admiral of the United Kingdom', *The Mariner's Mirror*, vol. 14, June 1928.

Rodger, N A M, *The Wooden World: An Anatomy of the Georgian Navy*, Annapolis Md: Naval Institute Press, 1986.

Ralfe, J, *The Naval Biography of Great Britain ...* London: Whitmore & Fenn, 1828.

Sainty, J C, *Admiralty Officials, 1660–1870*, London: The Athlone Press, 1975.

Saxby, Richard, 'The Blockade of Brest in the French Revolutionary War', *The Mariner's Mirror*, vol. 78, February 1992.

Sedgwick, Romney, *The History of Parliament: The House of Commons, 1715–1754*, London: HMSO, 1970.

Stephenson, O W, 'The Supply of Gunpower in 1776', *American Historical Review*, vol. 30, January 1925.

Syrett, David, *Shipping and the American War, 1775–83: A Study in British Transport Organization*, London: The Athlone Press, 1970.

_____ 'The Methodology of British Amphibious Operations during the Seven Years and American Wars', *The Mariner's Mirror*, vol. 58, August 1972.

_____ 'H.M. Armed Ship *Vigilant*, 1777 – 1780', *The Mariner's Mirror*, vol. 64, February 1978.

_____ 'A Check List of Admiral Lord Howe Manuscripts in United States Archives and Libraries', *The Mariner's Mirror*, vol. 67, August 1981.

_____ *The Royal Navy in American Waters, 1775–1783*, Aldershot: Scolar Press, 1989.

_____ 'Home Waters or America? The Dilemma of British Naval Strategy in 1778', *The Mariner's Mirror*, vol. 77, November 1991.

_____ *The Royal Navy in European Seas during the American Revolutionary War*, Columbia SC, University of South Carolina Press, 1998.

_____ '"This Penurious Old Reptile": Rear-Admiral James Gambier and the American War', *Historical Research*, vol. 74, February 2001.

Syrett, David and DiNardo, Richard, *The Commissioned Sea Officers of the Royal Navy, 1660–1815*, Aldershot: Scolar Press for the Navy Records Society, 1994.

Talbott, John E, *Pen & Ink Sailor: Charles Middleton and the King's Navy, 1778–1813*, London: Frank Cass, 1998.

Thomas, Peter D G, 'Check List of M.P.s Speaking in the House of Commons, 1768 to 1774', *Bulletin of the Institute of Historical Research*, vol. XXXV, November 1962.

Tomlinson, Barbara, 'The Battle Sanctified: Some Memorials and Relics', *The Glorious First of June, 1794: A Naval Battle and its Aftermath* (Michael Duffy and Roger Morriss, eds), Exeter: Exeter University Press, 2001.

Tunstall, Brian, *Naval Warfare in the Age of Sail: Evolution of Fighting Tactics, 1650–1815* (Nicholas Tracy, ed.), London: Conway Maritime Press, 1990.

Warner, *The Glorious First of June*, New York: Macmillan, 1961.

Webb, P C, 'The Rebuilding and Repair of the Fleet, 1783–1793', *Bulletin of the Institute of Historical Research*, vol. 50, 1977.

Willcox, William B, 'Too Many Cooks: British Planning before Saratoga', *Journal of British Studies*, vol. II, November 1962.

_____ *Portrait of a General: Sir Henry Clinton in the War of Independence*, New York: Knopf, 1964.

Index